AF327264

RAMON KELLEY PAINTS PORTRAITS AND FIGURES

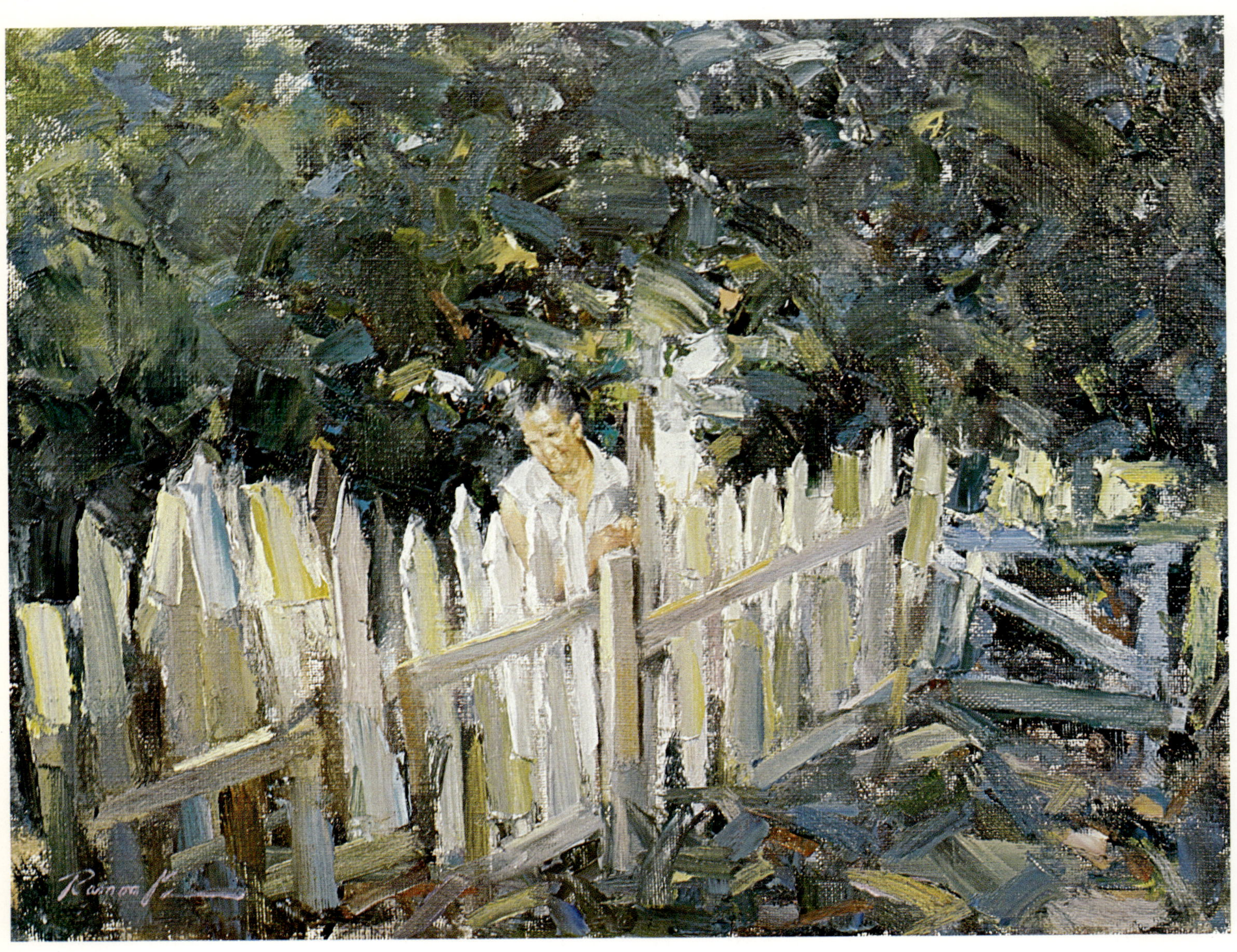

My Mother. *Oil on canvas, 12" x 16" (30.5 x 40.5 cm). I took advantage of the medium texture of Belsize canvas in the free brushwork of this sketch. It's an impressionistic painting, done in the backyard of my family's home in Cheyenne, Wyoming. I painted the picket fence with a palette knife. With palette knife and brush, I applied paint in a dappled way to suggest sunlight coming through foliage. To concentrate attention on my mother, I made the figure and fence near her the lightest area of the painting.*

RAMON KELLEY PAINTS PORTRAITS AND FIGURES

By RAMON KELLEY and Mary Carroll Nelson

WATSON-GUPTILL PUBLICATIONS/NEW YORK

PITMAN PUBLISHING/LONDON

First published 1977 in the United States and Canada by Watson-Guptill Publications,
a division of Billboard Publications, Inc.
1515 Broadway, New York, N.Y. 10036

Library of Congress Cataloging in Publication Data
Kelley, Ramon, 1939–
   Ramon Kelley paints portraits and figures.
   Includes index.
   1. Kelley, Ramon, 1939–   2. Painting—Technique.
3. Portrait painting—Technique.   4. Human figure in art.
I. Nelson, Mary Carroll, joint author.   II. Title
ND237.K442N44   751.4   77-9919
ISBN 0-8230-4505-6

Published in Great Britain by Pitman Publishing
39 Parker Street, London WC2B 5PB
ISBN 0-273-01151-0

Manufactured in Japan

First Printing, 1977

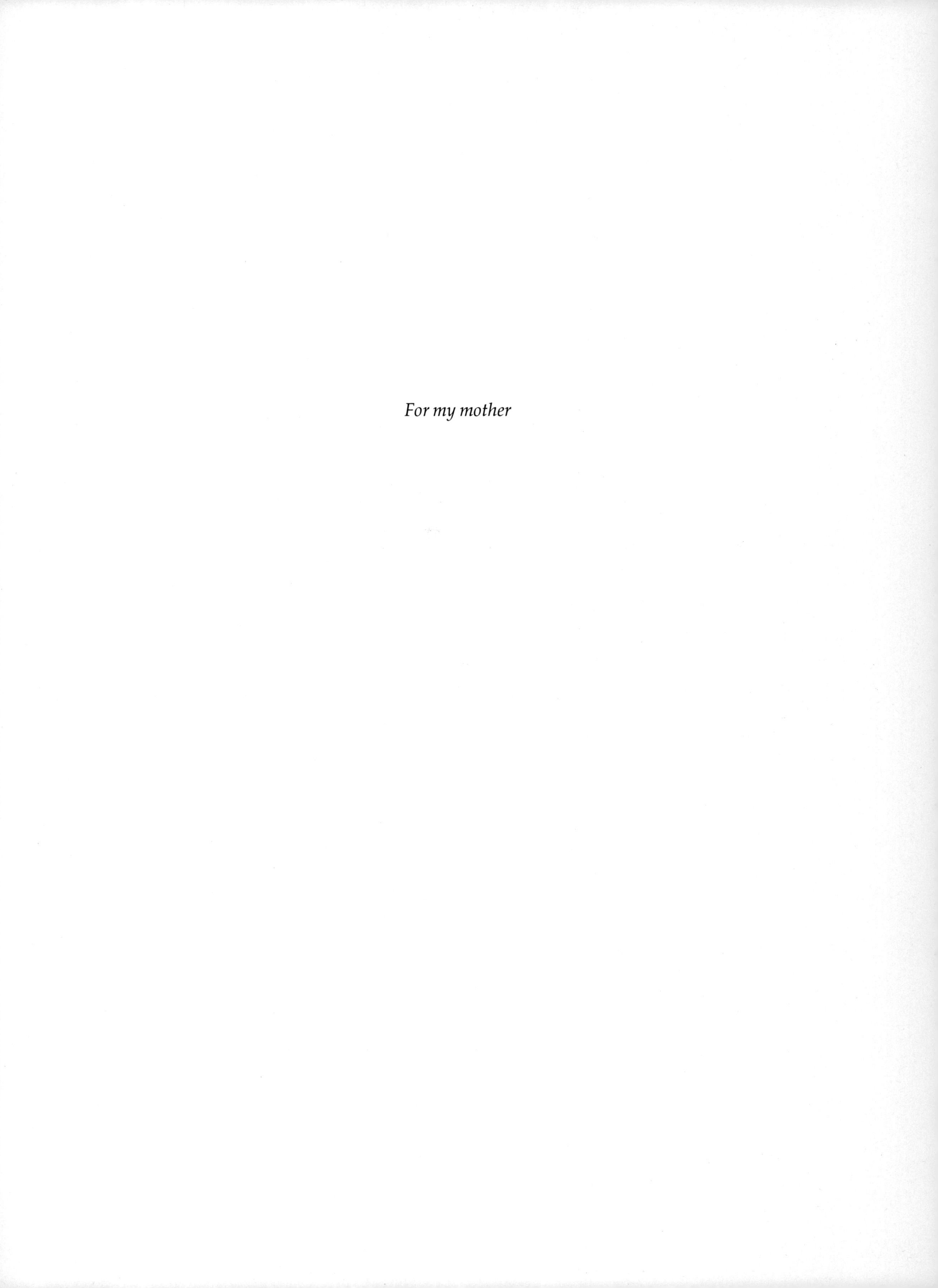

For my mother

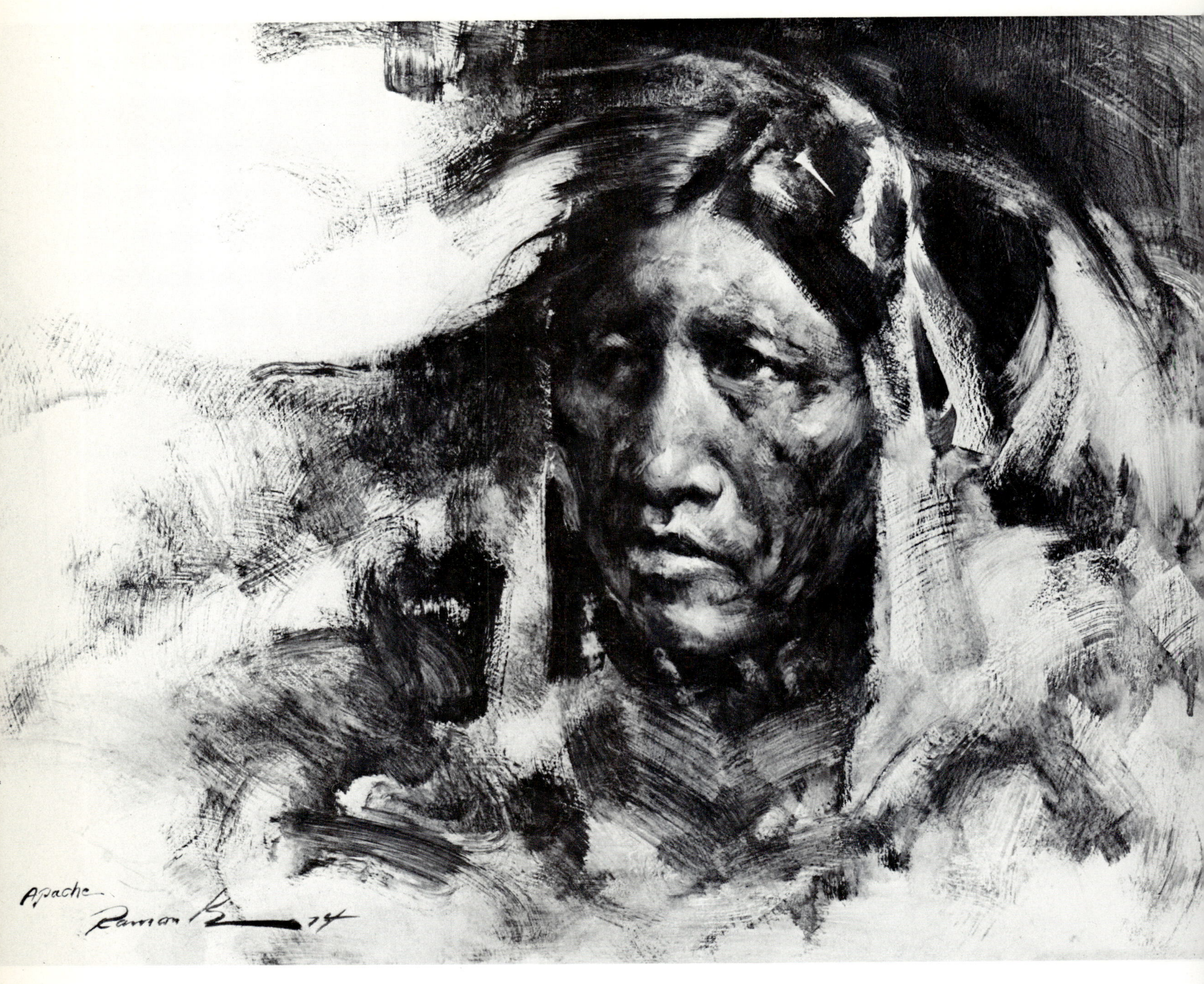

Apache. *Oil on Masonite, 12" x 16" (30.5 x 40.5 cm). The surface of this board was primed with acrylic white paint mixed with acrylic modeling paste for texture. This is an oil wash, done in burnt sienna alone. As a discipline, I enjoy working in a single color; it focuses my mind entirely on values. In some area, I diluted the paint with turpentine and handled highlights much the same way as I would a watercolor —wiping out some with a rag or scraping them out with a razor blade.*

CONTENTS

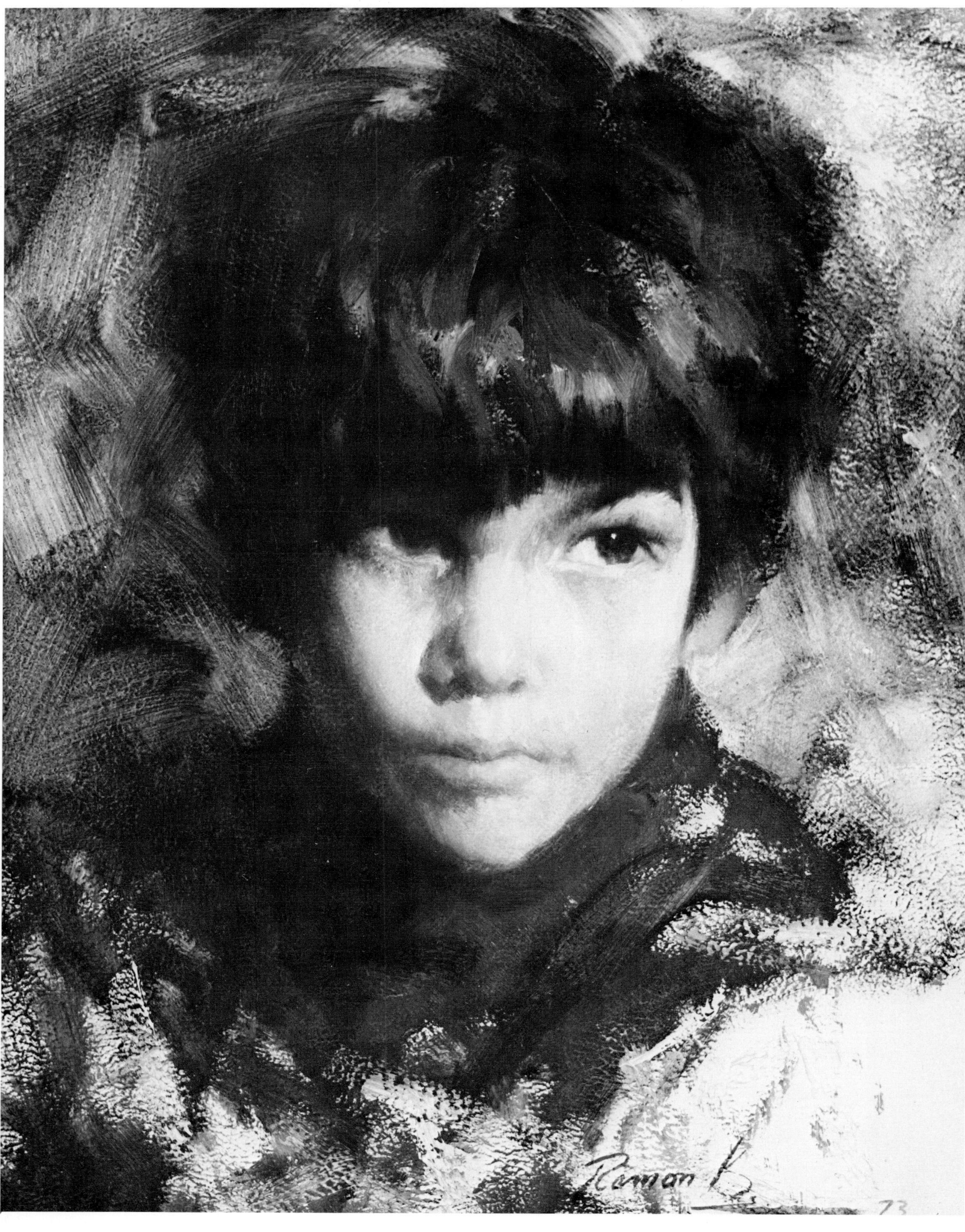

Raman
73

ABOUT RAMON KELLEY

Adam. *Oil on Masonite, 12" x 16" (30.5 x 40.5 cm). This is a painting of my son Adam, and I wanted to achieve a likeness as he was then—at age seven. I textured the ground on this panel with Liquitex gesso. While it was still wet I stippled it with a sponge. To capture the soft quality of a child's skin, I had to be careful not to make the halftones too dark on the lighted side of his head. I used rougher brushstrokes in the hair. The background was handled in an interesting way: I laid down wet colors and then removed some with a clean rag dipped in turpentine. The dark blue sweater balances the dark hair and frames the face. I painted the sweater with a few heavily charged strokes. In the bottom foreground, drybrush strokes add variety.*

It's 9:00 AM and Ramon Kelley is going to work. He tells his wife he'll see her later, steps out the back door of his fine, turn-of-the-century house in Denver, walks eight feet, and enters his studio. Once he locks himself inside, he's ready for another day at his business. For Ramon Kelley, that business is art.

Ramon is a bantam of a man, black-haired and dark-eyed. He radiates a calmness that conceals a turned-on, energetic nature. Still in his thirties, Ramon excels in a variety of media: charcoal, pastel, watercolor, acrylic, oil, and modeling in wax, not to mention lithography.

He has a voracious appetite for learning, so his studio is not only a work center, it's also his school where he stores his collection of art books on shelves close at hand. Old bound copies of *The International Studio* vie with contemporary books about little-known, but superb, Russian painters—page after page of colorful portraits and landscapes. Kelley sleuths for these volumes every time he goes to New York. He also owns many books devoted to masters of the recent past, like Anders Zorn of Sweden and Italian virtuoso Antonio Mancini.

Speaking of his books, Ramon Kelley says, "I try only to caress them—to keep them clean." But he spends hours looking at them—not reading them: Ramon Kelley educates himself through his eye and the spoken word. Other artists teach him. Gallery owners teach him. Museums teach him. He teaches himself.

Art history is his primary teacher. "I'm a great borrower," he says, meaning that he empathizes with certain painters of the past and views them as his masters. It was an early exposure to the art of Nicolai Fechin—a brilliant Russian emigré who settled in the Southwest—that fired his interest in becoming an artist. He relates best to those artists with a love for the human subject; colorists who paint zestfully, impressionistically, with soft edges and a lush surface. Ramon doesn't just look at a painting: he devours it. If he can't see the original, books bring museums to him.

There's nothing in Ramon's life story—prior to the early 1960's—that would lead one to suspect his later accomplishment in art. He grew up in the middle position of ten children whose father was a hard-working man of Mexican-Irish descent and whose mother was Mexican-English.

The Kelley clan lived in Cheyenne, Wyoming, a poor family who knew that the value of a dollar was the work it took to earn it. As a youngster, Ramon Kelley shined shoes for the airmen stationed near

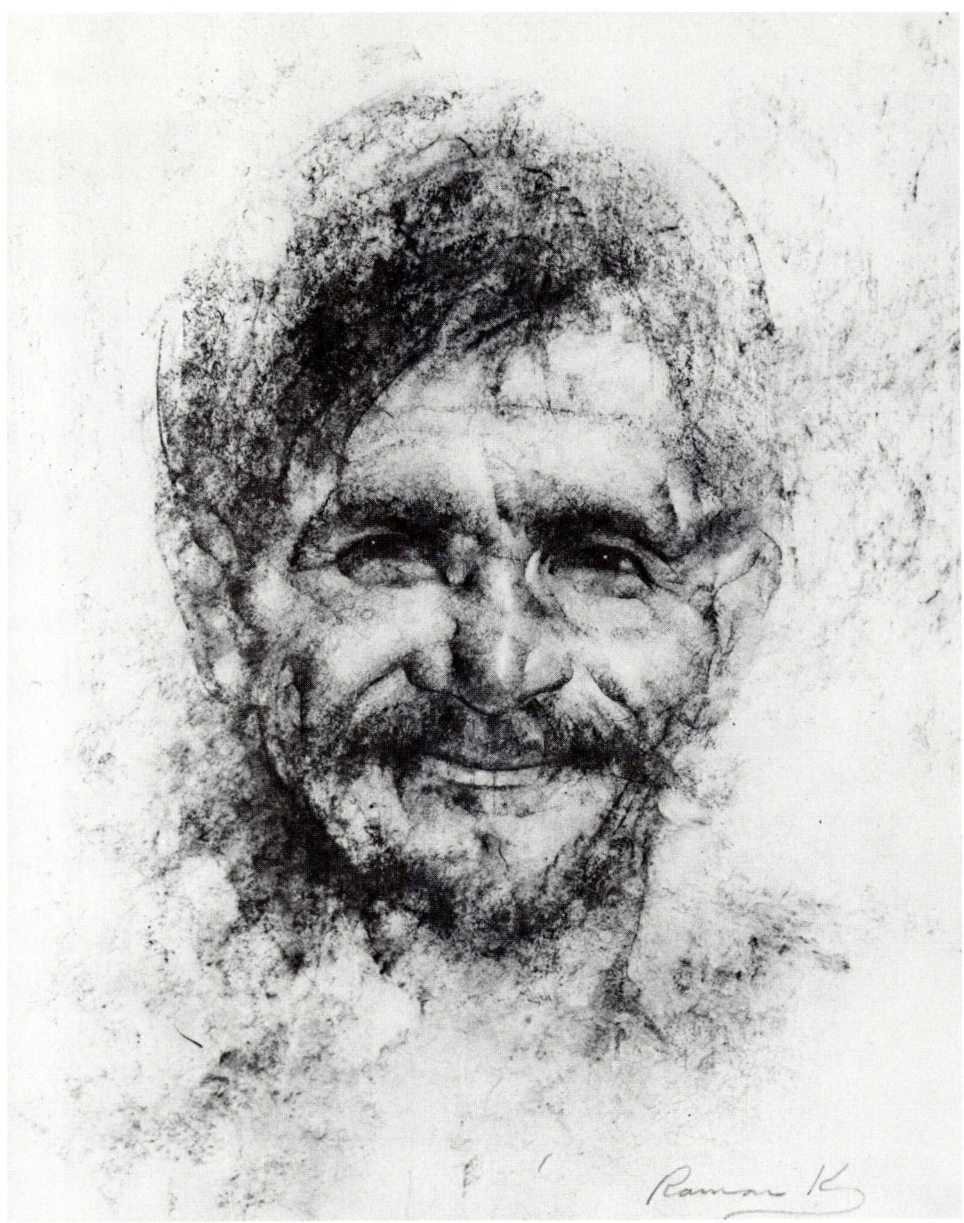

Happy Mexican. *Charcoal on rice paper, 13" x 10" (33 x 25.5 cm). This portrait drawing was my entry into the professional art world. In 1965, on a Mother's Day trip to Taos, this was one of the drawings I showed to Jane Hiatt, the esteemed art dealer. Her approval of it started my career.*

town; worked on a ranch; was a shag-boy in used-car lots; was a hotel houseboy; and delivered poultry to restaurants. He quit school after the eighth grade from lack of interest. Several of his teachers had encouraged his talent and he's still close to them, but he had no idea of pursuing art then. Instead, when he was old enough, he joined the navy for a four-year hitch.

That tour of duty gave him an opportunity to visit museums around the world and thus began the education that he continues today. When he was released from the service, Ramon went to Denver and spent a grand total of less than nine months in the Colorado Institute of Art. Ramon was fascinated by one class—life drawing. Though he'd found his subject, he still hadn't found his career.

For a few years, on the strength of his rapidly gained ability to do layouts, Ramon worked for ad agencies and earned a living for himself and Mona, whom he married in 1963. It was the birth of their first son, Adam, in 1964 that propelled Ramon Kelley into daring to be a full-time creative artist.

On Mother's Day, 1964, he went to Taos (the town of the admired
Fechin) to see if some dealer would handle his work. He took a half-
dozen, well-framed, charcoal character studies that he'd done at night
after working all day for the agencies. The first day in Taos was one of
discouraging turndowns. But on the second day he met Jane Hiatt, esteemed owner of the Village Gallery, one of the Taos landmarks. In her
day, Jane Hiatt has known and aided many Taos greats, including
Nicolai Fechin and Leon Gaspard. When Jane Hiatt saw his drawings,
she expressed her approval by accepting the unknown Ramon Kelley
into her stable.

Within a year, she had developed a clientele who wanted his drawings. But one day she told him, "Ramon, people want to see what you
can do with paint."

Ramon remembers, "The word *painting* scared the hell out of me. I
really just hoped to be a great 'drawer.' When I first started with color, I
used a warm pastel stick—like ochre or burnt sienna—and added a
suggestion of color over the charcoal drawing. Then I got a little braver.
I didn't know then about color temperature; I always used warm colors.
Pretty soon I began using all the colors I could in a painting.

"If you can paint in three colors, you know what you're doing. I love
color. I'm almost a hog about it. I won't say I've learned it all—it's the
way I'm *learning* color that's exciting and that I can share.

"I'm not known for painting little blondes. Me, I like warm tones,
nice ochres in the skin. Put a cool color near it and it tends to sing a
little more.

"You know when you paint an Indian in hot, earthy tones—then you
put a note of cobalt blue in there, it's just going to zing.

"I enjoy painting people—so I enjoy painting Indians as much as
nudes and children of different races. The coloring has a lot to do
with it."

His curiosity led him to try other media. In 1971, he bought a few
tubes of watercolors and painted a study of a Black boy, *Little Mack*
(page 39). The painting was accepted in the 104th American Watercolor
Society Exhibition and won the Helen Gapen Oehler Award. It is
characteristic of his career that his first try at something is a winner. His
work was accepted in each successive show thereafter, leading to
Ramon's election to AWS in 1975. He was selected as a National Juror
of both the 1976 and 1977 AWS Exhibitions.

He's also known as a pastelist and was one of the first members of
the newly-formed Pastel Society of America, begun in 1975. Painting in
oils and acrylics with brisk brushwork, Ramon asserts the same direct,
impressionistic style he brings to his drawings. He's done lithographs
and has modeled portraits cast in bronze. There's an assured, solid
form in all his work: in each medium, he takes conscious pleasure in
developing the rich surface.

Ramon finds it stimulating to work in a variety of materials and to do
varied subjects. He fears getting into a rut from repetition. Although he
may paint a favorite model often, he doesn't recreate the pose, color,
and size in the same medium.

He doesn't do tons of sketches and preparatory things. He jumps
right in and goes with it, alla prima, relishing the joyousness of the
approach. Sometimes he'll pull off a 4" x 5" (9 x 12.5 cm) piece he calls
"a little gem" and that might be his product for the day. Other times,

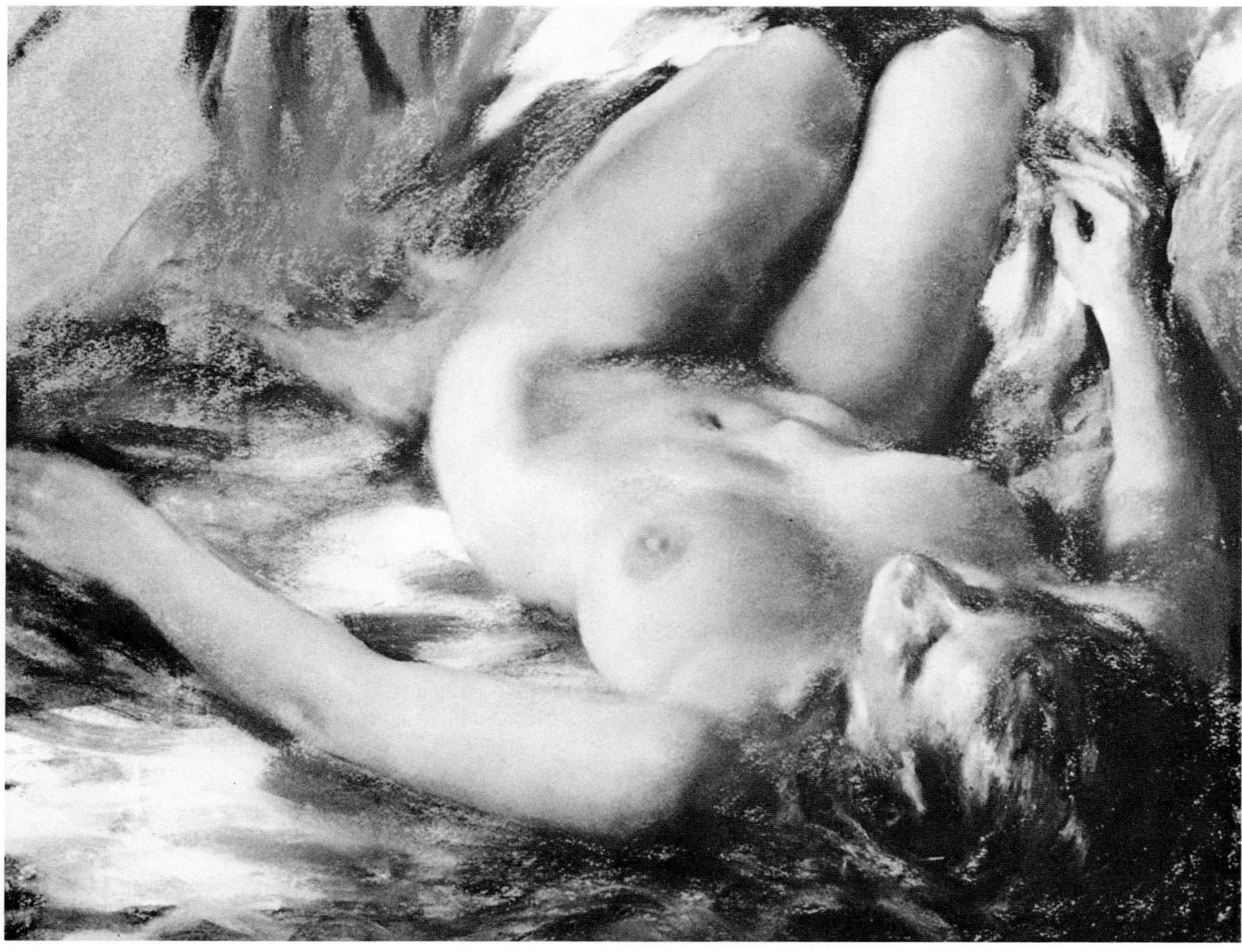

Nude. *Pastel on paper, 14" x 18" (35.5 x 45.5 cm). I was standing above the model and only three feet away, so this figure is greatly foreshortened. At such an extreme angle, one part of the figure often appears too small and another seems too large. So the artist must adjust the form to make it look correct. I rely on my intuition about the pose rather than on an academic formula. For example, I added to the size of the thighs because they seemed too small; I also made the left arm larger to exaggerate its nearness. The result is an interesting composition in which the space is almost completely filled by the figure.*

he might spend sixteen hours on a painting, working straight through, and that will be his day's work. He tries to complete something every day.

Completion is almost a "method" with Ramon. He doesn't often carry a sketchbook for incidental work, although on his travels he may do some reference studies and take photographs. Ramon is basically a studio artist. When he draws from the model, the results are modeled color and telling line—finished work, despite the speed with which it's done.

He fears too much success—too heady a rise in recognition. Though he's a prolific painter, a steady creator, he fears becoming a production artist and "peaking out" because of too much exposure. "Sargent, Homer, and Eakins never peaked out," he comments revealingly. Ramon takes the long range view of his career and resists the fleeting thrills of mercurial popularity. "I'm a one-man operation and a one-operation man," he says. Painting is everything he does and all he wants to do, all his life—not in response to a current fad. It's timelessness he strives for in his work.

People are the stuff of Ramon Kelley's art. Those people who matter most to him are his immediate family: Mona, their sons Adam and Ben, their little girl Lea, and myriad relatives from both Ramon's and Mona's families—Mona has ten brothers and sisters. Many members of both

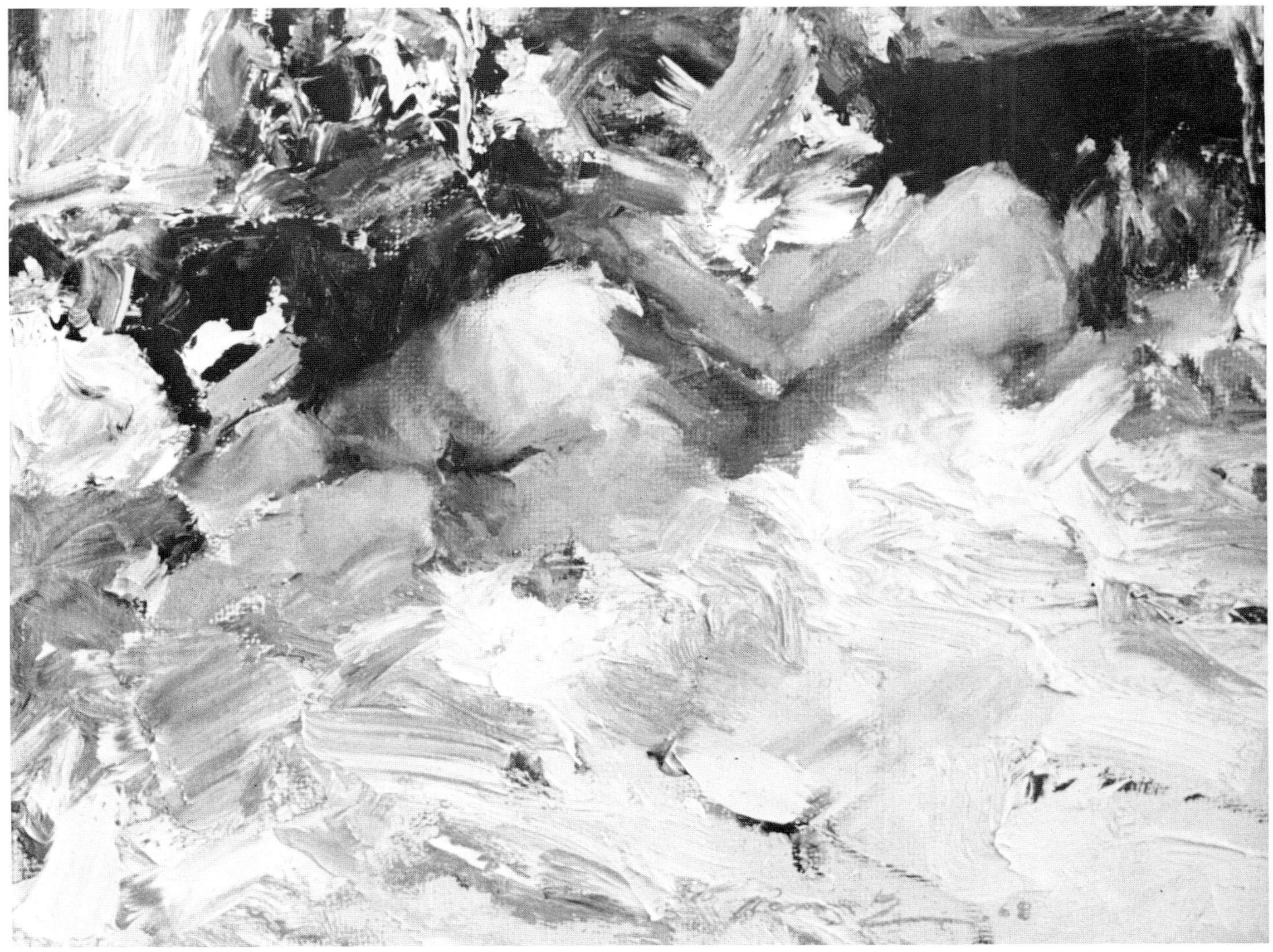

Nude. *Oil on Masonite, 9" x 12" (23 x 30.5 cm). This alla prima oil was painted from life in an artist friend's studio. Working quickly with a loaded brush, I established my composition and the pose simultaneously, stressing a simple diagonal. My major effort was directed toward pulling the figure out of the background. Though abstract, the background still had to suggest reality and not dominate the figure. With artistic license, I ad libbed the two dark areas—one behind the model's head and another behind her hip—to give a sense of space around the figure. A prominent feature of this painting is texture, made only by application of paint to a smooth board. Notice the variation in the size and direction of my brushstrokes.*

families live in Denver. They all make their way into Kelley's work. The artist's deep emotional ties to his family are most clearly revealed in the tender portraits he has painted of his children.

He claims with typical humor, "I could have become a little mobster." That idea is quickly dispelled when he begins talking about his childhood. "We didn't have a lot of possessions. It never occurred to us to ask for things like a bicycle, but we had good things—like homemade oatmeal cookies instead of hamburgers and cokes. We liked to do things together. We're very close. The best thing about growing up like that was that I always had a good sense of values." Highest on his list of values is the family; second is his career.

Ramon is no stranger to prejudice. He knows at first hand what it's like to be rejected simply because of his Mexican heritage. He's not bitter about it. In fact, it's one of the reasons he's attracted to and can capture the pathos and dignity in the human face. Sympathy for and understanding of his own people—of the Indians, of Blacks, of any person he paints—give substance to his character studies. It's not the wrinkles and folds of the skin that he's painting; it's the sense of life in the person that he focuses on.

Coming as he does from a people who know how difficult life can be, socially and financially, Ramon says, "I can't *afford* to be mediocre at what I'm doing." The first time he tried to give up the security of a

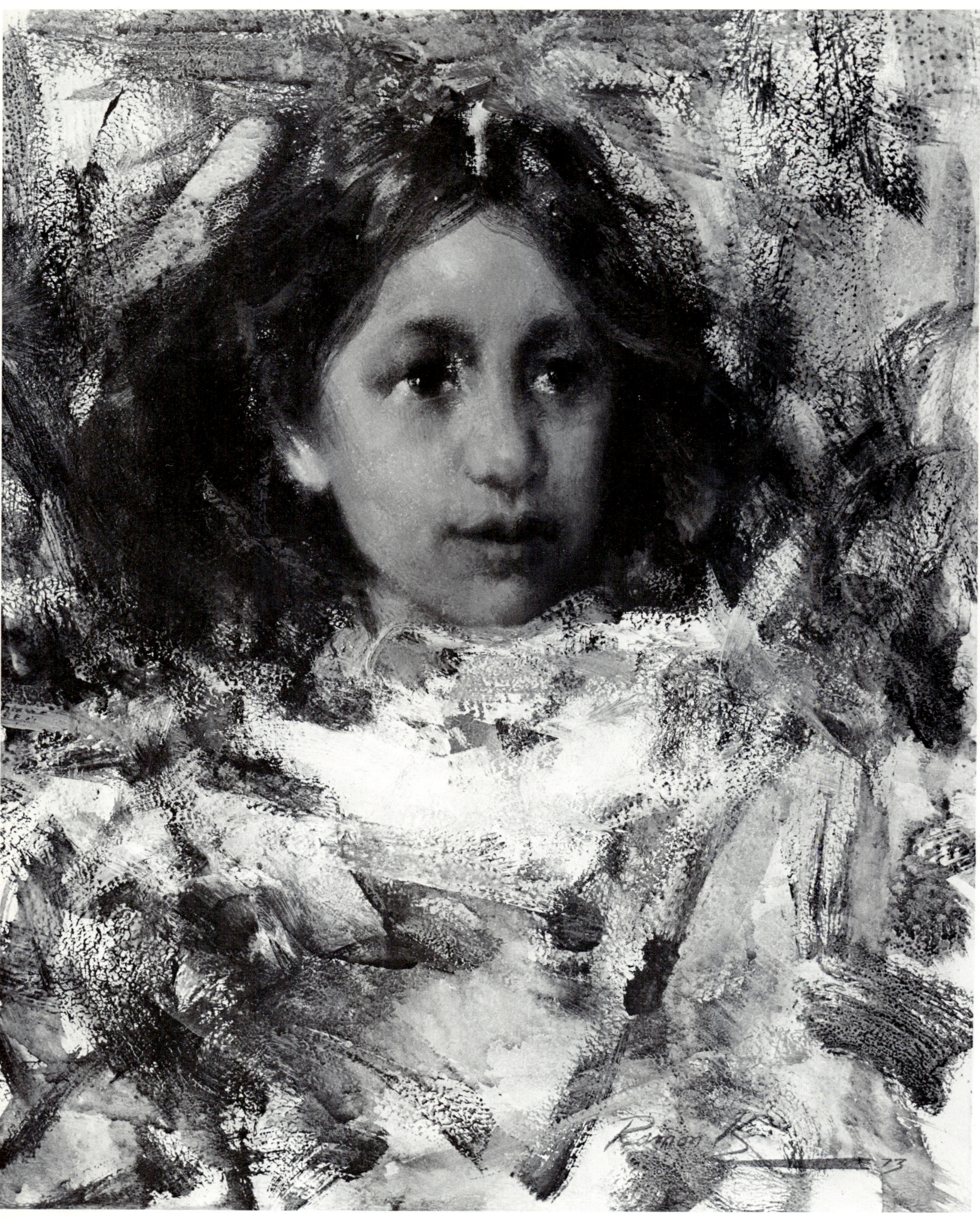

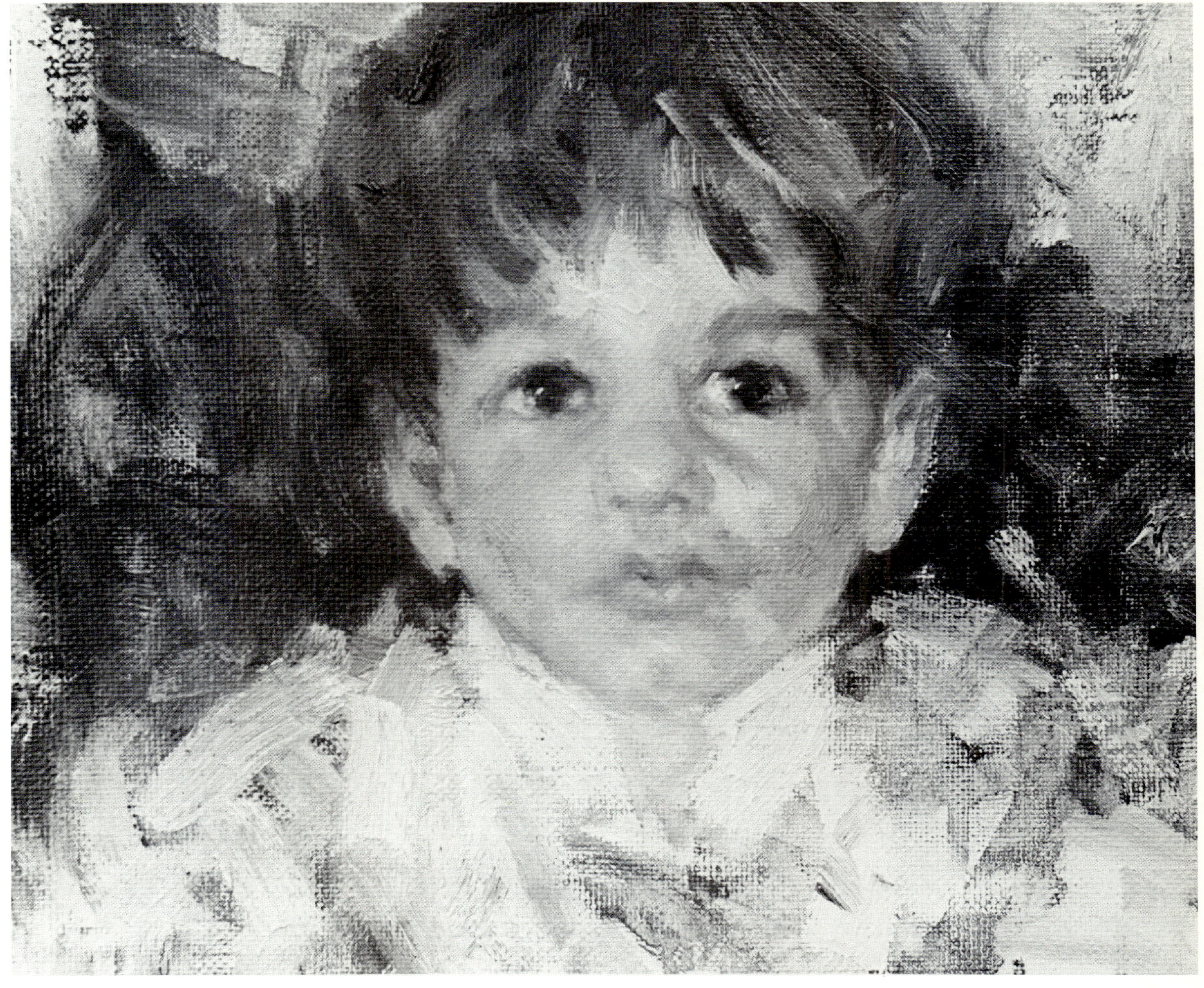

Pink Lace and Red Ribbon (left). Acrylic on Masonite, 18" x 14" (45.5 x 35.5 cm). Collection of the Frye Museum of Art, Seattle, Washington. Although this was painted in acrylic, it's a good example of my watercolor technique. I painted washes on the background and the bottom of the blouse with a bristle brush. I also used the bristle brush to scumble drier strokes in those areas. For the hair, I first painted light washes, then worked back into them with definite brushstrokes of a medium-size bristle brush. Because an acrylic ground is impervious to water, it's possible to wash out areas of the painting that are still wet. I did this on the left background and in the part of the model's hair. There's an impasto area on the blouse. The face is in shadow and is painted more densely in layers in a style more closely resembling an oil painting technique. There's a spirited quality in the spontaneous combinations of washes and opaque areas.

Ben (above). Oil on canvas, 8" x 10" (20.5 x 25.5 cm). This portrait of my son Ben was done when he was three years old. At that age, a child can't sit still; so I painted this from a photograph. In this alla prima oil painting, I used an approach similar to the one I use in pastel. First I painted washes in turpentine-diluted oil paint, using alizarin crimson and raw umber. I used a number 6 filbert to paint the shirt and background and a number 2 filbert for the face. I deliberately set up a contrast between the rough, wide strokes of the larger brush and the soft, more delicate brushwork on the face.

salaried job, he learned that, "I didn't understand anything about the business end of art. What do you do with a painting once you've painted it?" Learning about marketing has been as important to his career as learning to paint. There are many artists who have talent, but who don't comprehend the techniques of marketing. "I'm a businessman," Ramon says, and he works hard at it.

Basic to the success of a good businessman is the need for something fine to sell. When he's at work on his art, Ramon refuses to think about money. "When you walk up to your board," he says, "you have to love it just like your wife. You let it come out like music. You let it be natural.

"I'll finish a painting sometimes and I'll feel so high, just for a second, I'll think of all the great works in my books and feel I've reached that level. But then I can fall flat the next time. This keeps you honest; one fine painting doesn't make an artist. It's good for you to make mistakes."

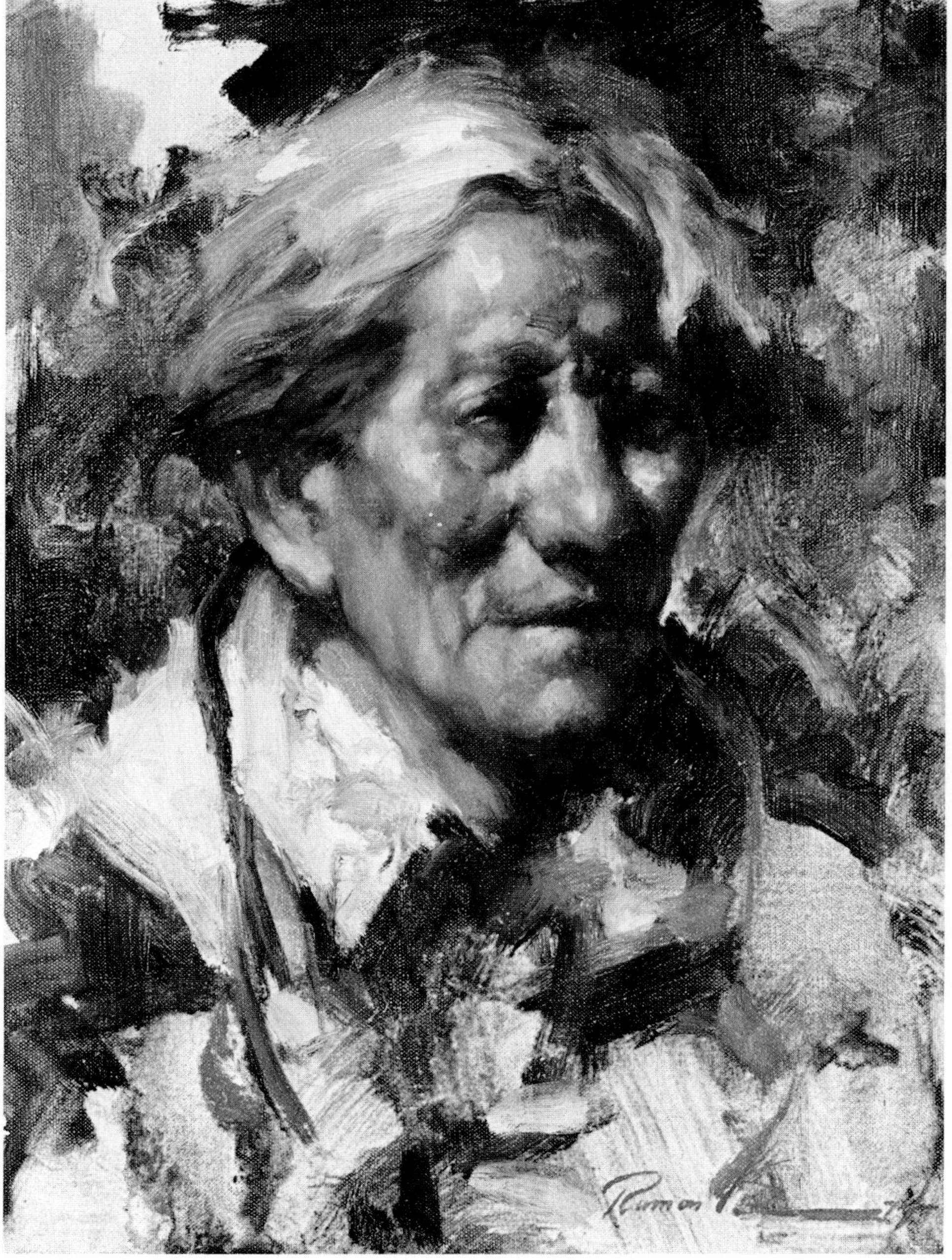

Indian in Blue Shirt. *Oil on canvas, 12" x 9" (30.5 x 23 cm). Against a transparent background of veiled colors achieved with thin overlays of washes, I painted the head with several layers of delicate brushwork. The background and foreground are made up of somewhat rounded, small shapes. Because the face is essentially a collection of molded features, the entire painting can be seen as an interlocked pattern of forms moving in different directions. Heavier pigment is used on the hair, on the left forehead, under the left eye, and on the left side of the collar. In the shadows the paint is more transparent, whereas in the light it's more opaque and built up.*

His normalcy and balance allow Ramon to pursue both his creative goals and his career without confusion. He's developed professional patterns to living that aid his career. He travels several times a year to search for subjects, capturing new faces and places in sketches and photographs for future reference. Experts in framing, lighting, and brochure-making also have a part in the business of being an artist; he cultivates those other businessmen who are necessary to a career. Although the Kelley family lives in an unaffected way, banquets, jet planes to New York, awards and honors are all accepted and enjoyed without self-consciousness as a part of the artist's life.

Continuous practice at the easel gives Ramon a chance to keep exploring, to keep learning. Each finished piece is evidence of his pleasure in trying new methods, new surfaces, new combinations. His work has an identifiable Ramon Kelley handwriting of vigorous brushwork, made dynamic by contrast in direction. Usually he surrounds his subject with abstract color, value, and texture that enclose the subject harmoniously

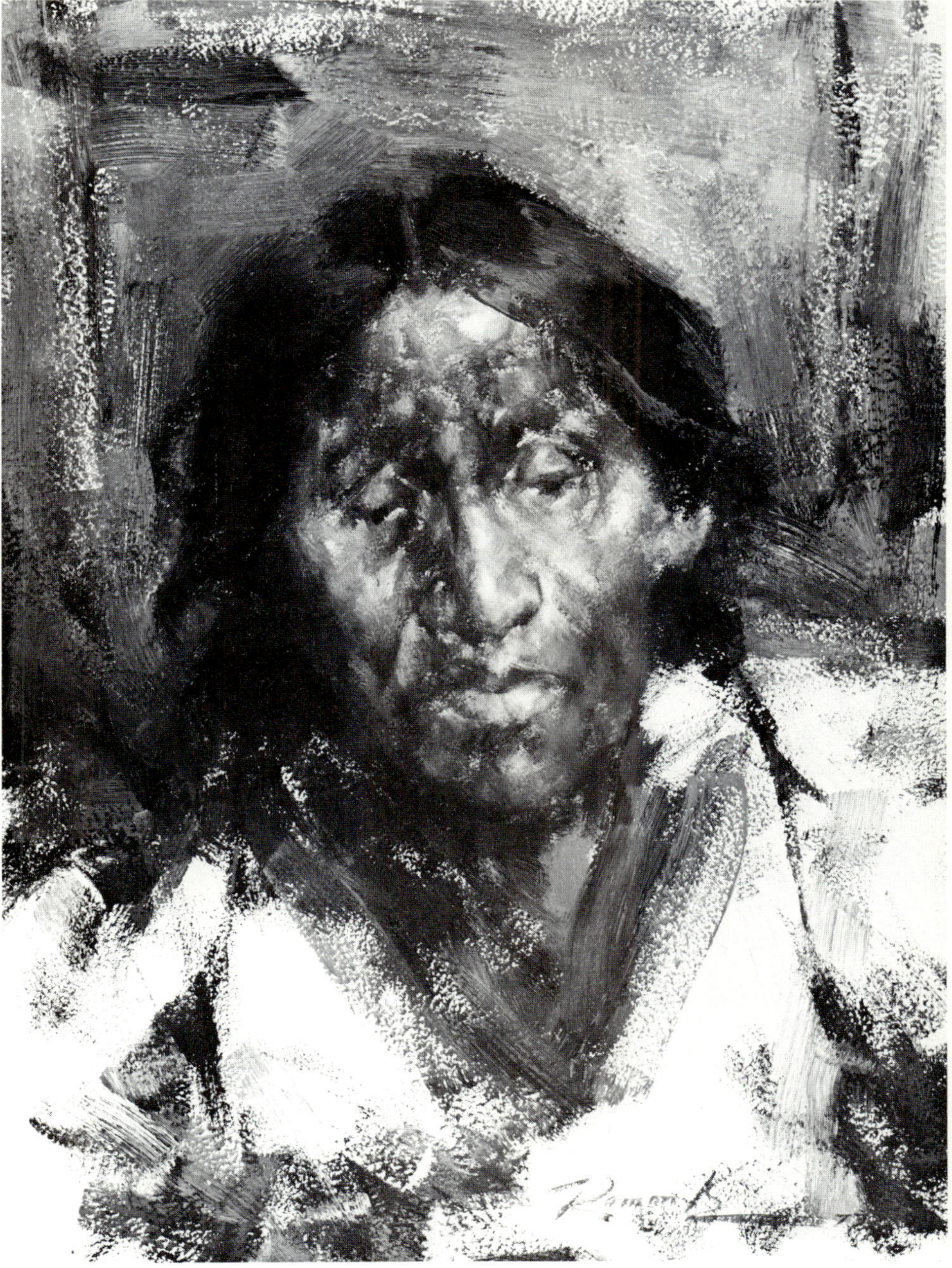

Taos Indian. *Acrylic on Masonite, 16" x 12" (40.5 x 30.5 cm). After priming this painting with acrylic gesso, which I textured heavily, I painted layers of washes, some of which are still visible. Not all areas of the board were covered —the white of the shirt is the white of the priming. The background is washed on in several layers of thin color. On the face, I built up the features, using an oil painting technique —that is, thicker paint with medium instead of water. I even feathered the strokes on the face. In a large part of this painting, I applied loose washes in a technique that more closely resembled watercolor.*

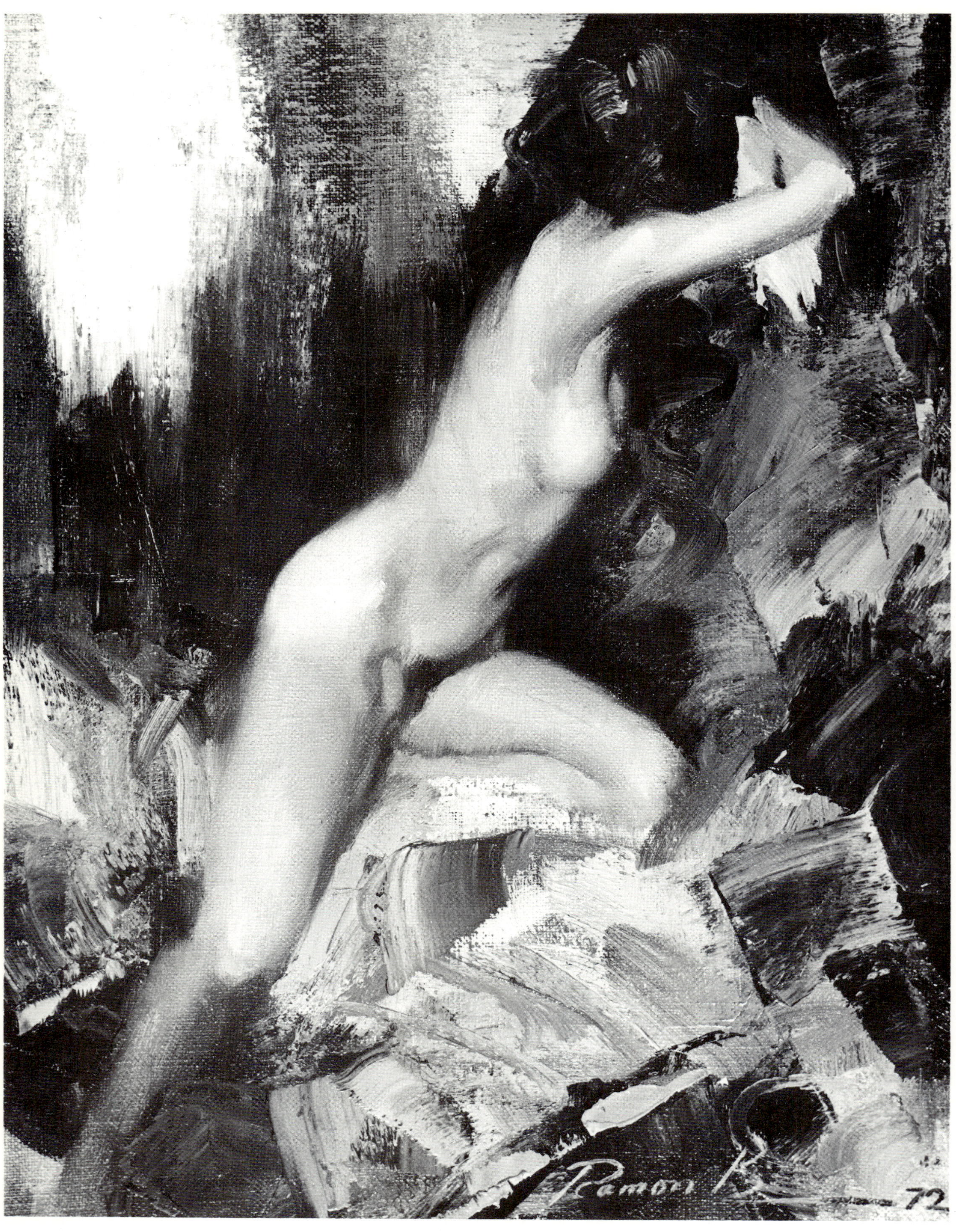

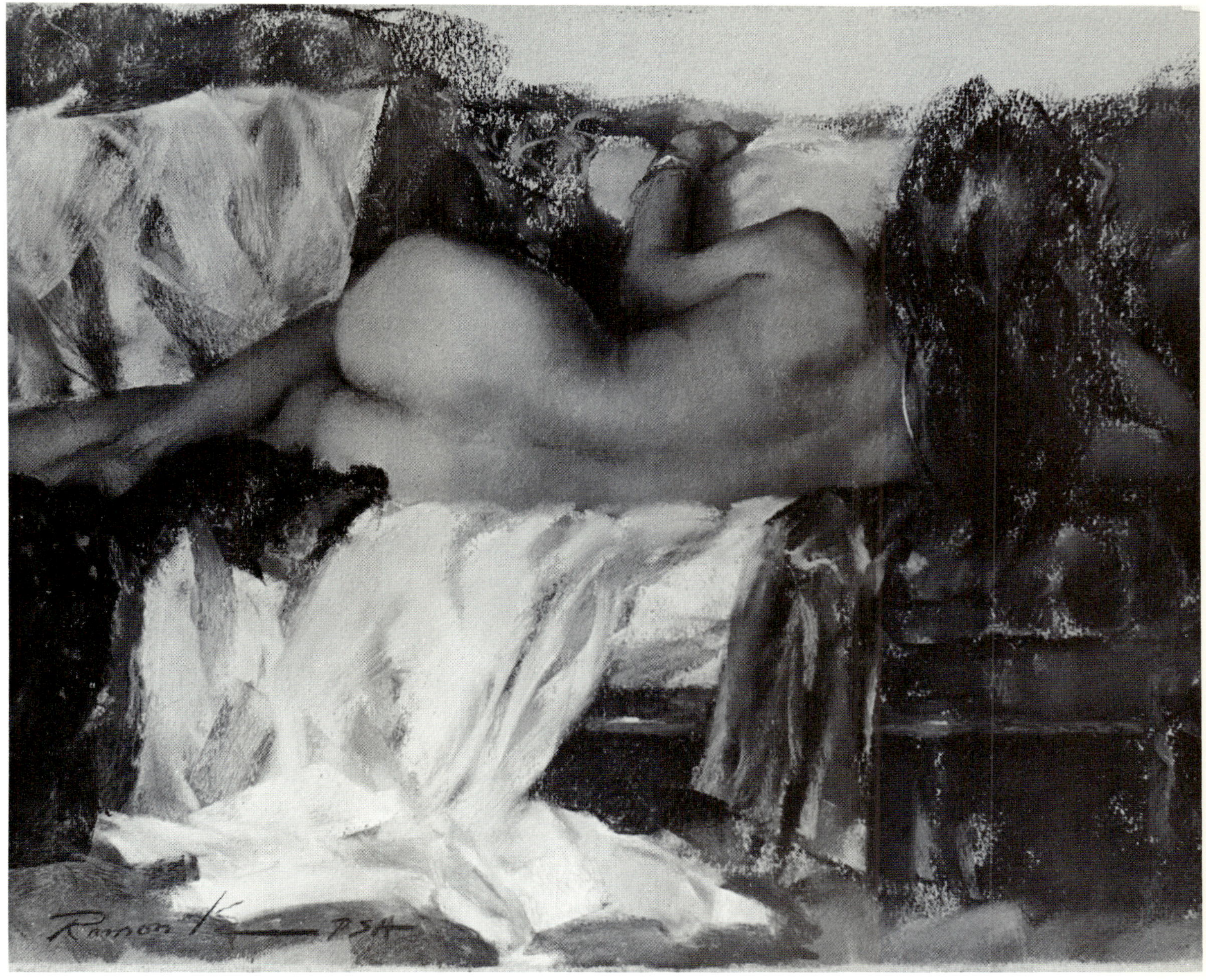

Theo (left). Oil on canvas, 12" x 9" (30.5 x 23 cm). Theo was painted from life in one sitting. Unusual background colors of purples and blues worked effectively with the warm flesh tones. This pose was a strenuous one for the model to hold, so I worked fast and finished the background and foreground areas with a palette knife. Notice the drybrush textures to the left of the model's head. They add their texture to the variety of rough and smooth brushstrokes and palette knife work.

Nude (above). Pastel on paper, 9" x 12" (23 x 30.5 cm). In this small pastel done in the studio from life, I've emphasized a strong, horizontal line. Notice the V-shape set up by the lines of drapery that converge at the bottom and frame the model. There's an intentional contrast in textures between the smooth flesh and surrounding drapery. The shadows in the drapery are cool against the warm tones of the model.

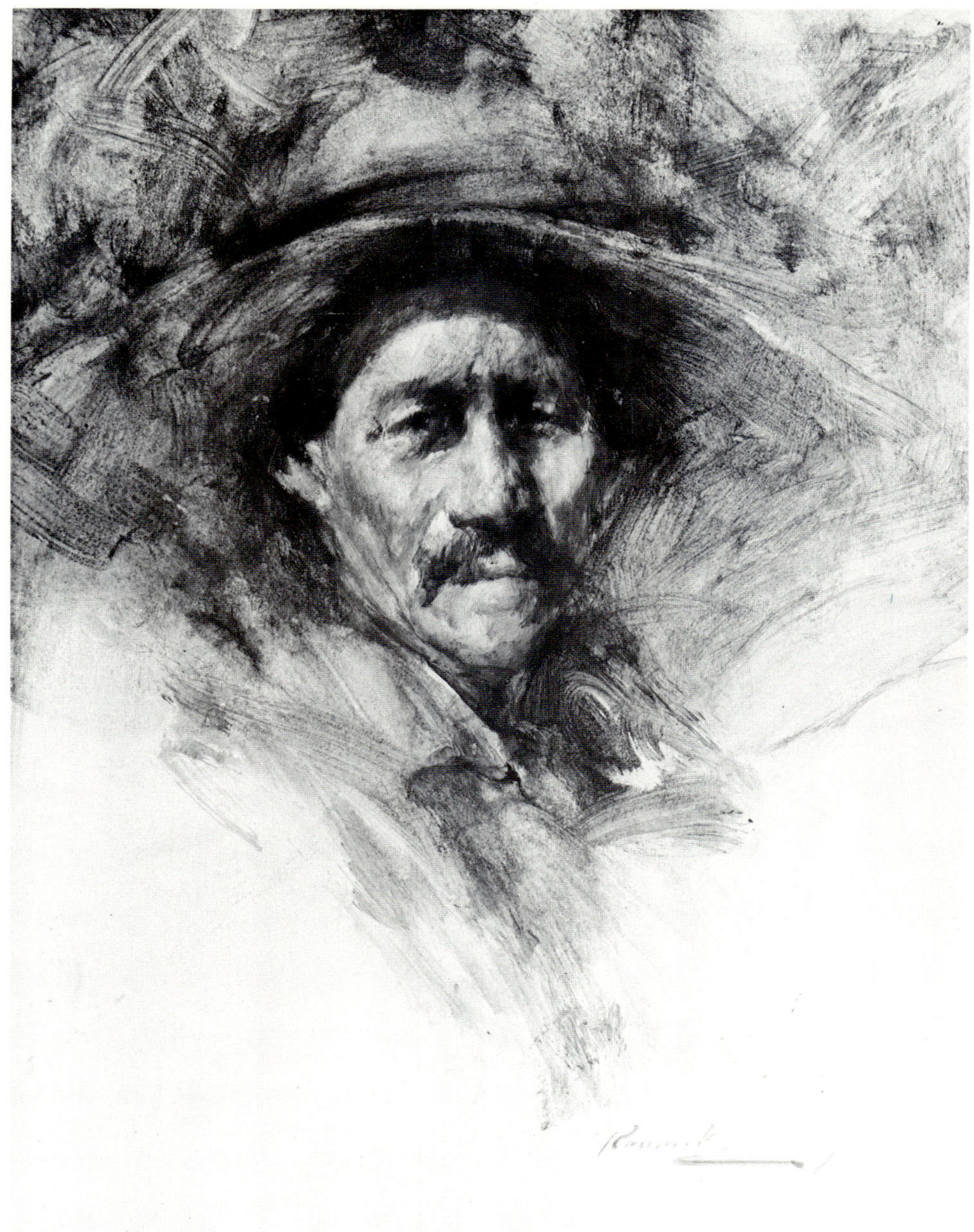

Mexican Farmer. *Acrylic watercolor on illustration board. 18" x 14" (45.5 x 35.5 cm). This painting is based on a pencil sketch and photograph taken in Mexico. I purposely used acrylic rather than traditional watercolor in order to achieve certain effects in this acrylic watercolor. Acrylic stays put and dries so fast that each layer can be seen as a separate entity —not fused as in a regular watercolor. This also means that brushstrokes retain their identity in this medium, and I dragged the brush in such a way that the quality of the bristles is visible and makes a pattern especially evident in the upper half of the painting. The brim of the hat cast a definite shadow on the model's forehead, enabling me to play interesting highlights on the face. Acrylic watercolors are more difficult to work with than traditional watercolors, as it's almost impossible to lift out areas after the acrylic has dried. So areas to be lifted out must be carefully planned and the wiping-out executed quickly. There's a transparent glazed quality to acrylics that's not possible to get in either oil or watercolor. Darks in the hair are particularly transparent. Drybrushed, scumbled, and dragged strokes are laid over the transparent washes in the hair to texture it.*

but do not constitute an identifiable setting. This prevents a dated look. His subjects are real people, but not too closely tied with our rapidly changing era. Their faces and clothes have a kind of permanent validity. The Taos Indians and the peasants of Mexico appeal to him. When he does a scene, rather than a figure, he chooses a village or market over the more urban subject. And, of course, a nude is forever.

The energy in Ramon's work and the emotional impact of his models give the impression of an artist who works only from his heart—in the white heat of a creative urge. That is only partially accurate; he's always working things out and guiding his hand with decisiveness, so his head is involved in his work.

Even his dress, while working, reveals a person with a professional approach. He wears street clothes to paint—neat, trim, with dress shoes, not the crepe-soled boot one often sees on the working painter.

Kelley in his studio resembles the dentist in his office. He's set up a studio that really works. It used to be the carriage house of the home he has recently bought in Denver. Later it became the garage, with chauffeur's quarters on the second floor. Today it's a luxurious, orderly place, with a personality. Everything he needs to paint in oil is housed in the main studio on the first floor. Materials for pastel and watercolor are upstairs. His studio is his private retreat and he doesn't expect any casual interruptions. Sales and business are handled by his galleries: the studio is strictly for creative work.

Mona and Ramon have found antique pieces of furniture that solve practical problems of storage and lend charm to his workday. One of the finest of his scrounged items is a huge piece of milk glass that once graced an old drugstore on Denver's Larimer Street. The glass serves as a palette for his oils. It rests on an 1886 drugstore cabinet with extra tubes of paint in its many little drawers. An antique dental cabinet holds his pastels. A model's platform supports a Victorian couch; alternatively, there's a worn, comfortable barber's chair where Ramon likes to sit—smoking his pipe and studying his newest painting.

Ramon tracked down an expert to equip his studio with excellent lighting, so he can paint equally well by day or with artificial light at night. Professional paper-storage cabinets, racks, and plentiful work areas are fitted into his ample studio just where they are needed. It's an efficient place with a touch of glamour.

Artists younger than he have a special appeal for Ramon Kelley and he stops, at times, to share what he's learned with them or to critique their work when they ask him to. He recalls those who helped him and he's grateful for what they told him when he needed it. He can put his knowledge into words, and has a similar directness verbally and artistically. Besides sharing in his studio—sharing many of his books, innovations, and enthusiasms with other artists in the area—Ramon also conducts workshops.

For two years the Kelleys owned their own gallery and discovered the real nitty-gritty of the marketplace. ("There's not enough respect for the artist," he believes.) The gallery added to the family's security, but also sapped Ramon's creative energy and his time. He can now look back on it and say, "We all need to slow down. We must gear down and enjoy what we have. The young know this." He admires the simpler aims of the young people coming along behind him.

The easy-to-reach charm of Ramon Kelley rests on his integrity and lack of pretense. These essentials of his character nearly mask his rare talent and skyrocketing success. Because he's not overwhelmed by his talent and honestly wants to improve, grow, and share his work, his gift promises to endure—as much a wonder to himself as to those who've watched him progress in one decade from ex-sailor to top-ranking painter. If you should ask "Will success spoil Ramon Kelley?" the answer would have to be "No." He's got his feet too solidly on the ground.

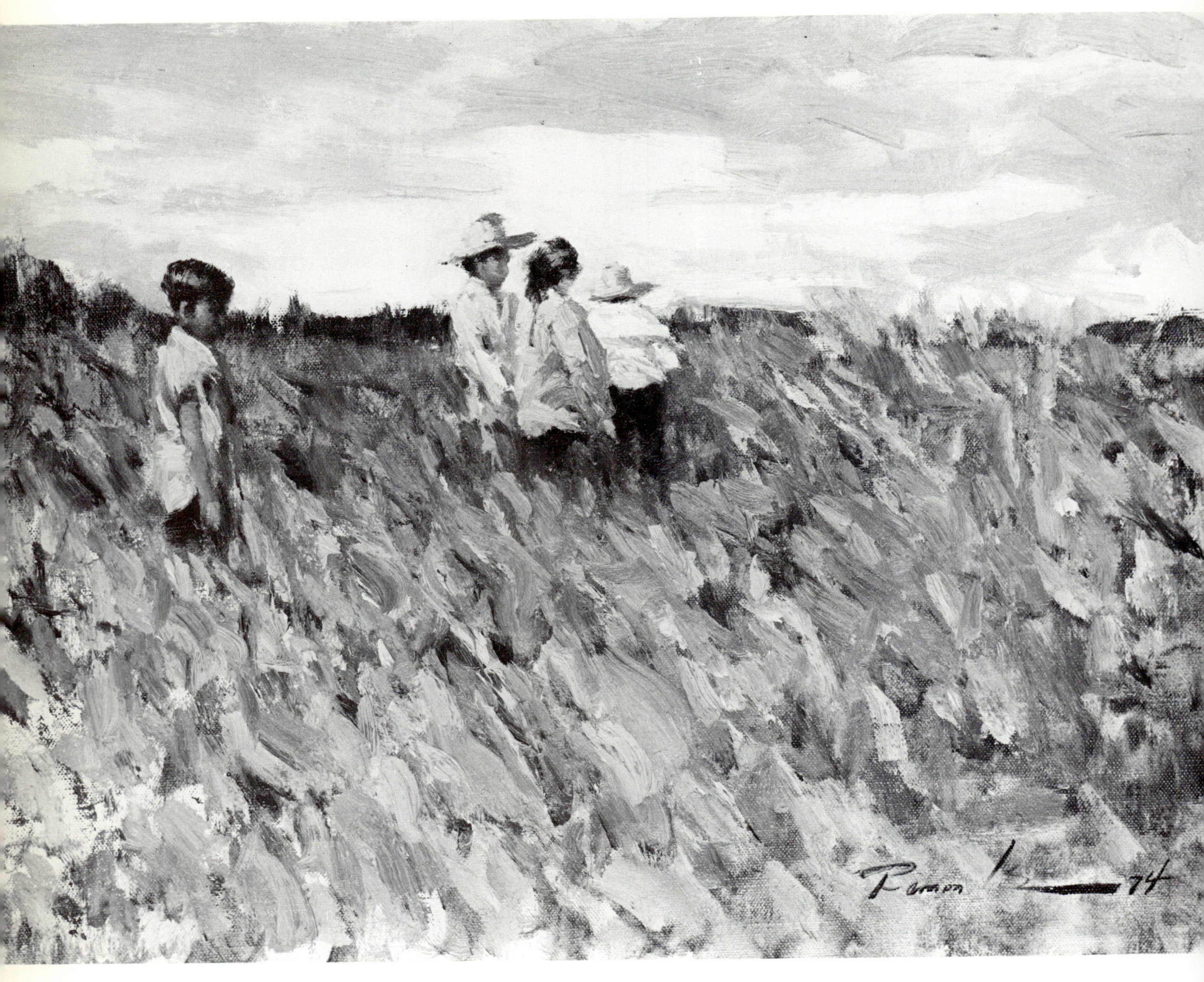

La Familia. *Oil on canvas, 12" x 9" (30.5 x 23 cm). While painting on location in Mexico, I spotted this family walking through a field. They were quickly gone, but I wanted to add them to my painting. So I revised my composition to include them by eliminating some shacks that were to have been my focal point. To capture the effect of a sea breeze on the field, I painted the vegetation fast with a medium-size flat bristle brush. I placed the brushstrokes all in the same direction, letting the figures walk into the wind. The sky was painted simply, with horizontal brushstrokes.*

RAMON KELLEY TALKS ABOUT PAINTING

Ramon Kelley is a self-taught artist who is constantly expanding his command of various painting media. In this interview, he answers questions about his own experience with pastel, watercolor, and oil. He also talks about his studio, professionalism, his philosophy, and his goals.

PAINTING IN MULTIPLE MEDIA

You're a multi-media artist. How did you branch out into so many media?

In my first gallery at Taos, New Mexico, I was accepted on the strength of my charcoal drawings and I really believed that I could be an artist with only one medium. That was all I exhibited. But after I began exhibiting, I realized soon enough that I'd have to learn to paint in oil. There was no way to avoid it. Soon one of my buyers who had several drawings asked for a painting.

I quickly did ten oils. Those were almost the first serious paintings I ever did in my life. I took them down to Taos and the director of the gallery rejected nine of them. When you stop and think about it, it's a miracle that she even accepted one! Well, since then, I've worked my head off learning to paint.

Even before I began painting, I was more or less coerced into adding color to my drawings. My earliest professional work was in charcoal or sepia chalk. I added color with pastel. I wasn't doing pastel paintings at that time—only colored drawings.

After I began to feel more in control of oil, I approached pastel differently. If you start working in a demanding medium, such as oil, it becomes much easier to switch to a less demanding medium. When I began to paint pastels, the knowledge of color I'd acquired from painting in oil was easy to adapt to pastel. The colors of pastel sticks are available in a pre-mixed range of values. I found color control easier in pastel for this reason; I could choose the color I wanted, rather than having to mix it as I did in oil. I also found it stimulating to change from oil to pastel.

Again, when I began painting in watercolor, I did it on my own—the way I've done everything—and I attacked it in a broad manner, laying in washes the same way I do in oil and pastel. I use bristle brushes rather than the customary soft sables. My approach worked for me. After the first watercolor, I became more and more confident with the medium.

I'm at the point now when I can go round and round from one medium to another. Painting in oil is the most demanding, though oil is still my favorite. However, I never find it laborious because, as soon as I feel that I'm getting stale, I change to another medium. I paint with acrylic, do lithographs, and sculpt a bit as well.

In oil painting, one builds toward the lights; in watercolor, the lights must be saved or washed off. Do you find it confusing to switch from one approach to the other?

Starting a watercolor, for me, is similar to the first step of an oil painting—that is, I lay in a wash. If I get a good wash down, then I have my watercolor. In an oil, I go back into the washes with impasto. In pastel, I often begin with watercolor washes too. Over the washes, I add pastel strokes boldly, which is like the impasto I use over the washes when I paint in oil.

In an oil, if I should want a light area, I can always add opaque white strokes. When I paint in my watercolor washes, there are usually nice light areas I want to save; but if I should cover up an area that I want to have in a higher key, it isn't too hard to wash or scrub it out.

Since my approach to the three media is really the same, I don't find multi-media painting confusing. I change media for variety and pleasure, but I try to retain a similar approach to all of them. However, I don't make formulas for myself or do exactly the same thing in the same way every time I paint. For me the act of creating a painting is getting a three-dimensional feeling on a flat surface—and that is the beautiful part of painting. I don't want it to become labor. That would show in my work and it would lose its zing. Changing media helps me to stay fresh.

Do you paint a series of paintings in one medium before changing to another, or do you constantly rotate from one medium to the next?

Yes, I do paint a series in one medium: then I change to another.

To prepare for a show, I start with oils because they require a longer drying time. Then I paint watercolors, and last, pastels. The oils and watercolors help my pastel painting.

When I'm not working on a show, I just paint with whatever medium I feel like. For me, this is a beautiful way to work. When I feel myself running downhill, I switch media. I feel sorry for the one-medium artist. A person can fall into a rut, working with the same style, subject matter, and medium. The work is exhibited and collected and every collector has one: so where does the artist go then? I feel lucky to be able to paint in more than one medium. It's fun!

You say that you mix watercolor and pastel. Do you ever mix any other media?

Yes, I mix pastel and watercolor, but that's almost all I mix. I *have* experimented. I remember one time I painted oils over acrylics, but that's a no-no because acrylics are plastic. They react to weather by expanding in warmth and shrinking in cold at a different rate from oils. Experimenting shows you what *not* to do, as well as what will work. I've tried putting washes under my Conté drawings, some low key and some high key. But mostly, I'm a direct painter.

Are you primarily a studio painter?

I was exclusively a studio painter until fairly recently. In 1973, I got interested in painting outdoors and I began teaching outdoor workshops every year. Painting outdoors makes you really see what's there and gives you an understanding of what the artists of the past— especially the French Impressionists—felt and saw. Trying to capture the color that's actually in front of my eyes is very enjoyable.

There's no reason to prefer one over the other—studio versus outdoors. But I *am* getting deeper into painting from life and painting outdoors. And I find it's a lot easier than painting from photographs, contrary to popular belief. When you can see your model or the subject, there it is: you just have to use your ability to capture it.

However, I do use photographs as supplements in studio work. Outdoors, I do direct sketching in oils and I take photographs. Then I come back to the studio to paint in a larger format, using both the photos and the sketches as reference. My oil sketch is my map for color.

I find it much too difficult to paint outside on a large scale. The light changes too rapidly. You almost have to complete the painting in two hours. Now, I don't really paint large pictures: 16" x 20" (40.6 x 50.8 cm) to 18" x 24" (45.7 x 61 cm) is usually a comfortable range for me. But even these sizes are too large, I think, for me to complete outdoors.

I also do a lot of still lifes; I set up my subject on the model stand and paint it directly as I would a live model. I prefer to paint figures from life, but I can't always do it. Sometimes a pose I want is too difficult for a model to hold for a long period, so I may use a photograph for it. If I can't get what I want from life, I do use photographs in my studio.

STUDIO AND EQUIPMENT

We recently bought a 70-year-old, four-story house in Denver. Beside it is a carriage house that I've had remodeled for my studio. We expect to live in this house for many years, so my studio is the result of considerable planning.

I had the left half of the two-story building gutted, removing interior walls and floor so that the ceiling of my main studio is 21' (6.5 m) above the floor. Large northern windows with adjustable shades are 18' (5.5 m) in height. They provide ample natural daylight both downstairs and also in my upstairs studio where I paint pastels and watercolors.

On the right wall are stairs made from old wood I had brought down from Steamboat Springs, Colorado; I've used other pieces of it for beams to give strength to the structure, for shutters upstairs, for a cabinet around the sink, and for a mount to house my banks of Criticolor fluorescent tubes. I have two 8' (2.4 m) banks that are hung 3½' (1 m) over my oil setup and another two 8' (2.4 m) banks upstairs over my pastel setup.

My downstairs studio is 20' x 21' (6 x 6.5 m). I have a Victorian fainting couch in one corner where models pose. An antique barber's chair is near my easel. I use it to take a break, smoke my pipe, and inspect my newest painting. In cabinets, one an ancient one from Mexico, I have supplies. My palette for oils is a big piece of milk glass, salvaged from an old drugstore, that covers an 1886 chest full of small drawers. I keep tubes of fresh paint in them. At the back of the palette I keep a tube of each color I use. My brushes are on the sides in pots or laid out ready to use.

There's a workroom on the first floor, under my upstairs studio. This is where I prepare my canvas, frame paintings, and do all the handyman things that an artist must do if he has a busy career.

Upstairs, off a small balcony, is a pleasant studio. I have a drafting table, ample bookshelves where I house my growing collection of art books, and a rolling table where I keep my pastels laid out ready to use. When I change to watercolors, I just lay my palette right over the pas-

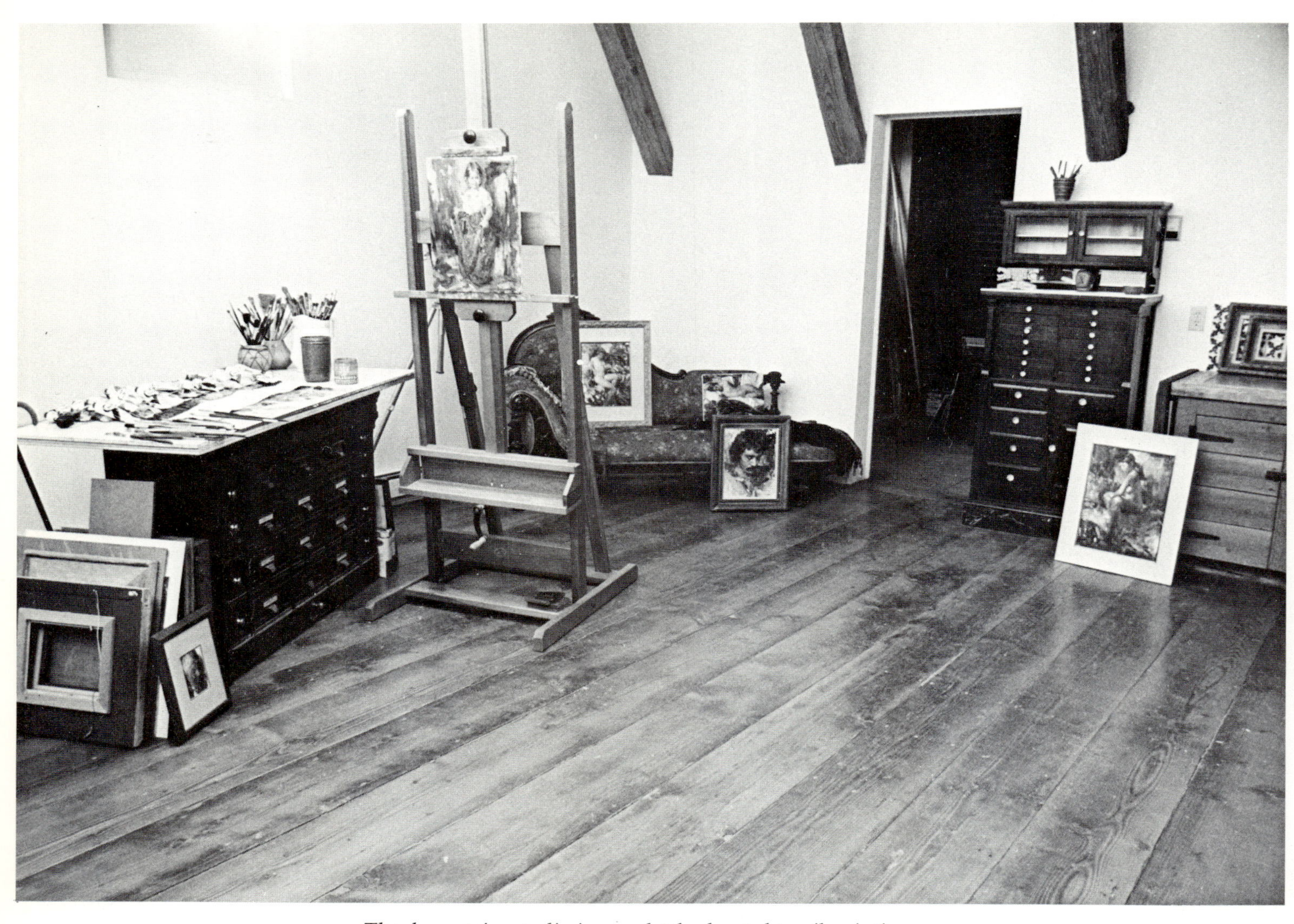

The downstairs studio is completely devoted to oil painting.

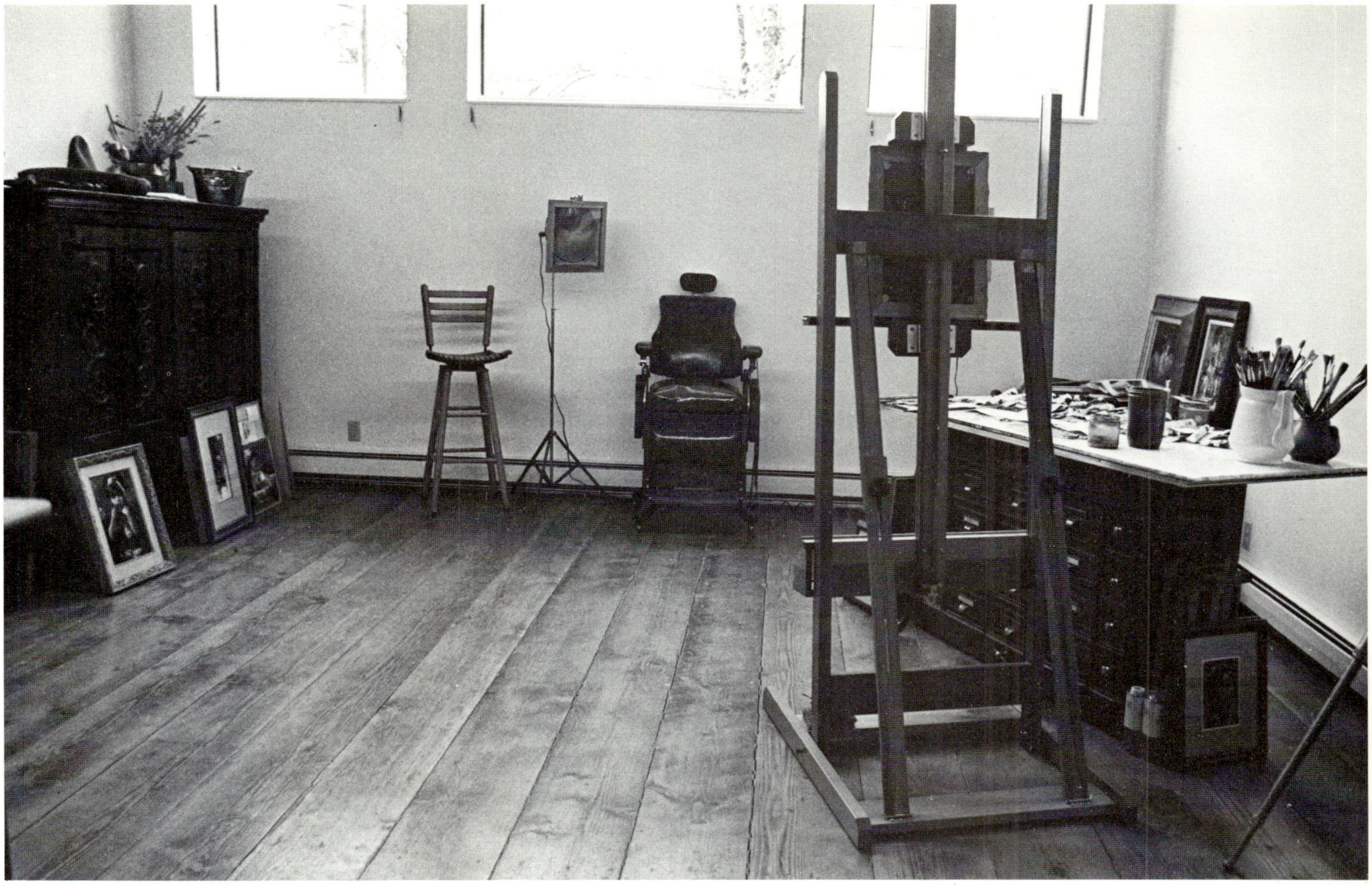

The oil painting setup and downstairs studio as seen from the opposite side of the room.

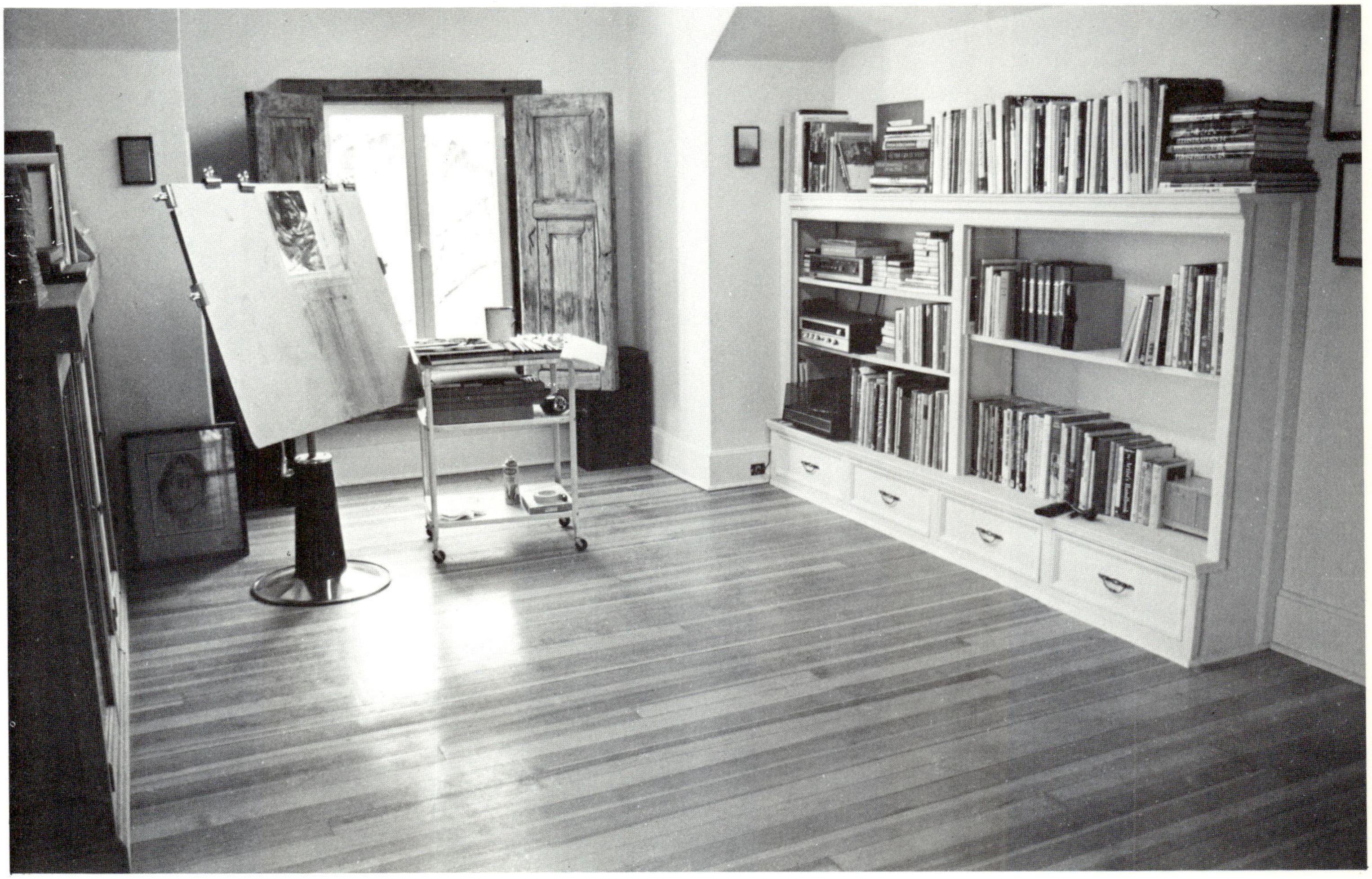

A view of the upstairs studio where Ramon paints both watercolors and pastels.

tels and start to work. In a closet under the eaves I have my files with a large collection of postcards of old-master paintings, past issues of *American Artist,* and correspondence. There is a bathroom on this floor also, and excellent southern light as well as north light coming from the balcony. My banks of Criticolor fluorescent lights (manufactured by Verd-a-Ray) allow me to paint on through the night without being troubled by deficient light. My stereo and classical music tapes are on the shelf. It is stimulating and soothing to me to have a background of music as I paint.

I've painted in bedrooms without an easel and I've set up several studios before. But this one is the most efficient one I've had, and it's also comfortable and attractive. The antique furnishings appeal to me. For the first time in my career, I'm free to just paint. I no longer have to be diverted by conducting my own sales; I'm not interrupted anymore. I spend so much time now in my studio that it's a pleasure to have one I like this well.

How did you select the lighting in your studio?

When I first started working, there was only artificial light in our apartment—warm or cool incandescent light. After we moved into our present home, I still used only light bulbs, but I soon found that they wouldn't do.

I did some research, made phone calls, and found the lighting I now have. This is Criticolor by Verd-a-Ray Corporation. The company manager came out and explained these lights. He put a small bank of Criticolor over my palette and I saw my oil colors for the first time under artificial light. The lights must be no more than 4' (1.2 m) from the palette. They come in 2', 4', 6', or 8' (0.5, 1.2, 1.8, or 2.4 m) banks.

I also have a lot of northern light from windows. During the day, I paint by this natural light, but I also turn on the Criticolor lights. That way, if I paint into the evening, there isn't much change in the light. Thus, my studio is equipped for both day and night painting, as Criticolor is as close to natural light as possible.

The small expense of these lights will make any studio well-lighted. It's worth noting that museums and paint manufacturers also use Criticolor.

What type of easel do you use and what would you recommend?

I have two easels. My watercolor easel is a standard, heavyweight aluminum easel with a tilting top and a lift. My oil easel is a good one, costing $350; it's sturdy and can hold anything from a small canvas to a really large one. I move my easels in and out of the same spot near my taboret.

But no one needs to spend a fortune on an easel at first. Before I had any equipment at all, I tacked my paper and canvas directly on the wall and painted on it. There's always a way around everything, even poverty. My first easel was a spindly little sketching easel that sort of walked around the studio with me, but it worked.

Most artists are handy with tools and can make their own easels. But when a person can afford it, a good professional easel is a delight and I do recommend it.

What's your preference in brushes?

I have quite a collection of brushes. I prefer my old, used, worn brushes to my new ones. Not only do the old ones have more character, but I've used them, bent them, and twisted them so long that they're almost a part of me.

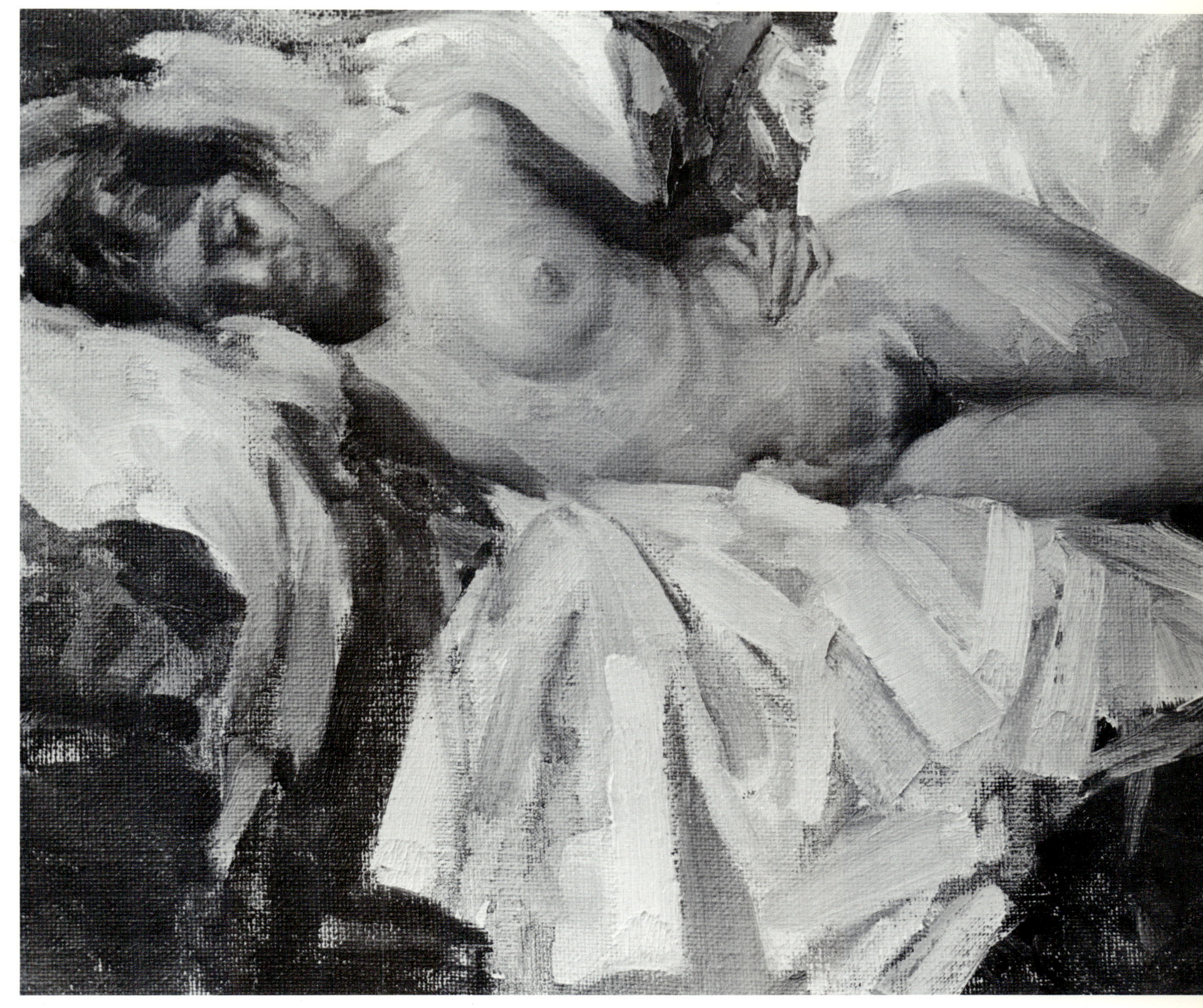

Nude. *Oil on canvas, 9" x 12" (23 x 30.5 cm). This was painted on Belsize, a pre-primed, English linen canvas whose rough texture adds interest to the painting. A photograph and a small sketch inspired this painting. There are only four major shapes in the composition. My intention was to get the figure to emerge from the drapery. The direction of the brushstrokes in the foreground leads the eye to the model. It's an easy painting to read. In all areas except the figure, the original strokes show in the final painting.*

I prefer flats for oil painting. They make a nice broad stroke or a thin line when I paint with the edge. I use numbers 3, 6, 10, and 12. I use filberts less often—I find them good for blending—in sizes 4, 6, and 10. I use small sables, numbers 4 and 5, for finer lines such as tree branches. I don't use sables in portraits. I don't use egberts—the bristles seem a bit long for me—and I don't use blenders.

For watercolor, I use oil brushes. I lay washes with a 2½" (6.5 cm) flat oil brush. For detail, I use smaller oil flats. Occasionally I'll work with a flat sable watercolor brush.

Of course, I buy a lot more brushes than I actually use.

PASTEL PAINTING

Could you describe your pastel painting setup?

The photograph below shows my setup for pastel painting. I have a stack of paper toweling on the far left. I buy this by the box in flat sheets, fifty pounds at a time. I use it in all my work to clean my hands, dust off, and wipe up. A can of Krylon workable fixative is just beside the towels.

On the left, below the fixative, are my hard pastels: Nupastels by Eberhard-Faber. I use them in linear drawings or for a detailed work. Notice that there are new sticks and also broken pieces. I use my sticks flat, rather than working with the tip. I think of the pastel as making a painting stroke, not a line. When I do need a line, I can sharpen the stick on sandpaper.

In the center of the table are my Rembrandt soft pastels. Again, new sticks are above, broken ones closer at hand. As I use up a chunk, I replace it from the new sticks.

You can see a stump next to the new sticks of Rembrandt pastels. Sometimes I use it for blending, but not often. I prefer to use the little finger of my right hand for feathering.

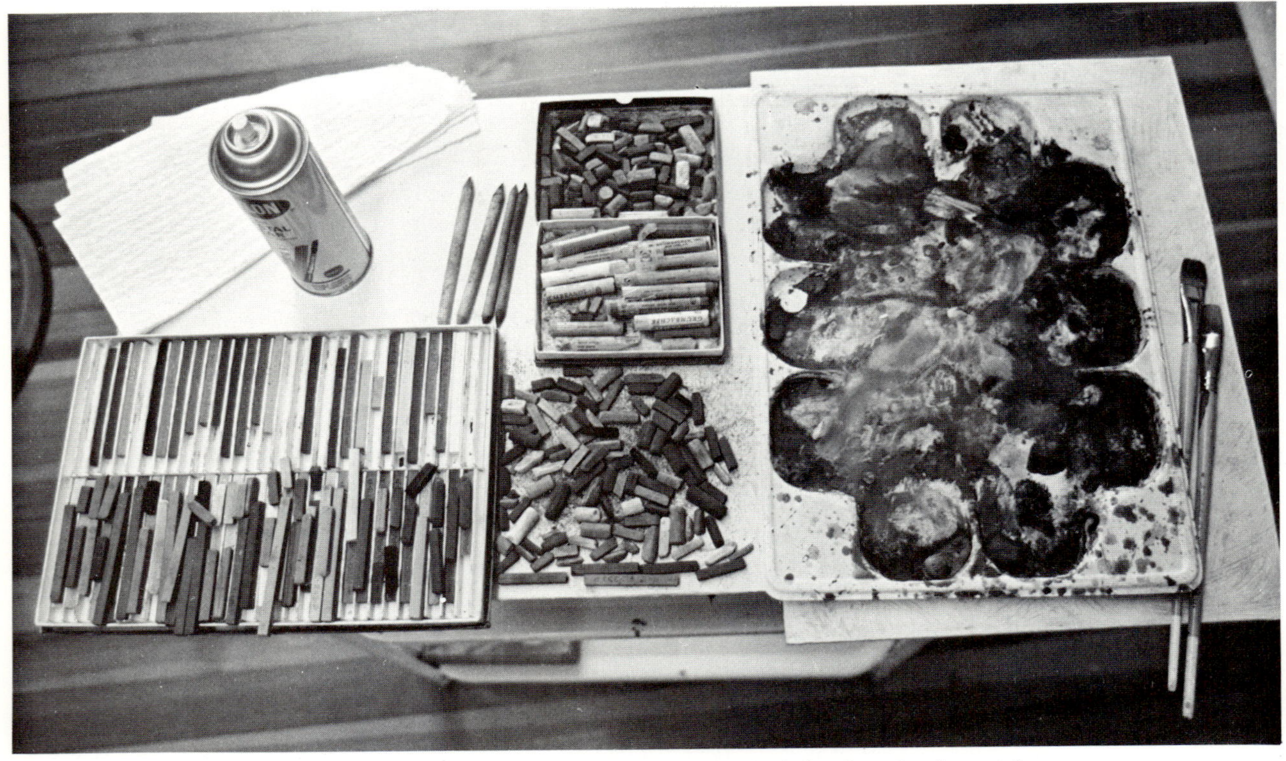

The setup for pastel painting includes both hard and soft pastels.

On the far right is my watercolor "palette," a white plastic tray. There are two nylon bristle brushes beside it. I often use watercolors as an underpainting for pastels, although not always. When I do lay a wash, I do quite a bit of scumbling with Grumbacher nylon bristle flats, sizes 8 and 12. These can really take the beating I give them when I lay in washes.

What type of pastels do you prefer and what colors do you buy?

As you notice in the photograph of my pastel setup, I use Rembrandt soft pastels. There's less binder in them. To me, they seem more like oils than harder pastels do. When I make a stroke with pastel, I want the color to imbed itself in the tooth of the paper as easily as the soft pastel does. I also buy the harder sticks, Nupastels, which are useful occasionally for lines and details.

In pastels, I buy two or three values of each single color. For example, I'll buy three values of cadmium red. The beauty of pastel is that colors are pre-mixed in a wide range of values, making it much easier for the pastel painter to get the shade he wants.

My palette includes:

Black	Ultramarine blue
Burnt sienna	Cobalt blue
Raw sienna	Cadmium yellow
Burnt umber	Cadmium orange
Raw umber	Vermilion
Terra rosa	Cadmium red
Viridian	Alizarin crimson
Phthalo green	Cobalt violet
Phthalo yellow green	White

When you're using pastels, do you leave the sticks wrapped? How do you keep track of which color you're using and which you must replace?

New sticks of soft pastel come wrapped in thin paper. I break off about an inch of a fresh stick, along with a small amount of the wrapper, and I use it up, absolutely down to nothing. Then I remove another chunk of pastel to replace it, still saving the wrapper for identification. I put out a new stick beside the old stick, so I never lose track of the color or its number. The harder Nupastels don't have wrappers. I just put a new stick next to the last clean chunk of a color, so there's a reserve supply waiting at all times. I keep a big supply of new sticks in drawers in a cabinet.

Familiarity with your own pastel palette saves a lot of frustration. It becomes instinctive to notice when a color is used up and needs replacing, and to break off another piece. It also helps to use a limited number of colors; there aren't so many to remember.

Pastel sticks must be wiped off constantly, as they pick up dust from the painting and from each other. I use my paper towels for this almost automatically as I paint. This keeps the color of the sticks clear and helps me find the little piece I need. The more automatically an artist learns to handle his equipment, the more energy he can save for spontaneous painting.

What types of pastel paper do you prefer?

I prefer the French Canson Mi-Teintes tinted paper and also Strathmore charcoal paper. They both have a good medium tooth. But my favorite surface is a rough, sanded, pastel paper mounted on sturdy board by Grumbacher, 22" x 28" (56 x 71 cm). I buy them in packages of half-a-dozen at a time.

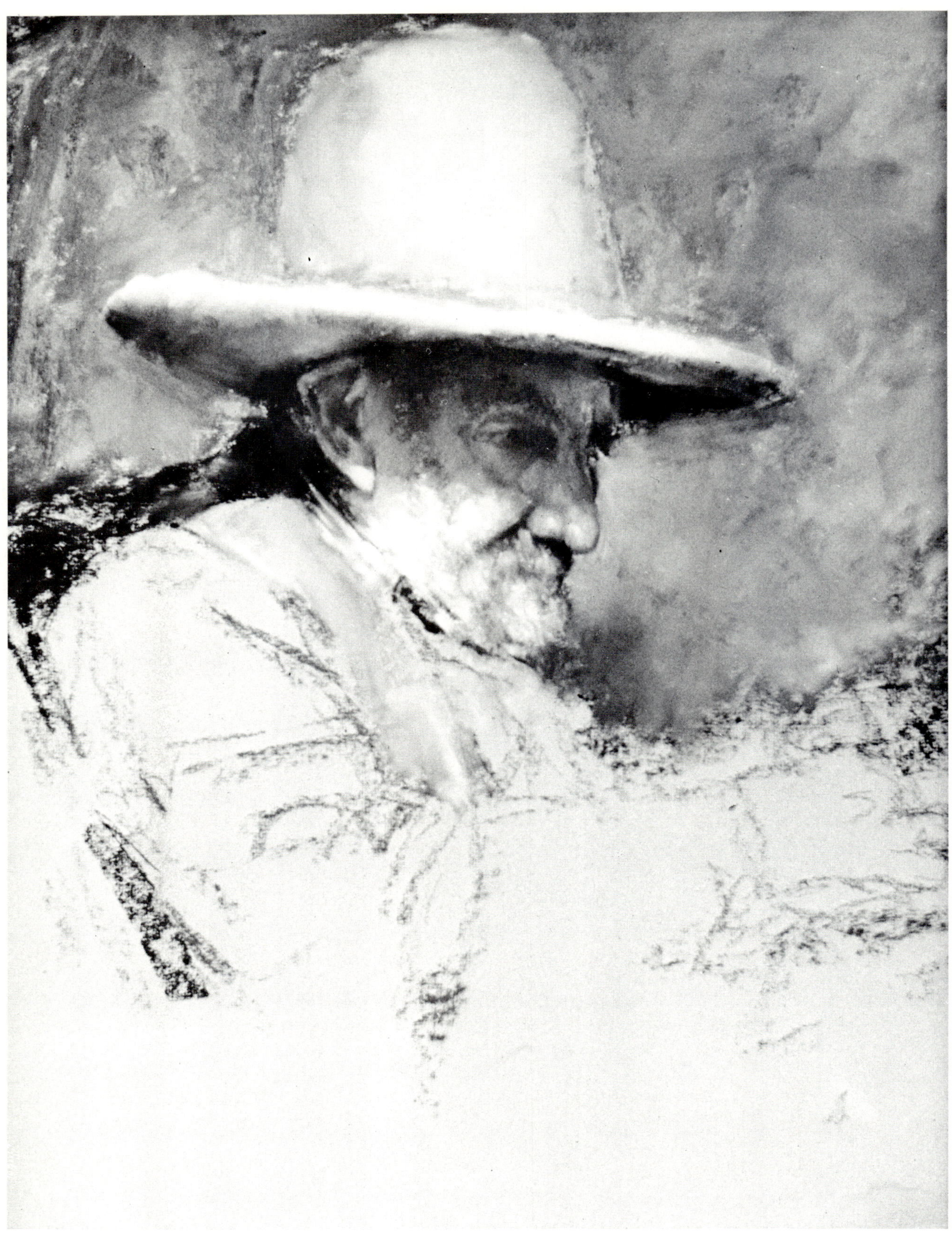

El Señor. *Pastel on paper, 20" x 16" (51 x 40.5 cm). I sketched this portrait of Grandpa Trujillo with the flat side of a 1" (2.5 cm) long chunk of raw umber pastel. I had to work rapidly because, at ninety-six, Grandpa found it hard to hold the pose. The shadow cast on the face from the brim of the hat was my key to the values in the painting—everything else had to be lighter. The light falling on the hat and cheek accentuates the shadow by contrast. Although the face and background are finished, the foreground is a simple sketch.*

Do you use fixative on your pastels?

I have two methods for painting a pastel. In one, I paint directly, without any buildup in layers, and frame behind glass—period.

In the other method, I do a quick layout and fix it. Then I paint another layer and fix that—proceeding in steps until the last layer, which I don't fix. I use a mouth atomizer to apply the fixative when I work like this. I use only the workable fixative. Fixatives come in a matte or gloss finish; I use the matte.

I keep my board slanted steeply forward. This allows the excess dust on the painting to fall to the floor, where it can be cleaned later. Painting on a vertical surface, into the loose dust, doesn't work well.

When the painting is finished, I hold the top edge with my fingers and give the picture a good smack against my old barber chair. Then I turn it upside down and smack it again. This loosens any specks of pastel dust that aren't adhering to the picture. This must be done before putting it in a mat or under glass—to prevent pastel dust from falling to the bottom of the mat.

How do you mix colors in a pastel painting?

When I paint with pastel, I hold the short, broken pastel stick in my right hand between my thumb and forefinger. I feather some strokes with the little finger as I move my hand over the picture. But I don't overuse feathering. In other areas, I lay strokes side by side and allow them to interact and "mix" visually. I change pressure so that some strokes fade out. Edges interest me and I try to vary them: firm in one area, blending and fading out elsewhere.

In pastel, other factors affect the mixing of color, too. Allowing underlayers to show through will affect color. Heavy impasto creates a different color effect than a delicate application. The tone of the paper itself affects the color placed on it.

What's your procedure in painting a typical portrait or figure in pastel?

When I model a figure or portrait, I think in terms of planes, and the first thing I go after is placement. Working on a head, for instance, I use broad strokes of dark sepia to suggest the head structure, eyes, nose, and mouth. The first strokes of color I put in are my darkest darks—on the hair, on the shadowed side of the head, in the shadows under the chin, and under the cheek on the lighter side of the head. I leave the areas of lightest value open.

In the second layer of color, I use a combination of colors—a warm and a cool—both darker than middle value. I stroke the colors broadly on the lighter side of the face, cranium area, cheek, and chin, allowing the darks of the underpainting to show through. I work on both sides of the face. In the shadows, I use cooler tones—especially under the nose and chin—to give an illusion of three-dimensional form.

On top of these layers go my middle values of warm colors. I lay a mixture of strokes in several colors on areas that are still open, but I save the highlights to be painted later.

This progression from dark to light is similar to the sculptor's way of building a form with clay. The lightest areas compare to the highest points—those which project furthest and hence catch the light. Highlights are most often found on the forehead, cheekbone, bridge and tip of the nose, upper lip, lower lip, and chin.

When I start a portrait in pastel, I often lay watercolor washes to model the form. When they're dry, I work over them with heavy impasto strokes of pastel.

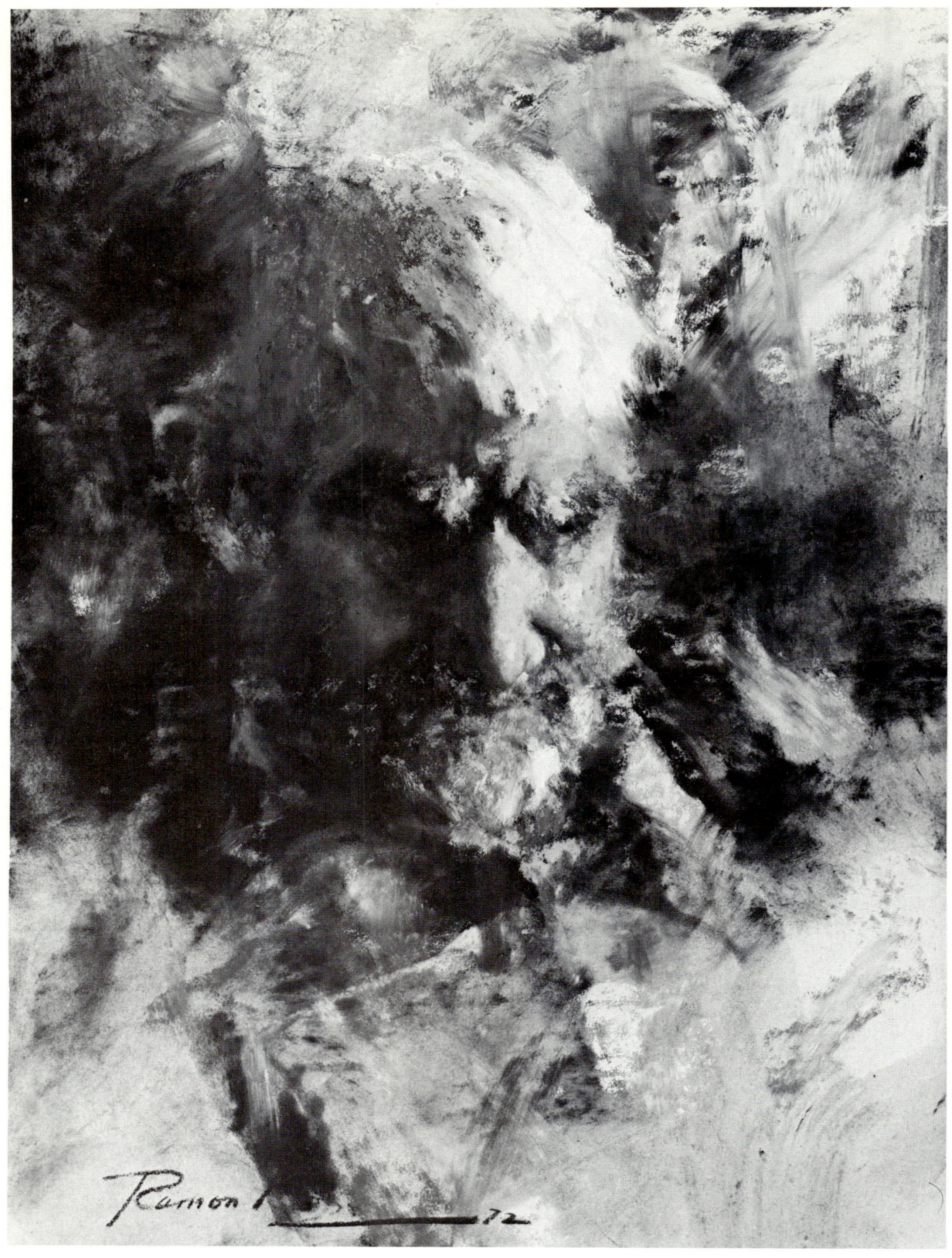

Grandpo Trujillo. *Pastel over watercolor on rough sanded board, 16" x 12" (40.5 x 30.5 cm). Working on a sanded board, I began by toning the surface lightly with a watercolor wash on burnt umber. I didn't try to cover the board completely—open areas can still be seen in both corners. In this impressionistic painting, all edges are soft. I was attempting a dramatic, chiaroscuro effect here with intense light on the hair and a strong shadow on the left side of the head. The face emerges beautifully from the soft, dark background. Note how the edges are defined on the lighted side of the face as they stand out against the darker background, while the contrast between the hair and the background above is more subtle. A color temperature contrast (not visible in this black and white photograph)—cooler on the hair and warmer on the background—separates the head from the background.*

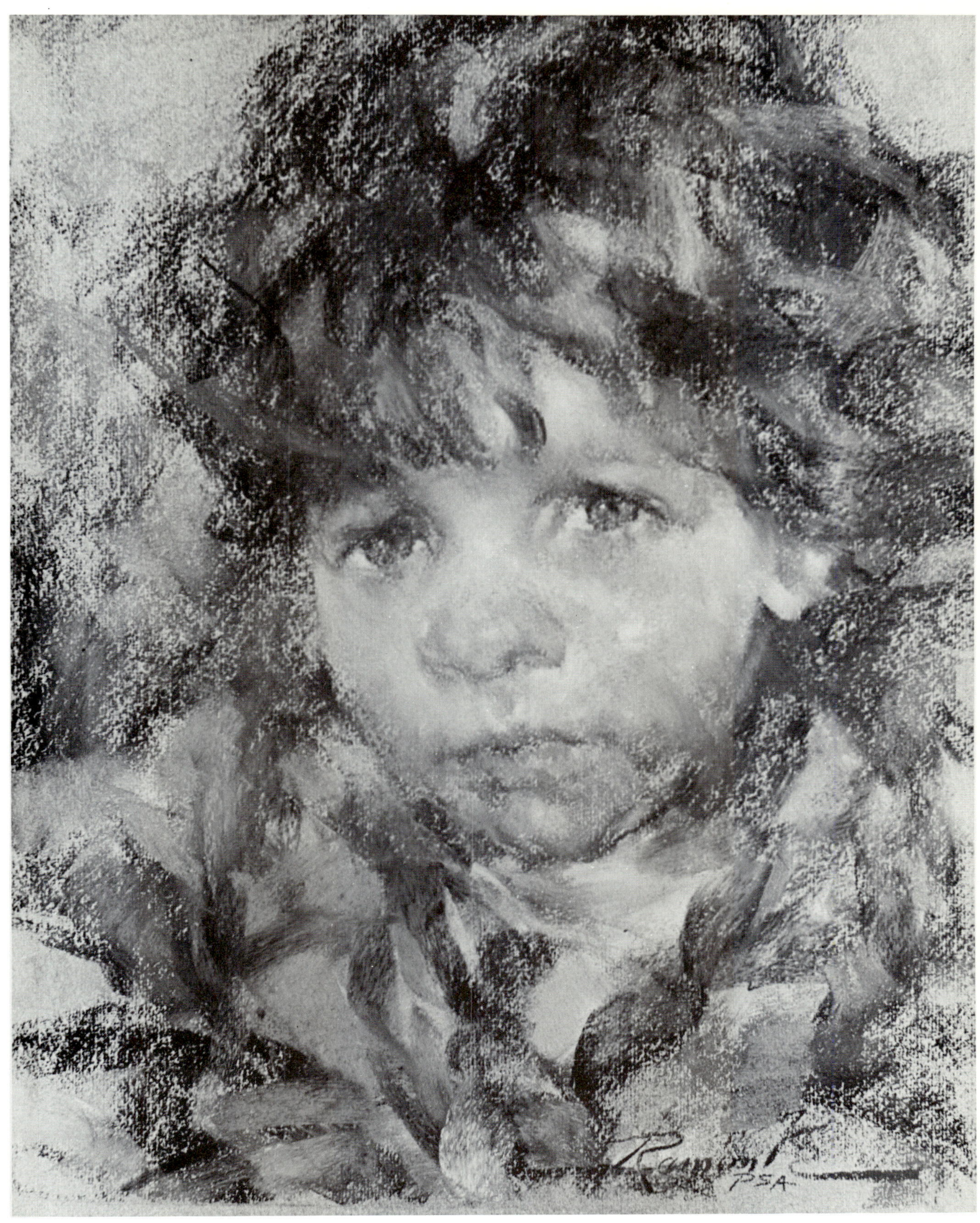

Ashley. *Pastel on paper, 12" x 9" (30.5 x 23 cm). Pastel lends itself to a variety of effects. In this painting, the hair, background, and blouse give almost a drybrush feeling. I handled it like a drawing, with the emphasis on facial features. There's an economy of means in the painting. Each area is extremely simple, but seen as a whole the painting reads as a shy three-year-old. This is a high-key painting in a limited range of values. It's more difficult to pull off such a work because there are no intense darks for contrast.*

I always say, "I lay down my first big basic mistake and then correct it, stage by stage, to the final painting."

In the underlayers, I make crude strokes and gradually refine them to build the main features of the portrait: the eyes, nose, and mouth. From these, I move to less important areas: the ears, hair, hands, drapery, and background. The first thing that catches your eye in a portrait should be the face. The rest should seem complete, but never dominant.

You often paint portraits. What are your goals in portraiture?

I'm not a commercial portrait painter and I don't do commissioned portraits. I choose a subject I want to do: Indians, Mexicans, children, or old men. An exact likeness isn't what I'm seeking, so much as the character of the subject, although I can be precise about a likeness when I want to be.

I make a strong effort to capture a mood or a feeling. I don't want to become so preoccupied with exactness that I forget to create the beauty of design or the rich brushstroke quality that makes a painting. In my view, paint quality takes precedence over likeness.

WATERCOLOR PAINTING

Tell us about your watercolor setup.

In the photograph below you can see a closeup of my setup for watercolor painting, which is in my upstairs studio. I have a large pot of water, tubes of paint, and a large plastic watercolor tray that I use for my palette on the table. This is the same table that I use for pastels.

My brushes are kind of an odd selection for most watercolorists. The brushes I use are as follows: Two nylon bristle brushes by Grumbacher,

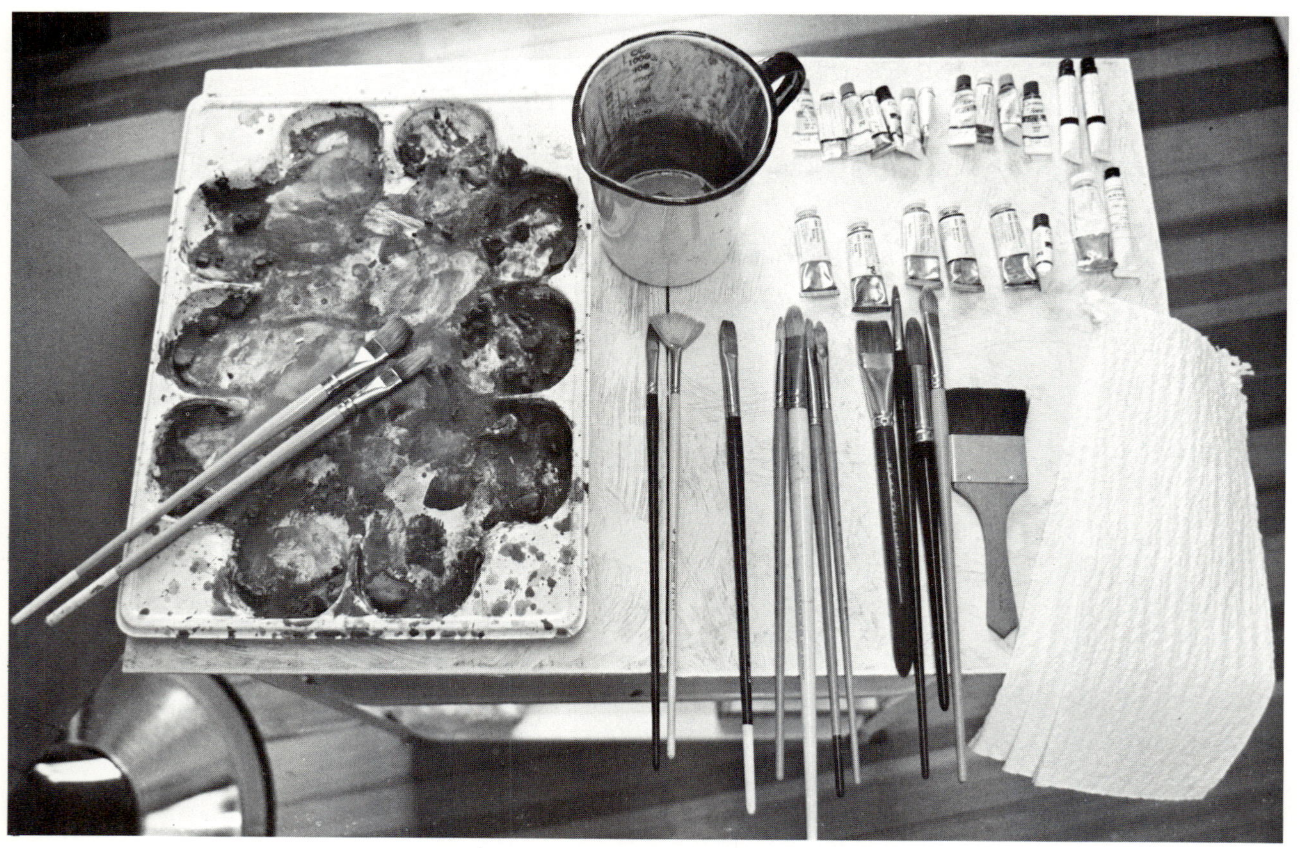

The supplies for watercolor are arranged neatly and efficiently in the upstairs studio.

numbers 8 and 12, which are in both this setup and in my pastel setup. (They're on the palette at the left of the photograph.) Then there are five filberts. I have a regular 1" (2.5 cm) flat watercolor sable with a chiseled handle, a Grumbacher number 1 oil sable, a Winsor & Newton number 18 watercolor sable, another bristle brush and a wide Japanese Haki brush with a short handle. It may seem unbelievable, but I paint my watercolors almost entirely with oil painting brushes. I keep a set of them upstairs and another set downstairs in my studio. It's the end results that an artist seeks—and I can achieve the kind of painting I prefer with these bristle brushes.

What's your water-color palette—the colors and brands?

I buy Chinese white and ivory black in large number 5 tubes. Most of my paint is Winsor & Newton in number 2 tubes. Here are the colors I buy in addition to black and white:

Raw sienna	Cadmium yellow
Burnt sienna	Cadmium orange (Permanent Pigments)
Winsor green	Cadmium red medium
French ultramarine blue	Winsor emerald green
Cobalt blue	Yellow ochre
Cadmium lemon yellow	Alizarin crimson

What type of water-color paper do you use?

I regularly use Arches 140 lb paper for figures. I choose the 300 lb for landscapes. In watercolor, I'm mostly a figure painter, but I've also done a number of market scenes in watercolor on Grumbacher sand board. This is a little harder to control than regular paper, but it gives interesting effects.

Do you stretch your watercolor paper?

I've never stretched or soaked my watercolor paper. I tape the paper to the drawing board, sponge the sheet to dampen it, and dry it with paper toweling. Then I'm ready to start. As I work, the paper will begin to buckle and develop mountains and valleys; I just run a hairdryer over the paper and it flattens out. After you put a good bit of water on the paper and go over it with a dryer, the sheet gets tight as a drum.

Many artists paint watercolors with their boards slanted at a slight angle. Do you do this?

I paint with the easel upright and the board straight up and down. I get a few runs, but it isn't much of a problem. I can't see the painting properly when it's flat or slightly tilted. I like to walk back and forth and look at my work as I do it; so I do all of my painting with the paper, board, or canvas straight up and down.

How do you mix colors when you're painting a water-color?

I mix colors in my plastic tray before I paint them on the sheet. But I also mix colors *visually* by overlaying one wash upon another. There *are* times when I can lay a single wash and that's all I'll want—so there won't be any layers over it. But most often I lay several washes over each other.

What's your proce-dure when you paint a watercolor?

In oil, I work toward the lights; in watercolor, I must reverse my think-ing, leaving the lights and highlights open, and working toward the darkest darks.

I go into the watercolor first with light washes. It's a fast medium and so I paint fast. I've practiced so much that it's natural for me to leave areas for the lights open where I need them.

I aim first for the basic, big, broad shape—either the face or the figure —in very light washes. I have no formulas, so I can't say that I use one particular color for the initial wash: it depends entirely on the subject. I hope to do something new each time I paint. I don't want to fall back on something I've done before, so I change in order to keep actively interested and avoid repetition. I might begin with a warm, very light sepia wash, or maybe a flesh tone.

If a live model is posing, I can see the shape in the first wash. When I look at the shape, I feel the way a sculptor feels when he looks at a stone: I can see something in it already. I know just where I need to put my darks and middle values to bring it out.

In the next phase, I lay in my middle tones on the hair, background, and some of the edges away from the light. These are cool areas. In the warm areas, I use middle tones of the flesh colors. To this point, everything is pretty broadly done with bristle brushes.

From here on, I can go more for detail, so I switch to a flat sable watercolor brush or a smaller size oil filbert. With the smaller brush, I can define the edge of the figure or the face, the eyes, under the nose, the center of the lips, the eyebrows. I touch in these linear elements here and there. These are my darkest darks, but they're not black. I might use a warm dark in one area and a cool dark in another.

At this stage, I've established a rough shape in color and I've defined it more with line and with dark touches. I've established my lightest lights and my darkest darks. At the same time, I've left parts open. I've been looking at the whole shape, not at details. I squint to see the *entire form* while I'm painting—that's what I work on capturing first.

Now I work on modeling. I don't necessarily paint more slowly, but I do paint attentively, working at firming up, searching for accuracy. I don't carry detail too far. I paint strong *suggestions* of things. I try to achieve this with the most limited amount of detail. By the time I get to the modeling stage, I'm close to finished.

I always work on the background and the figure simultaneously, so they're at the same stage of completeness. I play down the background, with the merest amount of description.

Before finishing, I study the painting. There's almost always something I want to scrub out and bring back to a lighter value. Maybe I'll want a highlight on the forehead. To lighten an area, I use a clean, damp bristle brush to loosen the pigment. Then I blot it with toweling. If necessary, I'll scrape out a highlight with a razor—on the tip of the nose or in the eye, for example.

OIL PAINTING

Now tell us about your setup for oil painting.

In the photograph on page 40 you can see the oil tubes set out in back of the palette, with the paint itself squeezed out on the palette, directly in front of the tubes.

The brushes I use are on the right. I use mostly filberts and flats, as well as smaller sables for the more detailed work. I have a few egberts for gathering more paint. These long brushes work beautifully for a long, loaded brushstroke.

There are a lot of knives in this picture, but the ones I use most are the straight-edged, round-tipped 2" (5.5 cm) knife and the 1½" (4 cm) elongated, triangle-shaped knife.

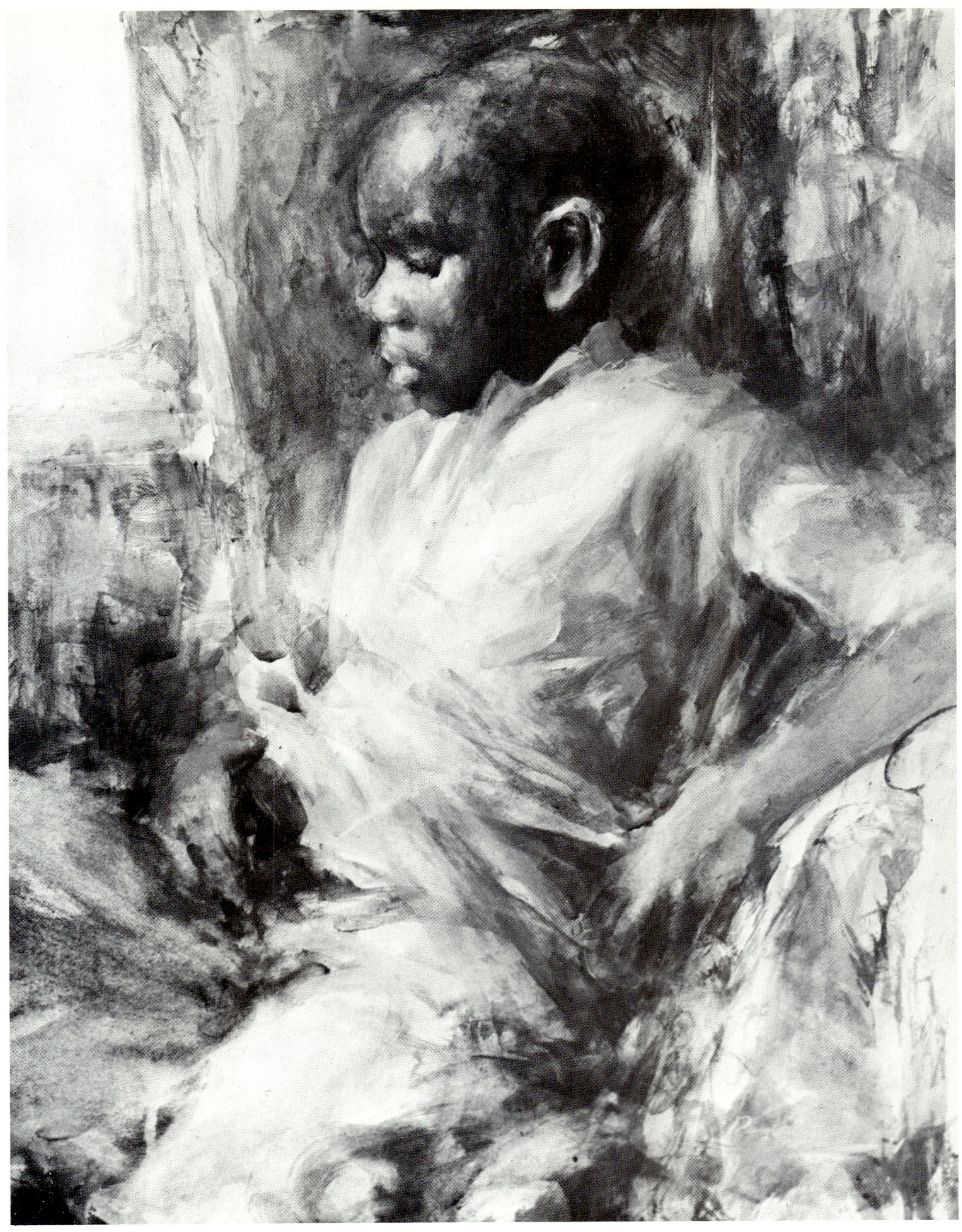

Little Mack. *Watercolor on illustration board, 20" x 16" (51 x 40.5 cm). This was the first watercolor I ever painted. I submitted it to the American Watercolor Society show in New York City in 1971 where it not only got accepted, but took a prize. Since I went at watercolor cold, without previous instruction, my first instinct was to handle it like oil paint. This led to very interesting results in the preliminary washes. After viewing the first stages of the painting from a distance, I was so pleased with the effect of the transparent underwashes, that I painted the entire picture transparently. I was using small- and medium-size bristle brushes. My aim was to create a three-dimensional form; therefore I was concerned with modeling and edges. Notice the strong profile of the face and the blurred edge of the trousers. Because I was painting on a board, not on paper, and because the surface was dry, the edge of the profile is sharply delineated. The more fused areas were done with overlaid washes. I saved the white of the board for the highlights.*

I keep turpentine in food jars. In the largest jar, I have a tin can at the bottom. The can is pierced with nail holes. When I wash my brushes in this jar, the sediment falls under the can; this keeps the turpentine clean. I clean my brush after every stroke. This way, every stroke is clean and the colors on the canvas are clean. After I swish the brush around in the first jar, I move the brush to the smaller jar of clean turpentine and finally wipe it on a towel. When I paint with oils, I keep the turpentine and towels off to the side on a table.

What's your oil palette—the colors and brands?

Here's my palette as I set it out from left to right:

Ivory black (Permanent Pigments)
Raw sienna (Permanent Pigments)
Burnt sienna deep (Blockx)
Terra rosa (Winsor & Newton)
Phthalo green (Grumbacher)
Viridian (Permanent Pigments)
French ultramarine blue (Permanent Pigments)
Cobalt blue (Permanent Pigments)
Cadmium yellow light (Permanent Pigments)
Cadmium yellow (Winsor & Newton)
Cadmium orange (Permanent Pigments)
Cadmium scarlet (Winsor & Newton)
Phthalo yellow green (Grumbacher)
Yellow ochre (Permanent Pigments)
Alizarin crimson (Permanent Pigments)
Superba white (Grumbacher)

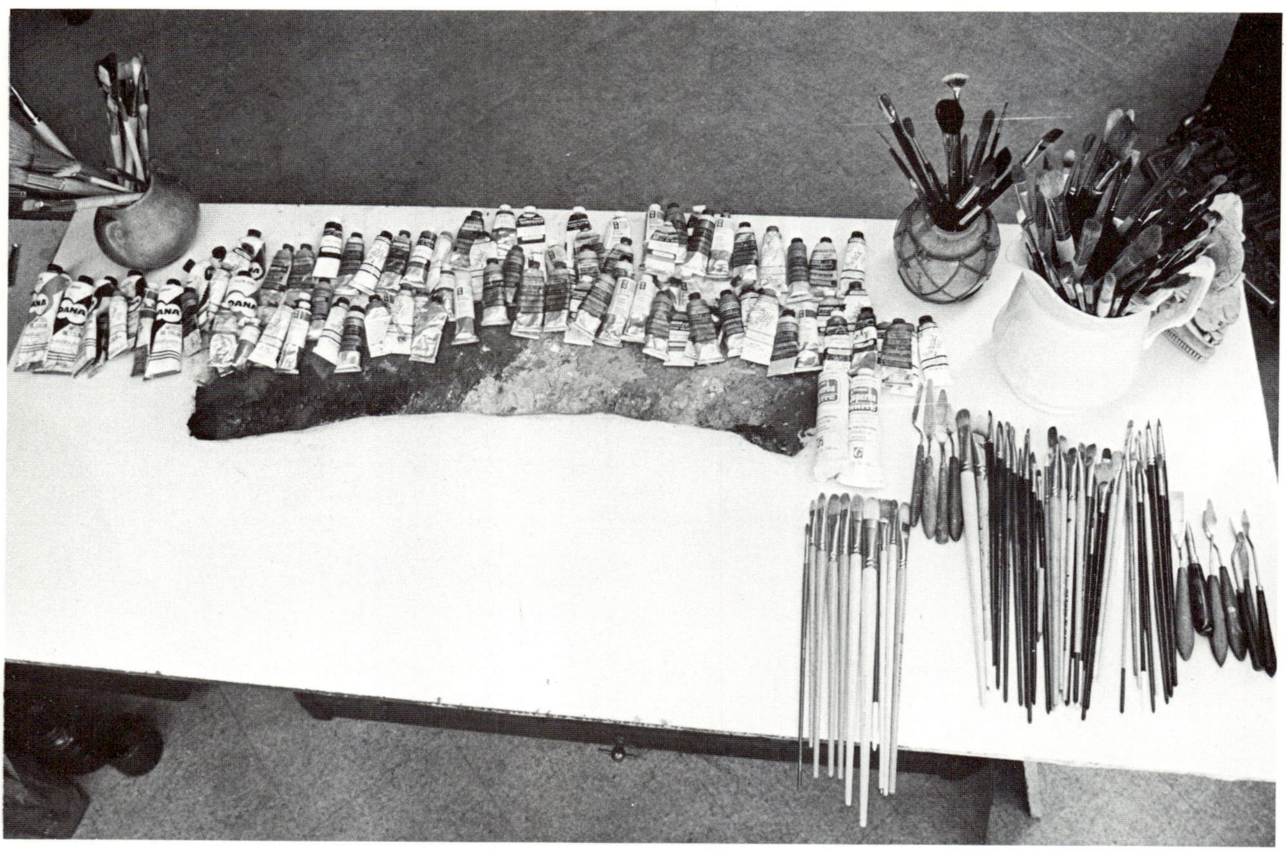

The oil setup is arranged on a large piece of milk glass that doubles as a palette.

What medium do you use with your oils?

I don't use any. I'm a stickler for permanency. I feel that anything you mix with oil paint breaks down its consistency so it's not pure anymore. In fact, I use turpentine only in the washes and to clean my brushes.

Do you mix color on the palette or on the canvas?

I mix my color on the palette. Sometimes I use a palette knife and sometimes a brush. I mix only enough for a stroke or two, then I clean my brush and mix another color for one or two more strokes. I frequently need to stop and scrape the glass clean again.

Do you ever lay glazes in oil painting?

I don't glaze in the Renaissance manner, but I do work with transparent layers occasionally. For example, I'll begin with washes and paint across them with a transparent color to let the underlayer show through.

Do you ever paint with palette knives or your fingers?

Absolutely yes. I use whatever it takes to achieve the right effect. I like to break up the textures in my work, so I use knives, fingers, or take a little swipe with a rag.

What size canvases do you prefer for oil paintings?

I don't paint "giant-sized" canvases. My largest is approximately 28″ x 34″ (71 x 86.5 cm). I'm more at home with 8″ x 10″ (20.5 x 25.5 cm), 9″ x 12″ (23 x 30.5 cm), and 16″ x 20″ (40.5 x 51 cm). In these small shapes, you get such juicy little gems, whereas, the bigger ones sometimes lack POW!

What painting surfaces do you prefer? How do you prepare them?

I use both canvas—a good quality of gray Belgian linen—and Masonite panels.

As a matter of fact, I've just prepared forty Masonite panels. At the lumberyard, I have untempered Masonite cut to standard sizes: 8″ x 10″ (20.5 x 25.5 cm), 11″ x 14″ (28 x 35.5 cm), 9″ x 12″ (23 x 30.5 cm), 12″ x 16″ (30.5 x 40.5 cm), 16″ x 20″ (40.5 x 51 cm), 18″ x 24″ (45.5 x 61 cm), and 20″ x 24″ (51 x 61 cm). I sand the boards before priming.

I prime both panels and canvas the same way. Rabbitskin glue comes in powdered form, in sheets, or in chunks; I like the powder. The directions for mixing are on the box; it isn't hard to do. I use this glue to size the board in two coats—it dries very fast. I then sand this very lightly with fine sandpaper.

On the dry rabbitskin glue, I paint a layer of white. I use Grumbacher flake white and add turpentine to make a thick, pasty mixture. With a 2″ to 4″ (5 to 10 cm) brush, I work this into the surface. I'm happy with the texture of the brushstrokes. It's important to make sure that the white binds properly, so I scrub it onto the surface. This has to dry at least a month before it's ready to paint on.

I prefer to prepare my own surfaces, as I like to vary the textures. I stretch raw linen on stretcher bars in the same standard sizes I use for Masonite panels. The linen is all stretched and ready before priming, of course.

What's your procedure in painting a typical portrait or figure in oil?

I'm an alla prima painter. I do very little preliminary work when I paint. To me, alla prima means that I lay down my brushstrokes directly and finish the painting in one session. This is a lot more difficult than working out sketches and underpainting and then following a slowly developed plan.

In oil painting, I try to cover the surface, not save any whites. My oil procedure has more in common with pastel than with watercolor.

Oil painting is a building-up process. It's a dark to light medium, comparable to a sculpture made of wax or clay in that it's an additive process: modeling is done by adding to the shape and working *toward the highlight*—that area that projects furthest forward. In a watercolor, the painter "carves away" from the lights to the darkest darks. I have no trouble making this mental switch from one mode of thinking to the other.

I paint in oil on a variety of surfaces—primed linen or Masonite. For portraits and figures, I use a finer surface than I would for a landscape.

With a diluted turpentine wash, I first lay in the basic shape. The color I pick depends on the subject—for a little black boy I'd use a warm wash.

Once the form is blocked in, I study the model and decide on which area to accentuate. In each view of a nude, for example, I accentuate only one aspect of the model. This is time-tested, traditional. There *are* artists who finish every part of the painting equally, but I'm not one of them. If the figure is a back view of a nude, I might stress the derrière and subdue all the rest.

During the middle stage of the painting—after the block-in—I model with paint toward the highlights. I work all around the painting, on the

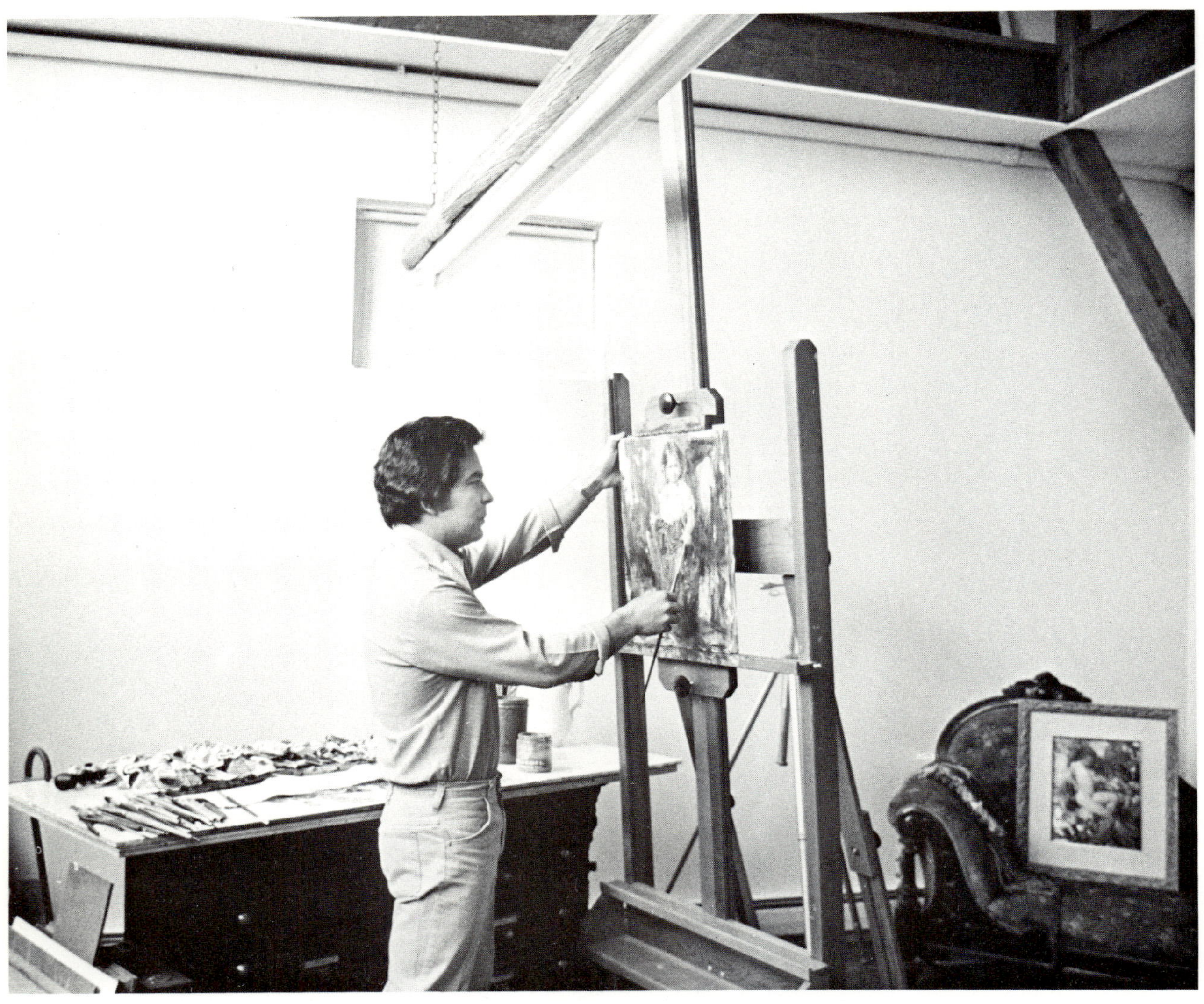

The artist at work in the oil painting studio downstairs.

figure and on the background, balancing colors, including a touch
of the background colors on the figure and vice versa. My aim is to create
a suggestion of form with beautiful colors, not to work on the painting
in too detailed a way.

After I feel that the modeling is complete enough, I paint the highlights. Under fluorescent light, they'll be warm on a light subject, while
on a dark subject (a Black or an Indian) I use a cool highlight. Natural
light creates cooler highlights.

My final procedure is to go in and hit the picture here and there with
a touch of color—perhaps a cool blue in the background and on the
figure. At the end, I study the painting to link up the colors; I add little
touches of almost pure color. In a very high key painting, I can add a
pure white or a pure black if the painting allows it; but on a middle
value painting, I couldn't use a pure white because it would create too
much contrast and be too distracting.

When I teach, I recommend that a student lay in washes boldly, but
put on impasto strokes slowly. I think this gives more zing!

There are some paintings that require more time, but my work looks
as if it were done quickly. I don't work days on a single painting. If I
can finish it in one session, I try to do so. I need to stay with it and try
to get it right on the first try. If this means painting through the night,
then I do it.

WORKING WITH THE MODEL

**Do you prepare for
painting by
sketching?**

I do charcoal sketches from the live model every chance I get. But I'm
trying to learn to draw with the brush while I paint. Learning to draw
in paint has done more for my painting than hundreds of small
sketches could do.

Some artists have learned to sketch exceptionally well. They're fantastic draftsmen, but they just aren't very good painters. There's so
much involved in the creation of a painting besides drawing. You
have to put all these things together—composition, color, texture. It
isn't wise to put too much emphasis on only one aspect of the art
of painting.

If I concentrated too much on the sketch, I couldn't let myself go and
paint naturally. It's beautiful to paint instinctively and see that a picture
is starting to sing. I'm trying to let this happen to me. I go up to my
board and let myself go—to see what comes out. The first painting
might be a mess, but with sustained practice and faith, you can go on
"automatic pilot" and paint. The paintings will just roll out like music. I
always remember what John Singer Sargent said about watercolor: "I
have abandoned all fear of the medium."

I'm no longer concerned with just the preliminary warm-up sketch.
My sketches are made directly on the canvas with strokes of paint. Over
those quick strokes go the heavier impasto and, with luck, I'll finish the
whole painting with bravura brushwork.

**When you begin a
figure painting, do
you have a pose in
mind? How do you
go about posing the
figure?**

I learned from still life painting that the best result comes from the
best setup you can come up with. So it takes me about half as long to
set up a figure painting (or a still life) as it does to actually paint it.

I have the model change pose constantly until I find one that suits the
composition or format—the setting that I've arranged for the model on
the stand.

I don't have a definite plan in mind when the model walks in. I get my ideas from having her move around until she falls into a pose that clicks and I say, "Yes, this is going to be the painting." Once that decision is made, then the pose is maintained until the painting is finished. The position is marked so the model can take breaks, of course, but she returns to the same pose until I finish.

Do you practice drawing from the model?

We do hire a model for sketching classes—artists get together to do this. To keep in practice, to train your hand and eye to be coordinated, you have to draw from life. But since I believe that you must take your drawing ability into painting, I like to sketch from the model in oils. In this way, I'm practicing drawing and painting simultaneously.

You're well known for paintings of the nude figure. Do you ever work from photographs when doing figure paintings?

I do sometimes work from photographs of difficult poses. For simpler poses—easier ones for the model to hold, such as simple standing, sitting, or reclining poses—I use a live model.

I find it much easier to paint from the live model than from the photo. When you work from life, everything is there in front of you: the proportions, the color, the light, and the values. You don't need to make compensations, as you do when working from a photograph. All photographs distort somewhat, so the photograph requires more brainwork from the artist: you must handle the light, color, and value in the photo so that they seem lifelike. There, working from a photo takes far longer, as you must rely on your mind and your memory, rather than just observe and paint the live model. That's why I always prefer to paint from life.

You frequently paint a beloved model, such as your wife's late grandfather. Can you explain how your portraits of him continue to inspire you, although he's no longer living? Are your favorite models related to you?

Quite a few of the people I paint are close relatives or friends. The subject to concentrate on is always the one you know best.

There are portraits in my studio of my two sons, Adam and Ben. I also paint my daughter, Lea, a lot. It's a joy to paint my own children because I know them so well and it's easy to get a likeness. I have a new subject now in the baby my sister takes care of, Stephanie. I've seen her over and over again while she plays on the floor or lies on a bed.

Sometimes I see an interesting character walking down the street and I'd love to be able to paint that person. Perhaps I can arrange it, but the person is still a stranger at first, and I must get to know him.

Now, Grandpa was a great-looking man and I was as close to him as my wife was, although he was her grandfather, not mine. I painted him often and I even did some wax studies of him. I also took a number of photographs of him. Altogether, I've managed to collect a great deal of material on him: I still find him a fascinating subject.

You're a colorist and most of your work is warmly colored. Would you discuss your preference in coloring, especially in a model? What appeals to you?

I began by painting Indians, Mexicans, and Blacks, not because I'm interested in ethnic portraits, but because I like the coloring of their skin. I respond to hot colors, such as the skin tones of a Taos Indian. The purples, browns, and ochres in black skin are magnificent, I think. It's a terrific challenge to paint a Black or an Indian—more so for me, anyway—than to paint a white person.

PAINTING TECHNIQUES

What's the role of the background in your plan for a painting?

By painting freely on all parts of the work, I try to develop a background as a harmonious addition to the figure. The background is less important than the figure, but it can't be left to be filled in at the last minute. It has to grow right along with the painting. I think it's important to move all around the picture continuously and not focus on the figure exclusively. I like to leave the background undefined, but I don't want to create any definite separation of the figure from the background.

Do you accentuate the line at an edge or allow it to fuse?

Edges are important, but not outlines. There are no harsh outlines in nature. But fused edges are frequent in nature. I like to use the expression "hit or miss" to describe what I try to do with edges. Here and there, such as on a foreshortened knee, I define the edge of the kneecap itself. As the knee recedes, I feather the edge. The result is a "flow." Edges *stop* the free movement of the eye, so I use them carefully.

What advice can you give to a painter on control of values?

Trying to create this illusion of three-dimensional form on a two-dimensional surface demands gradations from light to dark. Contrasting values give the illusion of form. Usually an artist is taught to think of values as ten steps, from the lightest white to the darkest dark. It's a good plan for an artist to practice painting a value chart, using mixtures of white and black pigment only to gain mastery over value gradations. A few years back, an old artist friend (who's no longer living) told me that one of the best lessons in the control of value is to paint an egg. I thought that would be one of the easiest subjects in the world, so I rushed back to my studio and set up a still life with a couple of eggs. Needless to say, I fell flat on my. . . .

First of all, in painting an egg, you're looking at an object that has almost no color and such a simple shape that it's very difficult to make that shape look round and project toward you. So, from that time on, I've made it a steady practice to paint still lifes and practice controlling value with color.

I believe this practice has led me to look at a large shape in terms of a single value, rather than as a series of small value changes. I find the largest shapes I can within a form, simplify the form, and then reduce the number of value changes necessary to suggest it. For example, in a blouse or shirt, I'll search out the big areas to be painted with one color, one value. Your values depend on the light source—whether it's artificial light or natural light, such as the north light in the studio. A portrait most often has a light side and a dark side.

You seem to be more concerned with warm versus cool than you are with gradations of value.

I do find warm versus cool contrasts indispensable. It isn't enough for me to make a nice value study with a convincing three-dimensional shape. I want my work to sing. For this, a touch of cool on a warm surface or, likewise, a bit of warm on a cool area, adds excitement. It finishes the painting. Furthermore, the change of color temperature helps achieve modeling, as I explained a moment ago.

Do you pre-plan a high-key or low-key picture?

No, I let the subject matter set the key. I was once painting on location at Steamboat Springs, Colorado, on a gloomy, overcast day. I was painting beautiful white-faced calves on a snowfield. I toned the snow way down to create the gloomy day. There was enough white in the

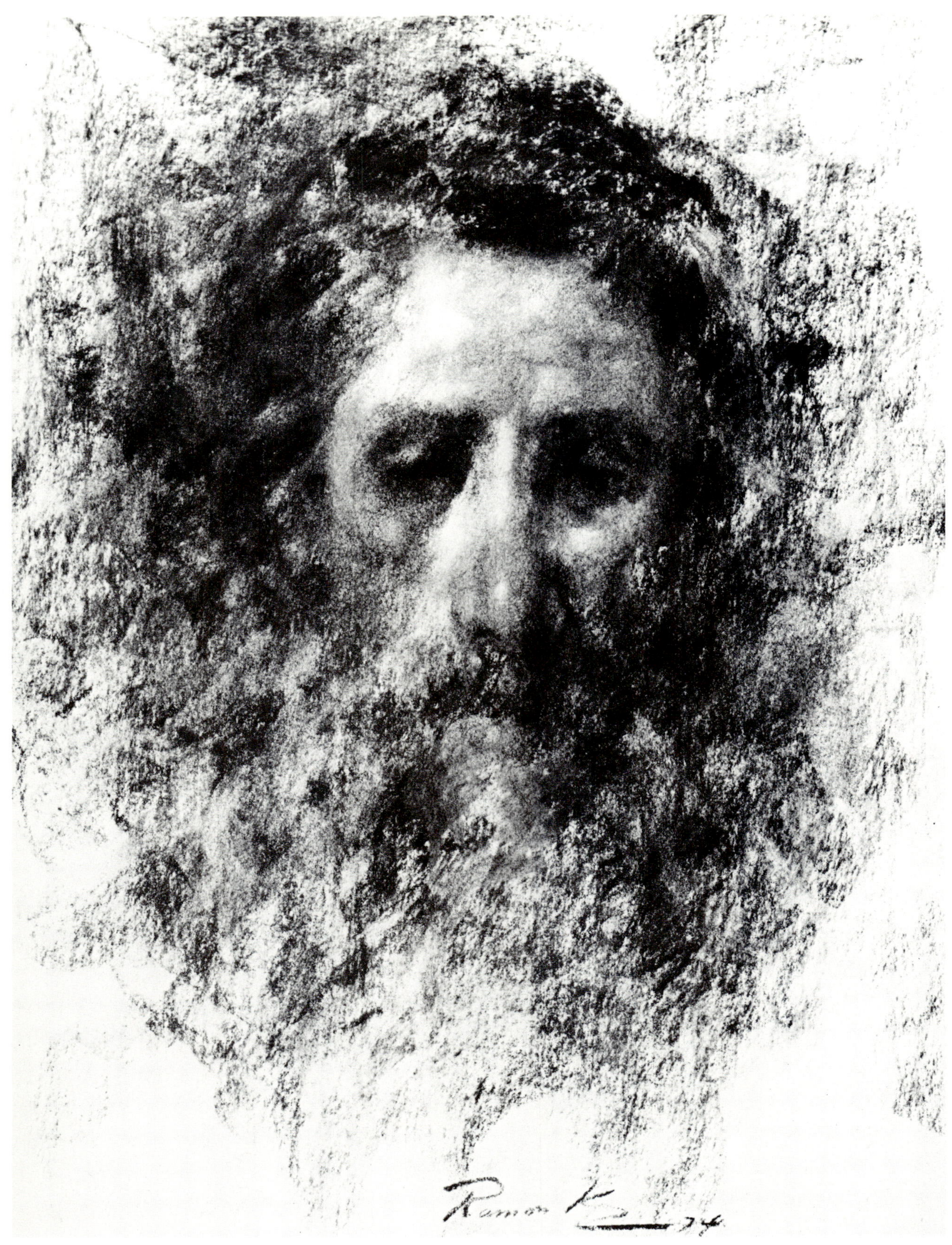

Study for Bearded Man. *Pastel drawing on rice paper, 14" x 10½" (35.5 x 26.5 cm). This drawing was done in burnt sienna pastel. I first toned the facial area, then immediately indicated the hair, beard, and background.*

By working broadly and loosely, I was able to complete the study in thirty minutes. Highlights were lifted with a kneaded eraser. Hair, eyes, nose, and mustache were strengthened with darker darks.

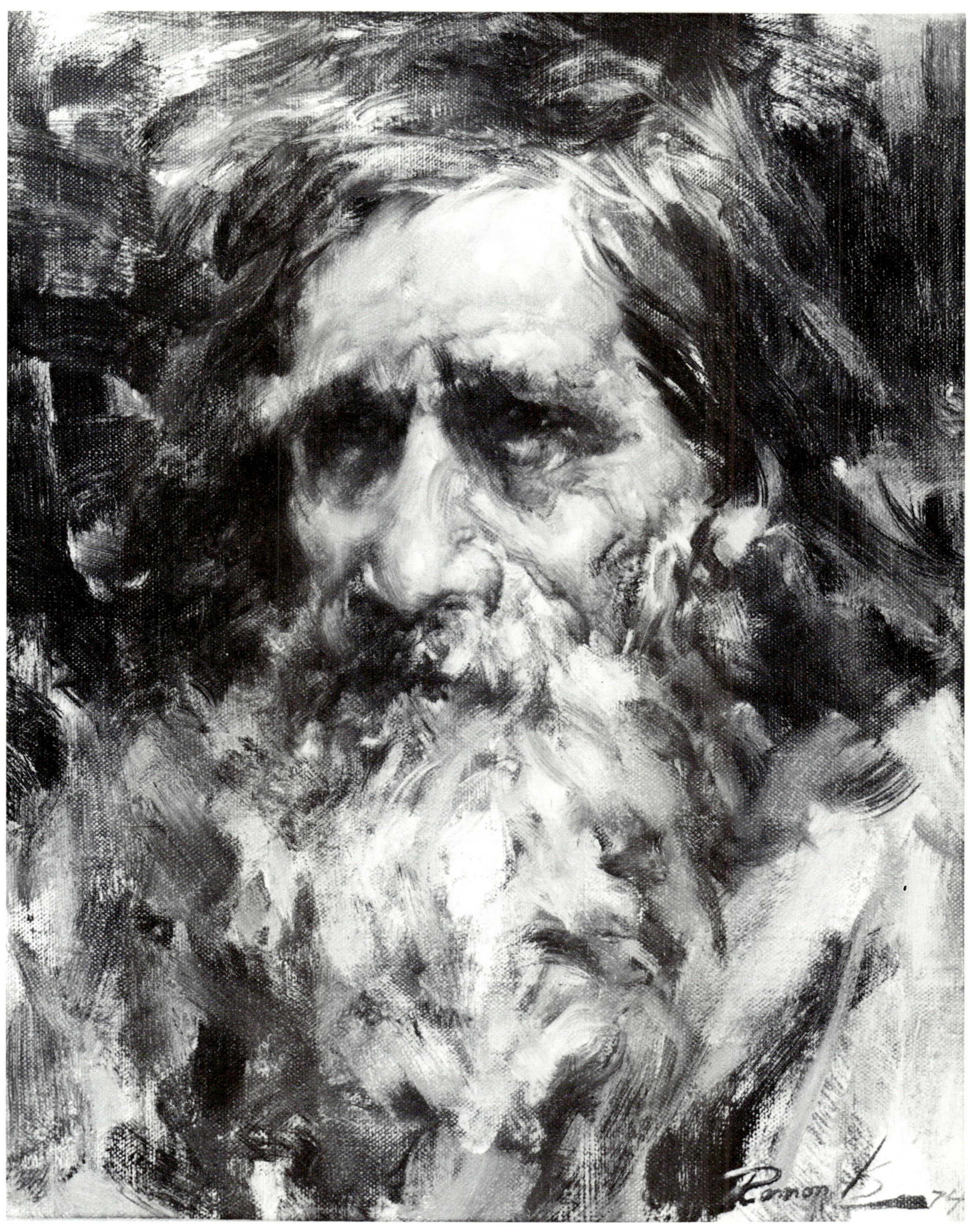

An Old Timer. *Oil on canvas, 10" x 8" (25.5 x 20.5 cm). I painted this on a finely woven linen canvas, which provided a smooth surface. There's no heavy pigment in the painting. With repeated color washes of oil mixed with turpentine, I built up the painting in layers. I wiped out highlights from the wet washes, as in a watercolor. The heaviest concentration of pigment is in the beard and mustache, where I added a few impasto strokes over the washes.*

calves' faces so that they stood out from the snow. I painted the calves warmer and the snow cooler to further accentuate the difference, but the key of the painting was low, even though one would think a snow scene might be high key.

In portraiture, of course, I paint in a low key when I have a dark model, while a fair-skinned person would dictate a higher key painting.

<table>
<tr><td>What's your approach to composition?</td><td>I prefer to speak about my figure paintings rather than my portraits because there's far more involved in composing a figure with a background and a foreground than in composing a simple portrait.</td></tr>
</table>

For example, in the painting of the reclining nude on page 139, there are many elements that must be composed harmoniously. I think of the figure as the main actor and the other areas as having supporting roles. My first concern is the placement of the figure. Though she's almost centered in the canvas, the slightly diagonal line of her pose adds some tension and interest to the basic design. The triangular shape of the bent knee and arm varies the horizontality of the model. The model is the dominant form. There are four other large shapes that suggest drapery over soft bolsters. These forms are simply defined and painted broadly, in dramatic contrast to the more carefully modeled figure.

My goal in composition is to make pathways for the eye leading to the subject. The darker areas of the background create these directional lines. Lighter areas near the figure attract the eye, and so do the small areas of warm color above and below the figure. Broadly painted strokes—in all the lesser areas—are directed toward the figure. I want the viewer's eye to move freely around the painting, but to return again and again to the figure.

Many of my decisions about composition are spontaneous additions made during the act of painting. My design here includes five basic forms placed in a slightly slanting *H*, crossed by strong diagonals. This makes a stable framework for the composition, but I believe the paint application—the color, the value contrasts, the direction of the brushstrokes, and the suggestions of form—is what makes the composition work. I'm more involved in these considerations than in formal design principles.

PROFESSIONAL ADVICE

What does the gallery owner expect from an artist?

The gallery owner has a right to expect that the artist will bring in new work regularly and that it will be professionally framed—with the screw eyes and wire already in place and ready to hang.

There must be a good understanding between the gallery and the artist—a businesslike relationship, rather than a friendship. Sometimes a gallery will prevail upon friendship to try to get an artist to furnish more work than the artist can really produce. This is a trap to be avoided. It leads to *turning out* paintings, not creating them. Therefore, I urge the young artist to keep things on a business basis.

I try to keep at least eight or ten paintings at each of my galleries at all times, so that the gallery can offer a reasonable choice to a buyer. When I take my work in, I get a consignment slip for my own records and for the gallery. If necessary, I move my paintings from one gallery to another: I don't leave them in a gallery more than six months. I've been very lucky: I've never had to move my work more than once before it was sold. But I still follow this six-month rule so that the work in any gallery isn't stale.

I find that I can't supply more than three good galleries. Other artists might be able to produce enough to supply more. My job is to paint the pictures, crate them, and ship them. To do that much is to do a lot. An artist can't afford to spread himself too thin.

Today, 40% is a fair commission. A few galleries charge only one-third; if an artist should find such a gallery, he's wise to affiliate with it because the profit for the artist is that much greater. When a gallery is well established and doing a good job for the artist, then 40% isn't too much. After all, the gallery pays its overhead and makes its profit from the commission. If the gallery promotes the artist well—and this is one thing the artist has a right to expect—then the 40% is justified.

What would you advise on framing paintings?

Let me begin by discussing the matting of a watercolor or a pastel. You don't want to put glass in contact with a pastel or a watercolor. If you do, there's danger of *foxing*, or mold stains. To prevent this, I separate the painting from the glass with a mat. But most mat boards aren't 100% rag and there are acids in these boards that will eventually stain a painting. I cut a thin sheet of museum board, which *is* 100% rag, to match the mat and put it between the mat and the painting.

I also cut two vents in the backing board to allow air to circulate behind the painting. This helps to prevent the collection of moisture.

Now about frames in general. I began my career using expensive frames, and before long I owed the framer a fortune. I learned that in the beginning you can't afford the most expensive frames. Unless you're subsidized, you should learn to *make* frames. It's obvious that the frame has to go with the painting. For example, the linen liner, if you use one, shouldn't be lighter than the painting or you'll see the liner before the painting. The frame should enhance, but never overpower, the painting. I know now that if a painting is priced at $300 and the frame has cost $50, then the package must cost $350. You must get your money back in order to continue framing your work. If you're a professional and you are asking a high price for a painting, then the frame must be of high quality. A good frame definitely increases the value of a painting.

What sort of records do you advise the beginning pro to keep?

He should start immediately to write down on a card or in some other convenient form, the title of each work, the size, and the medium. When a work is sold, he should record the date and the price at which it was sold. I used to keep the name of the buyer on the card, but some galleries won't furnish that information any more because a few artists have abused the dealer by using the names and addresses to sell directly to the buyer and bypass the gallery. I can understand the gallery's reluctance to furnish the names of buyers to the artists.

For taxes, an artist must have a complete record of what he's sold. He can use the same card system he uses to keep track of his work.

Should an artist maintain a slide file of his work?

I don't recommend that an artist who's just beginning his career go out and hock his brushes to buy a camera. But as soon as he can afford it, I think an artist can benefit by taking his own photographic record of his work.

I have an old file cabinet from the 1880's—with twenty-one drawers

in it—where I keep my file of transparencies. I take 2¼″ x 2¾″
(5.5 x 7 cm) color transparencies of my paintings, especially of what I
consider major works. I also shoot black and whites and keep prints
on file. When I get a letter from someone who's interested in the
purchase of a painting, I can pull out and send him a print, all titled,
dated, and priced. I file by title and medium.

Maybe it's just as well not to have *every* early painting I ever did on
film; it might be discouraging to look back on them all. But an artist
does need to see how his work is progressing; for this, a photographic
file is essential. It can be done with 35mm slides, but I find the larger
transparencies more useful because they can be used for color reproduc-
tions more easily. You can also make a good file of black and white
prints only. Every professional artist eventually *must* start keeping a
photo file.

<table>
<tr><td>How should an artist go about getting the necessary publicity?</td><td>Most of the publicity an artist gets should come through his gallery. If an artist is having a show, it is up to the gallery to publicize the show in the locality of the gallery. Newspaper coverage is free, but there's also promotion in the form of brochures or invitations to the show. This should be paid for by the gallery. If an artist is making money for a gallery, the gallery occasionally should buy space in national art magazines such as American Artist, Art News, or Art in America. This is very expensive, of course, but it boosts the artist's reputation and thereby encourages sales, which is good for the gallery as well as for the artist.

Sometimes, when I can afford it, I myself will buy space in a national publication. I think it's good exposure and helps my career. I recommend this to other artists.</td></tr>
<tr><td>What advice do you have for a beginning pro about extending his market?</td><td>The beginning pro should literally take everything that comes his way and not be "proud." He should be flexible and enter the mall shows, the shopping center shows, bank shows, sidewalk shows—go any-where he can to gain exposure and become a self-supporting profes-sional. He needs to do this for survival!

At first, the beginning pro should find a local market, right in his own area. But he shouldn't be content with that. As soon as sales are fairly regular, he should try, slowly, to move into more distant markets, until he might have a gallery in the east, maybe one in the midwest, and another in the west.

The beginner has to start with very low prices to sell more and to build up a following of collectors who're interested in his work. An unknown artist can't ask outrageous prices; no one will buy. When I started, I sold many paintings all over the country at low prices. I built up my prices just a little at a time. I advise artists not to be discouraged if their old buyers begin falling off as prices go up; new buyers soon will develop—buyers who are in a higher income bracket.</td></tr>
</table>

TALENT AND TRAINING

<table>
<tr><td>Do you think talent is God-given or something we develop?</td><td>I didn't always think talent was in-born or God-given, but I've begun to change my opinion.

When I was a kid, I couldn't get anything across to my teachers. I wasn't able to express myself in words. I was poor in math and in read-ing, too. Other kids had the same trouble in my part of town. But if a</td></tr>
</table>

boy was a good ball player—even if he wasn't a good student—he'd play right through high school and into college. Well, for me, it was *art* that kept me going.

I'm inclined to believe that we develop the talent we have available to compensate for other things we can't do well. Art talent may have been born inside me—a "God-given" talent, if you want to call it that—but it took being ignored by teachers to bring it out.

As a self-taught artist, how have you mastered anatomy?

I remember reading an anecdote about the Russian artist Nicolai Fechin. He was asked if he had made thousands of anatomical drawings in art school. He answered that he *had* studied for years to perfect himself as an artist, he wasn't studying *anatomy*—he was *painting*.

I haven't drawn thousands of anatomical studies either, but I do have a good strong feeling for the figure. I study books about anatomy and I've drawn studies of bones and muscles, but basically I rely on my intuition and my feelings for the rightness of the form.

You've said that you admire the work of Nicolai Fechin. What other artists do you admire?

I do admire Fechin. We're very lucky to have had this great Russian-born painter working here. He's left behind some great work.

When I was in Naples and Rome in the late 1950's—while I was in the navy there—I discovered the work of Antonio Mancini, a 19th-century artist. I was just flabbergasted. I've been very much influenced by his work, his alla prima, bravura painting of people.

I've also chosen to paint people because I believe I know people better than any other subject. Moods, feeling, and character are what interest me.

As an artist progresses in his career, he develops new loves. We've all been influenced by different artists. If we all locked ourselves in our studios, we'd never advance. We must look at other artists' work and take from other artists—not to copy, but to borrow. The influences are always there. If an artist claims he hasn't been influenced, he's deceiving himself.

I've been fortunate that my career has taken me to New York to receive a few awards. When I'm there, I go through bookstores, one after the other. It's a hobby with me. I find books on artists people have never heard of, and I collect books of all types about many artists. I probably have one of the nicest collections of American and European art books. I continue to collect them because this is where I get my education. Never having gone to art school myself, I go through my books and study the paintings to help myself become a better painter.

Other artists I've become especially interested in are John Singer Sargent; the Swedish painter, Anders Zorn; and the Russian artists like Nicolay Kasatkin, Ilya Repin, Valentin Serov, and Abram Arkhipov. These are all figurative painters with a bravura style.

It's obvious that you have a very accurate eye and have spent many hours learning by looking, rather than listening to lectures. How do you do it?

Looking is the basic job of the artist. It's amazing how much the eye sees and the mind retains. An artist always relies on his memory bank as he paints, though perhaps unconsciously.

But the eye tends to be lazy and must be *taught* to see. It's possible to look without seeing. You have to look at everything with the painter's eye. Joachin Sorolla y Bastida was asked, "When do you paint?" He answered, "I am always painting, even while I am sitting here talking to you." I've always thought that was a magnificent statement. The true artist is always painting—in the mind's eye—even when he's away from the easel.

I try to check on myself occasionally to find out how much I retain of something I've looked at. Even at the breakfast table, I find myself studying the milk pitcher, the fruit, and the cups and saucers. How would I compose them? What colors would I use? Then, later on, I'll test myself and try to recapture the picture I had in my mind's eye.

You've referred to Sargent and Eakins as men who never peaked out. What do you mean?

Thoughts of peaking out must go through the minds of most serious artists. Even in my lifetime there are names of those who have come and are already gone. Their fame was quickly won and quickly lost. Yet, men like Sargent and Eakins did fantastic things till the day they died.

I'm trying to pace myself. At first, I wanted to do everything in five years—to be accepted by the academies and major societies and paint great paintings. I'm mellowing now. My great desire is to learn to paint and to continue to improve. If I can do this, the rest will follow. I'll wait.

If I'm lucky enough to be painting when I'm an old man, great! If everything comes too fast, what do you do for an encore? I hope things come little by little throughout the years, so I continue to strive and try to improve.

DEMONSTRATIONS

THE FIGURE IN PASTEL

One of my favorite subjects has always been the nude. In this first demonstration of a seated figure, I begin with a watercolor underpainting and then lay impasto strokes of pastel over it: this is my "mixed media" approach to pastel painting.

I often do tiny 4″ x 5″ (9 x 12.5 cm) pastel sketches that I like to call my "little gems." They usually serve as a guide for a larger finished painting, although, at times, one of them might stand alone as a framed work of art. I save most of them for reference. My inspiration for this demonstration was such a little gem, done from a live model.

When I do a small sketch, I may work directly from the live model, from a photograph of a model, or from a drawing I've previously made from the model.

In the small format, I think out the composition, colors, and values. When I do a larger painting, I follow the plan of the small one, but I have to add many new spontaneous touches and refinements to fill the larger format.

This painting is 22″ x 28″ (56 x 71 cm). I'm using a sanded pastel board in a warm ivory tone that harmonizes with the nude figure.

My watercolor palette for the nude is ivory black, alizarin crimson, cadmium red light, and viridian. I lay a broadly washed underpainting with a number 12 nylon brush—just enough to establish the sense of form and distribution of values, as well as the placement of the figure and the gesture of the pose.

My pastel palette consists of cadmium yellow, cadmium orange, cadmium red, raw sienna, alizarin crimson, viridian, and cobalt blue. I break my soft pastels into 1″ (2.5 cm) chunks and paint with the side of the chunk so that the width of the pastel strokes harmonizes with the watercolor brushstrokes beneath. After each stroke, I wipe the piece of pastel clean with a paper towel.

My goal in this painting is to capture the beauty of skin texture and flesh tones.

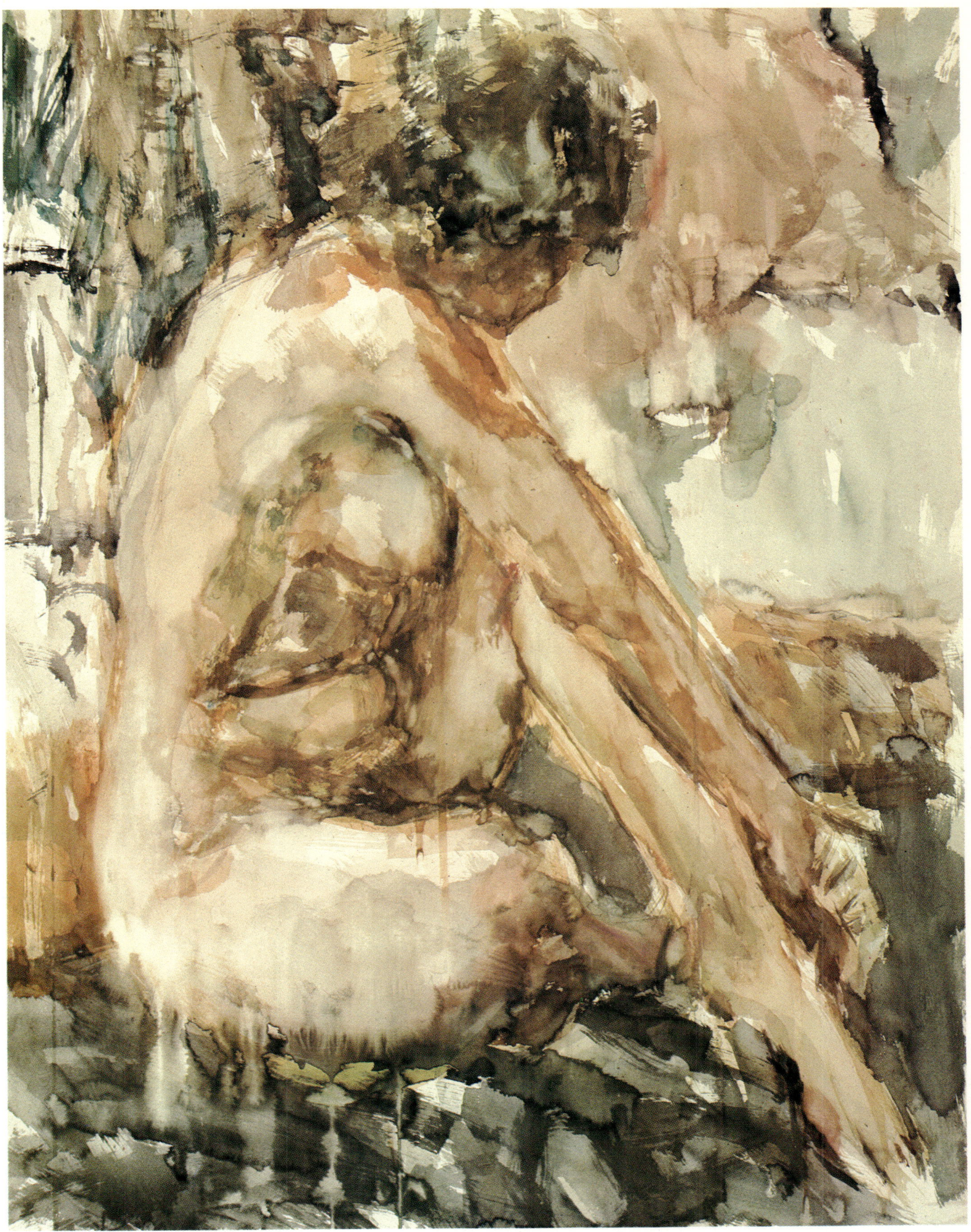

Step 1. The warm washes of the background, like the tones on either side of the head, are mixtures of viridian and alizarin crimson which yield warm neutrals. The cooler background tones, like the color at the left of the head, are the same mixture, but dominated by viridian. The figure, too, is modeled with warm and cool variations of this mixture, as you can see clearly in the forearm. The dark model stand is just broad strokes of gray. I've already begun to work over parts of the figure in pastel. Strokes of viridian chalk are brought down to establish the line of the back. I start to model the shoulder, the front of the torso, and the raised thigh with various tones of cadmium red and orange, alizarin crimson, and a few strokes of black (smudged into the warm tones) to sharpen the line where the torso and thigh meet. Soft pinks of cadmium red and alizarin crimson are stroked along the back and the right thigh to indicate the lighted areas.

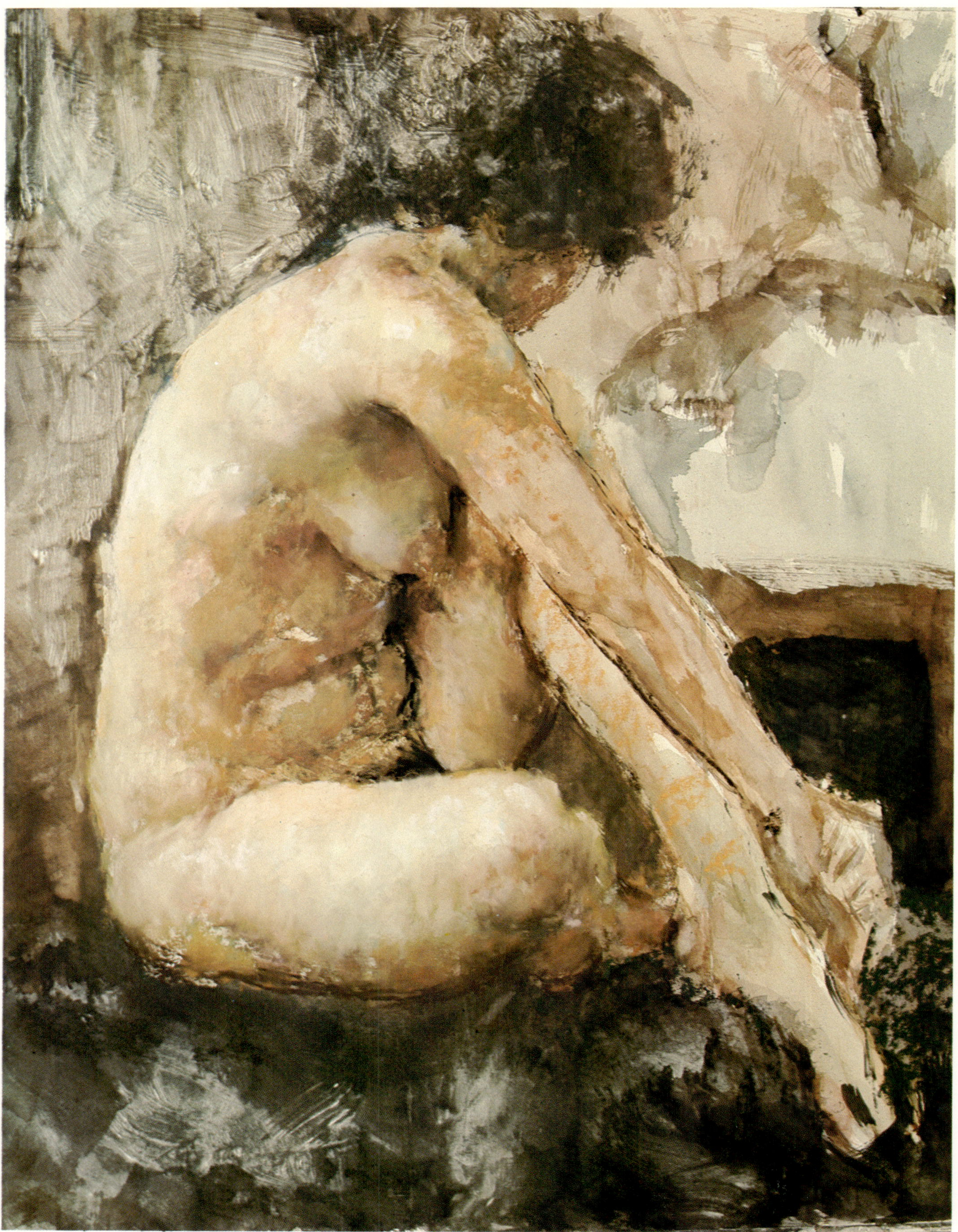

Step 2. Now I begin to strengthen the contrasts of the figure with the background, working in broad pastel strokes. I block in the orange drapery to the left and then strike back in with viridian to cool and animate the orange. The gray wash of the model stand begins to disappear under strokes of viridian, which clearly define the lower edge of the figure, who now sits more securely on the stand. The face is in shadow and all you can see there are a few dark strokes of alizarin crimson, cooled by a touch of viridian. For the shadow areas, I'm using pastels which are simply darker values of the watercolor washes. In the lighted areas, I'm using warm pinks made with cadmium red and alizarin crimson; notice the right shoulder and the right knee. The highlights on the shoulder, right knee, and the back are cool blue accents made with light cobalt blue.

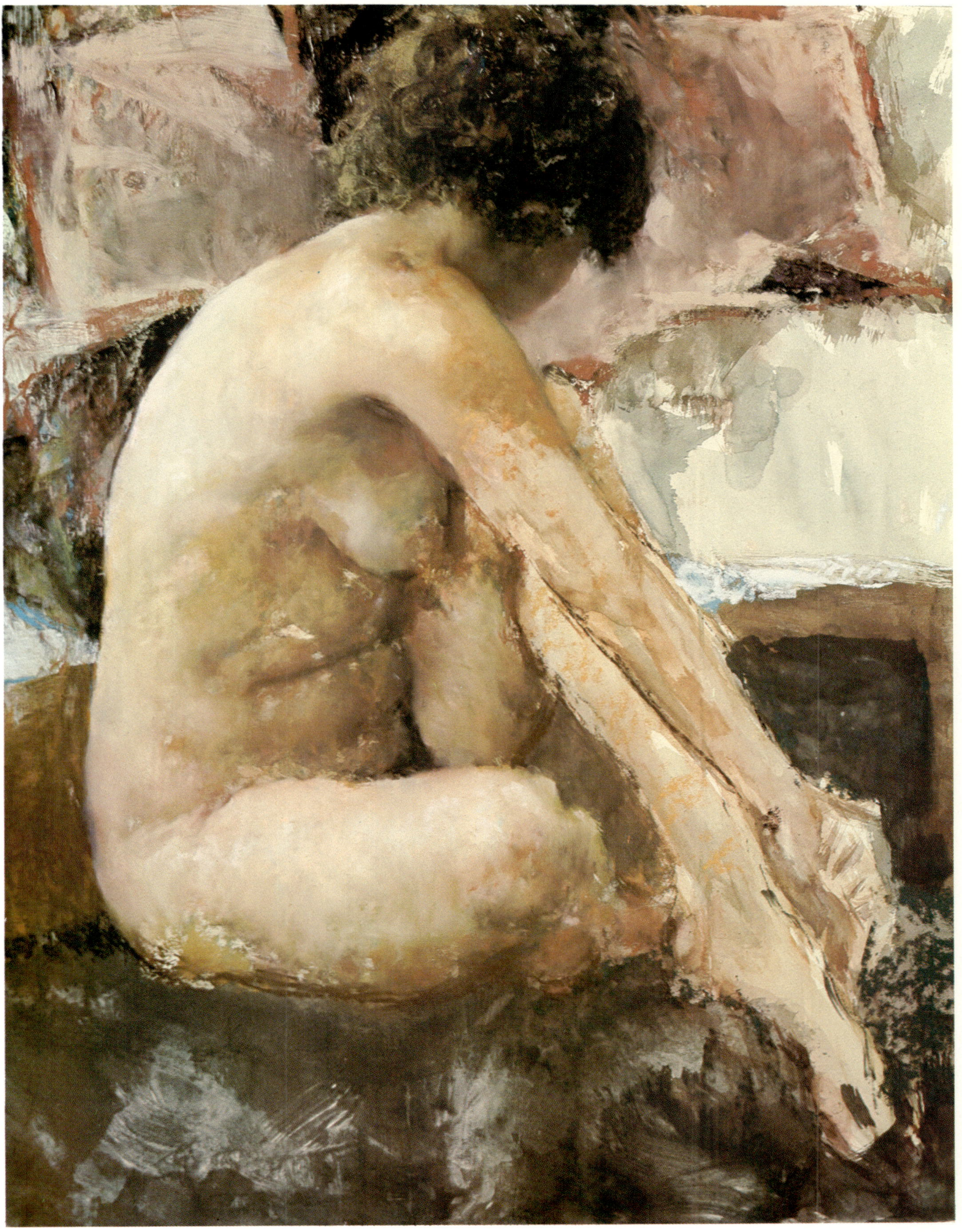

Step 3. At this stage, I concentrate on defining the figure and the background shapes more precisely. I build up the lights and shadows of the pink drapery behind the head, using particularly thick strokes for the lights. With a wet brush, I work back into the foreground drapery, melting the pigment into the paper and unifying the big shape into one solid dark. I add a strong dark at the left to define the back. I define the shape and texture of the hair with black, alizarin crimson, raw sienna, cadmium yellow, and a touch of blue. But above all, I concentrate on the torso, building up the lights of the back and thighs with soft pinks, and blending the shadows into the lights with soft touches of my thumb, but always avoiding too much polish to avoid making the color look slick.

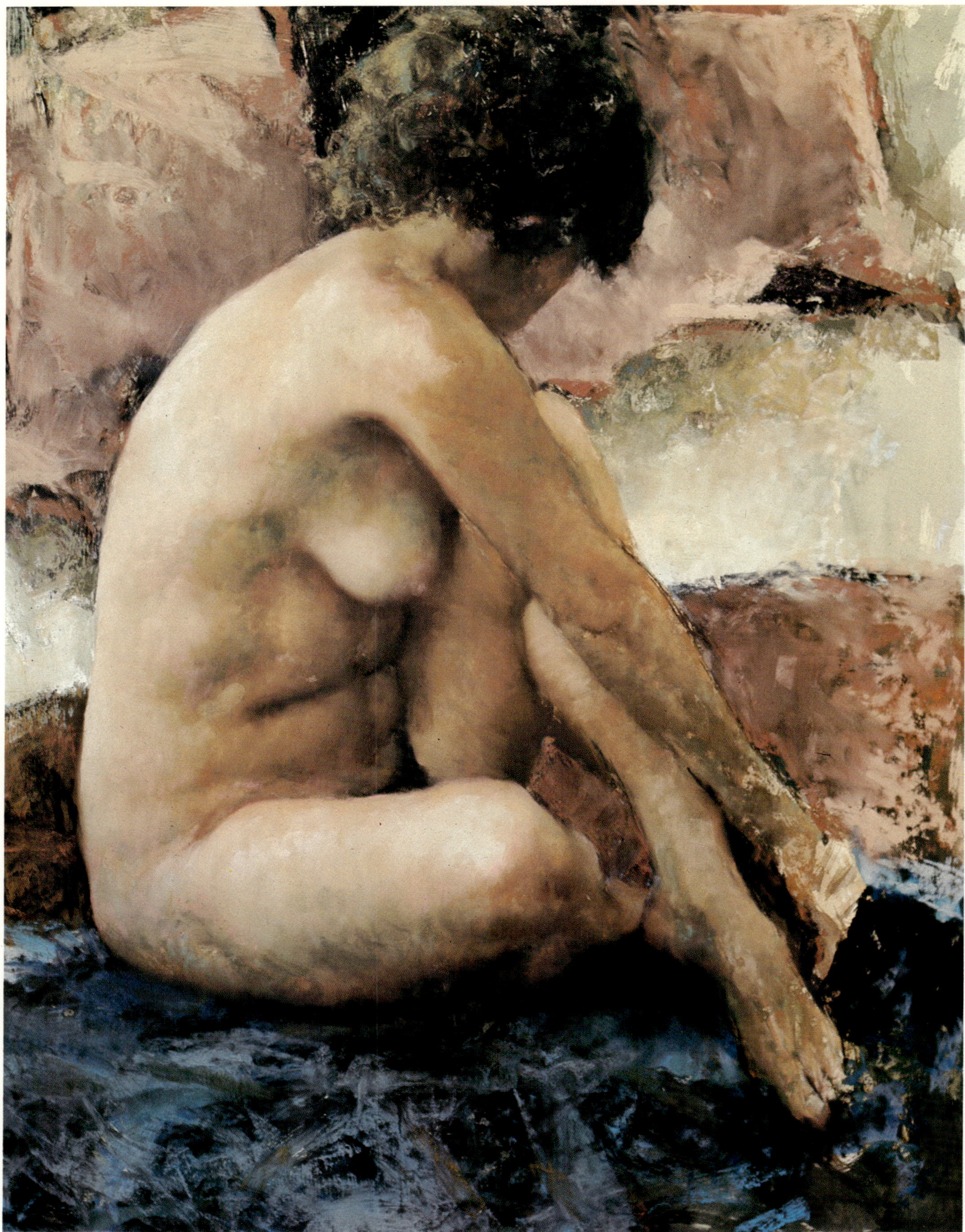

Step 4. At this stage, I emphasize color and definition, covering the watercolor washes with lots of solid pastel pigment. If I leave too much wash showing, the painting will look unfinished, especially on a sanded board. I really lay on the pastel vigorously, pushing it in with the stick or with a finger to cover the surface well. I work warm reflected light into the shadow of the face, add the highlight on the hair, and add a warm touch to suggest more of the ear.

I add a dense patchwork of dark and light blue strokes (plus hints of orange) to build up the drapery on the model stand. I also build up the lights and darks on the figure and blend the tones more thoroughly, so the forms become more three-dimensional. There are cool touches on the torso and right thigh, just where the light turns into shadow. Notice that I've decided to eliminate the distracting dark shape along the model's back.

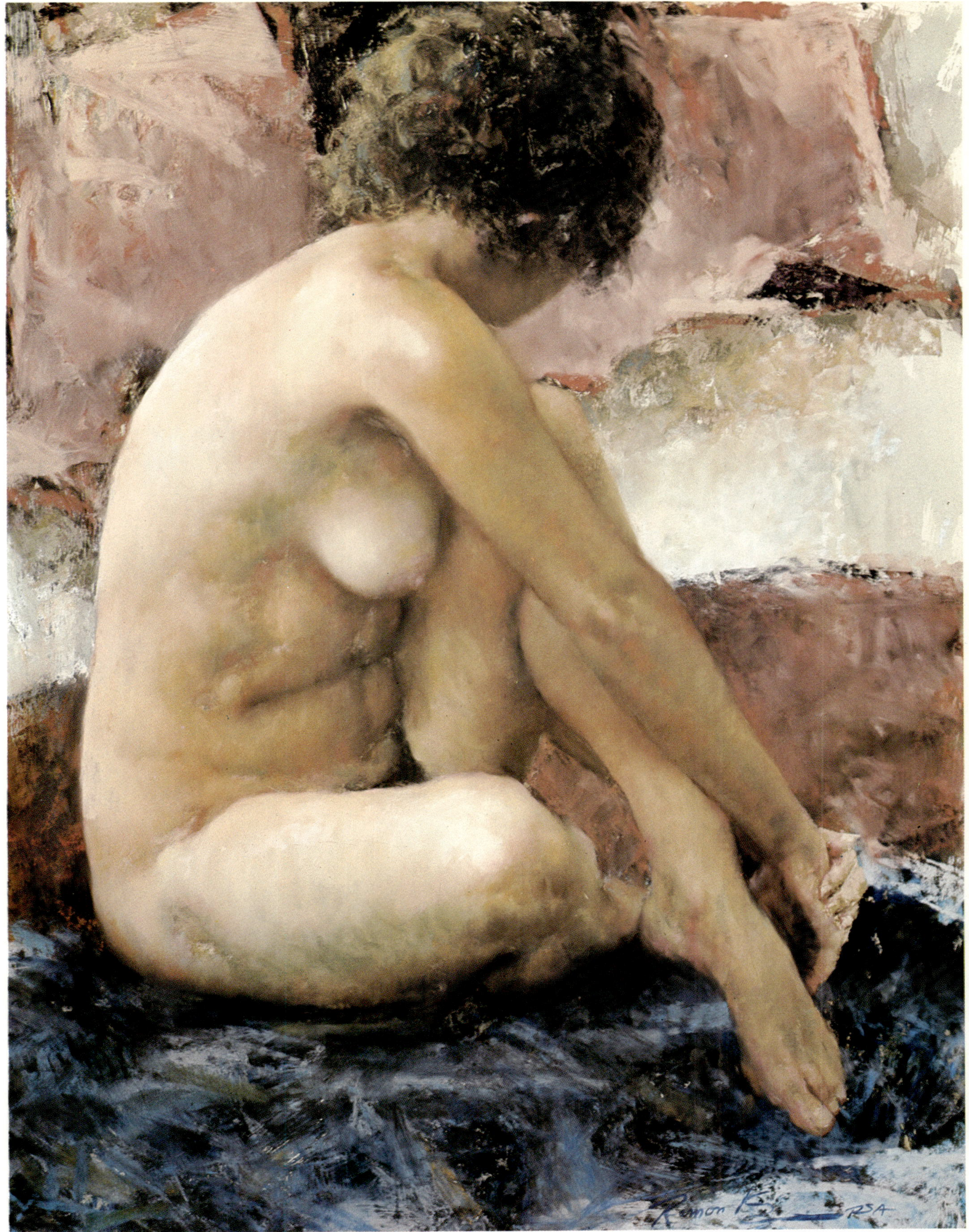

Step 5. Finally, I make the foreground drapery even cooler to contrast with the warmth of the figure, which now stands out more boldly. I build up the shoulder, arm, and left leg to model the forms more distinctly; finish the forearm; finish the hands with warm pinks, putting a shadow under the palm of the right hand; and finish the foot, adding the toes and the delicate modeling. Notice that I've darkened the raised thigh and lower leg, as well as the arm, so that the strongest light now falls on the back and the right thigh. You can see that I use particularly warm colors on the hands and feet; this is true to nature, since the blood is close to the surface in these areas. A last sparkle of light is added to the blue drapery to make it look less heavy. *Nude on Blue Drapery* was exhibited at the Pastel Society of America in New York City and in Mainstreams 1976 at Marietta College in Marietta, Ohio.

THE PORTRAIT IN PASTEL

The delight of a nude is in the beauty of flesh. In the first demonstration, I carried the modeling and smooth surface texture quite far to capture the softness and pearly skin tones of the model.

Now for my second demonstration, I'm doing a more roughly painted portrait of an old man from northern Mexico; his flesh tones are on the warm side. Where a shadow meets the light on a Mexican or Black face, there's a warm color right at that juncture.

There's color in the shadow, too. For example, a few strokes of blue in the hair help to make the portrait as colorful as possible. You have to be careful about adding such colors: too much and it's theatrical; too little and it's colorless.

In this portrait, I block in the forms with watercolor again, but I carry this watercolor underpainting as far as possible toward the finished stage. I'm seeking a rougher texture than in the first demonstration, so my technique is somewhat different, with more active handling of the pastel. The use of watercolor is a shortcut—it allows me to build the basic construction so that I can then work spontaneously in pastel for more gusto and crispness. I think of the watercolor as a map to go by.

This portrait is done on white French sanded paper, mounted on board. I prefer the mounted paper, as it simplifies framing.

My first wash is almost "no color"—a mixture of black with a touch of yellow ochre. My initial search is for placement and gesture, stated in a toned-down neutral gray wash of medium value. I use a ½" (13 mm) nylon flat brush, designed for painting in acrylics; it can take the abuse it gets from painting over sand.

This painting is done from life. I want to paint a realistic picture of old age—the grizzled beard and shadowed face in bright light. The model is wearing a red turtleneck, which I change toward the end of the painting to the loose cotton shirt worn in northern Mexico, since this seems to suit the subject better.

My pastel palette is alizarin crimson; cadmium orange, red, and yellow; cobalt blue; burnt sienna; white; and black.

I contrast warm strokes with cool to enrich the modeling. In each stage, accuracy of drawing is essential. You have to ad lib with the direction of strokes to activate a portrait; otherwise, it can be a static sort of thing. My vigorous final strokes of pastel are meant to produce an energizing effect.

This portrait of Tim Oteo is 14" x 11" (35.5 x 28 cm), and is done on white French sanded paper, mounted on board. I prefer the mounted paper, as it simplifies framing.

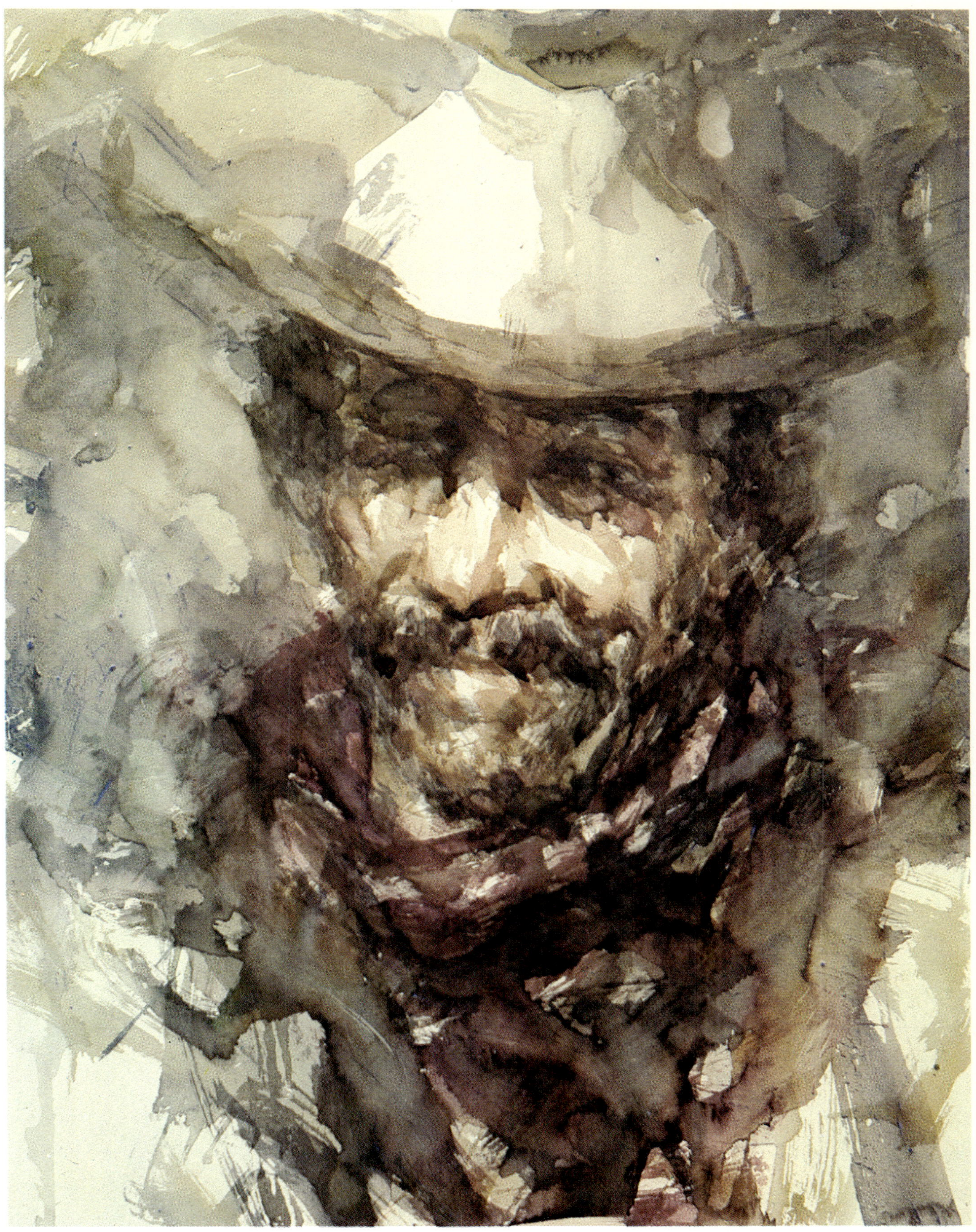

Step 1. With a neutral mixture of black and a touch of yellow ochre watercolor, I lay in washes that are cooler in the background and on the garment than on the face; to warm the face, I add more ochre. With alizarin crimson, I barely suggest the garment under the chin. I leave areas open to catch the light in the face, hat, and background. You'll see some linear drybrush over the clear, juicy washes. This isn't important to the final work, but it's important to me. I have to be constantly aware of some of the lines of flesh or scars in the face and of the textural differences of the face and clothes—or I may lose the whole painting. I'm always drawing at every stage of a painting.

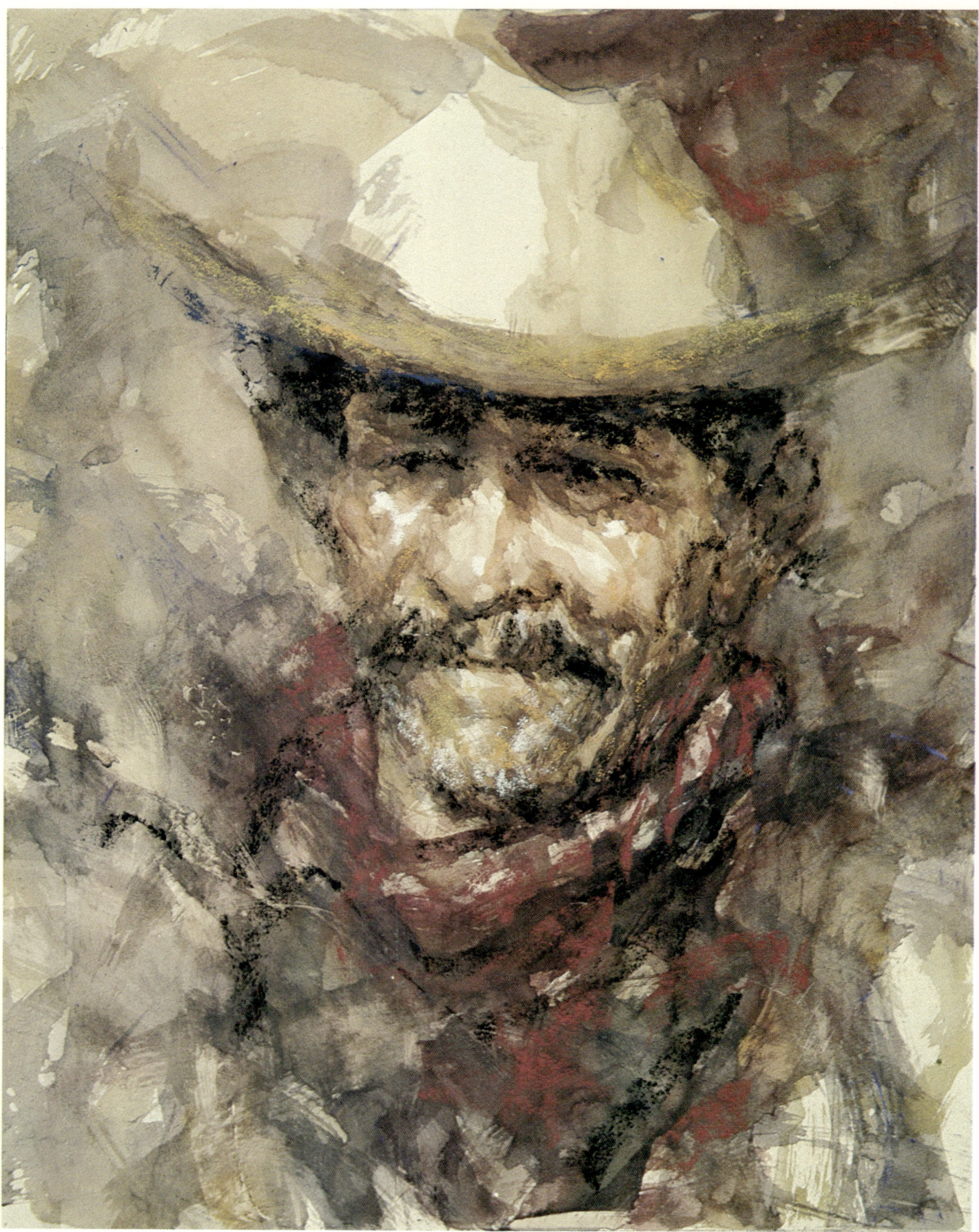

Step 2. My habit—which I recommend—is to work all over the board, never dwelling on any one area. I add alizarin crimson to the face with intentional, direct strokes, but I paint in on the shirt with a scumbling effect and I give a few scumbled licks of it to the background. Alizarin crimson, when placed over the dark underlayer, becomes grayed, which is what I want. Washes of pure color are pretty, but unnatural. I use cadmium orange and yellow ochre to warm the face. With the black and ochre mixture, I place cool tones under the eyebrows, on the hair, under the nose, and on the mustache and beard.

At this stage, I lightly indicate the darks with black pastel: the boundaries of the ears and head; the shadow on the cheek, the darks beneath the hat and nose, and some folds on the shirt. I place a few touches of alizarin crimson pastel on the shirt for color and add some white pastel strokes to the chin for the stubble.

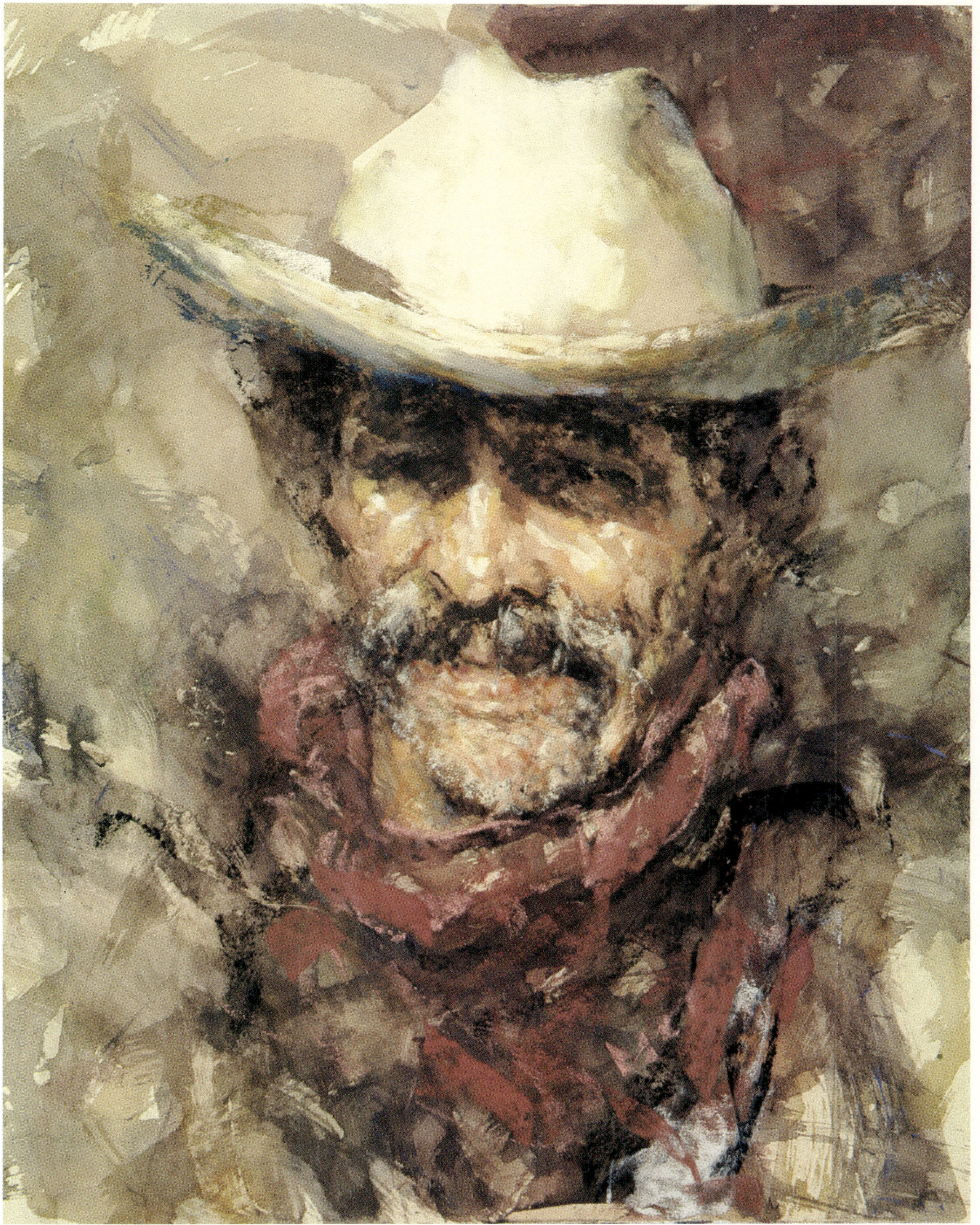

Step 3. My final watercolor washes are much darker values of the local color. (Local color is the actual color of an object, unaffected by such environmental factors as the lighting or reflected color.) I use cadmium red and burnt sienna in the flesh under the nose, on the cheeks, and in the shadowed areas. I bring out the cranium area with warm darks on the right side, under the brim of the hat. The darkest values in the painting are on the shirt. Because they're a known quantity, they act as a reference to which I can compare values elsewhere. For example, I can see that the face is not as dark as the garment. I give attention to the modeling of the eye sockets, the bridge of the nose, the ear, the chin, and the hat in these last washes. I now add a few light strokes of alizarin crimson pastel to the shirt.

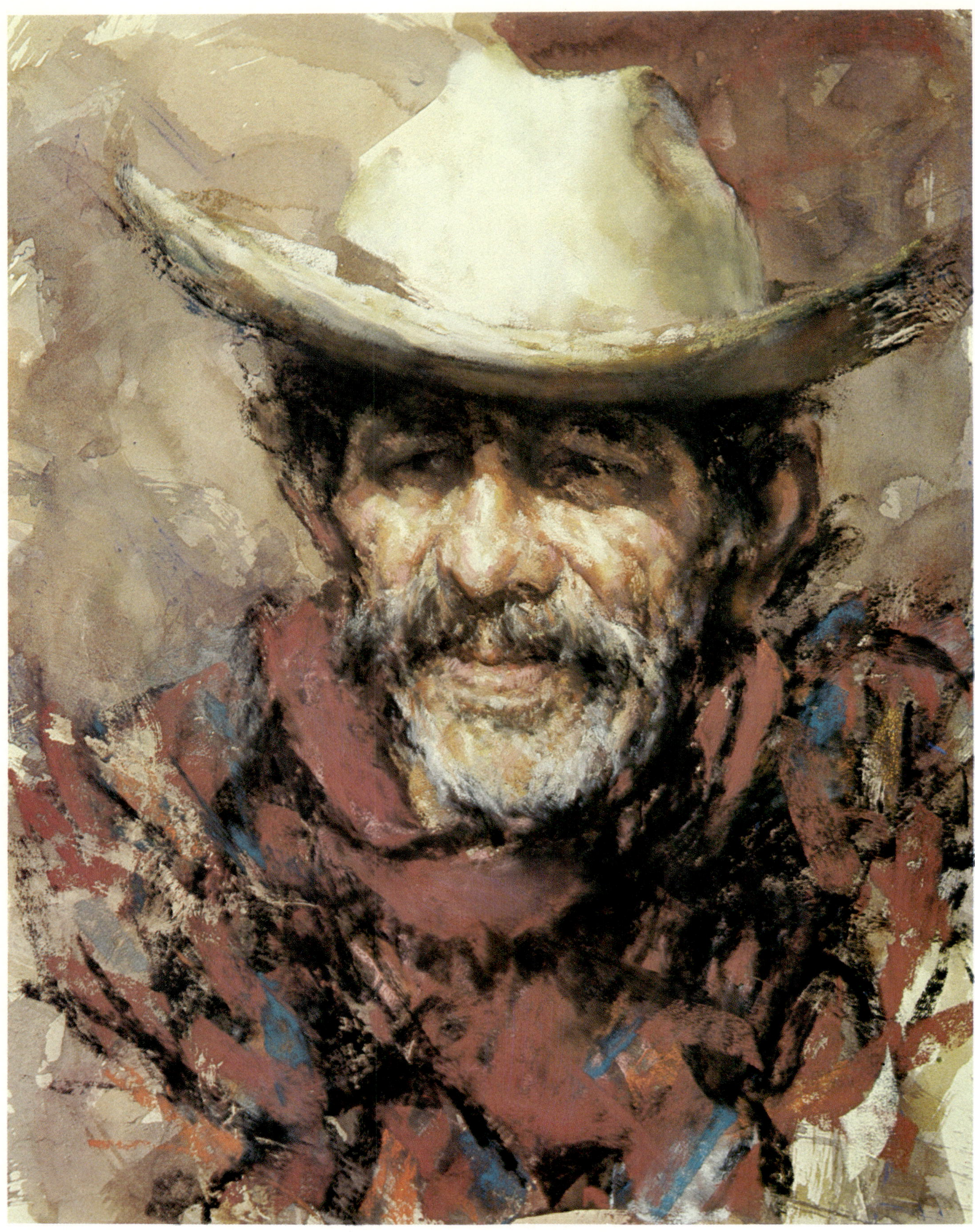

Step 4. I switch to pastel completely now, starting with black on the darkest darks, under the brim of the hat, in and around the eyes, under the nose and chin, and in the mustache and stubble on the chin. I add cadmium yellow to the hat and face, and stroke grayed alizarin crimson over the neutral washes in the background. Notice, in particular, the strong modeling of the lips. Also note that on the lighted chin, the warm flesh tones and the cool stubble of the beard are the same value, but their contrast in color temperature keeps them separate. I try to keep the painting crisp, with definite strokes of color, but I've learned never to paint hair with lines—it gives a "noodle" effect. Simply blocking in the hair as a mass is more realistic.

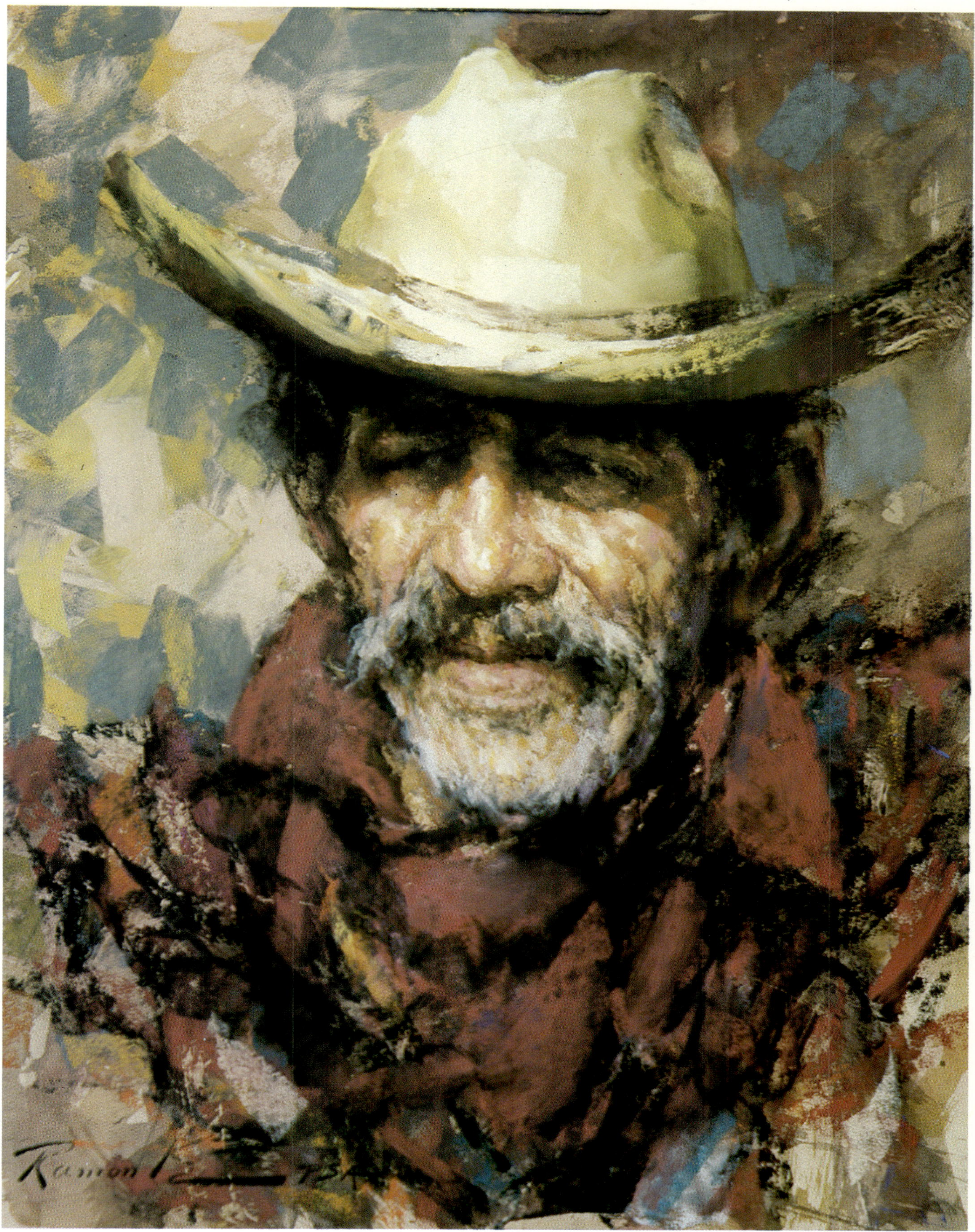

Step 5. In the final stage of the painting, I work on details of modeling and enrichment of color. With a hit-or-miss stroke, I make the band of the hat. I describe the right ear accurately, without overpainting it. I accentuate the strong light source by painting chunks of light into the background, using the piece of light cobalt blue pastel held flat. The edge of the lighted area is cadmium yellow. Under the chin, I use black and a curved stroke of blue around it. To cool the glint in the old man's right eye, I use a grayed blue, leaving some warmth on the bottom of this light; I add a touch of the blue to the left eye also. I change the turtleneck to an open-collared shirt with a few dark lines. Now all the colors in the painting are moving through the painting, every color setting up paths for the eye to follow. Warm and cool tones are in the background, the face, hat, and shirt. With a few gutsy strokes, I finish it off and add my signature.

THE PORTRAIT IN OIL

This portrait is a demonstration of an alla prima character study—simple, bold, and direct. In a larger figure painting such as *Stephanie* (pages 72–77), I try to get as much work as possible into the face before I go on to other parts of the painting. But when I do a portrait like this one, *Ernie*, I plan to build toward the final painting evenly, working all areas at the same time. But I'll hold back on refining any one feature until all the color harmonies are working well. The warmth of the face will play against the cool hair and background. I'll be using attention-holding aspects of the model—his mustache, beard, and open shirt—as focal points.

I'm using a ⅛″ (3 mm) thick Masonite panel, 14″ x 11″ (35.5 x 28 cm), of medium texture, primed with white lead over a rabbitskin glue size. I plan to let this texture show through in the scumbled effect of many strokes in the painting.

The palette I'm using is raw sienna, burnt umber, cadmium yellow, cadmium scarlet, alizarin crimson, cobalt blue, cobalt violet, phthalo green, ivory black, and titanium white. I plan to use cobalt blue, cobalt violet, and phthalo green for the cool areas; and cadmium yellow, cadmium scarlet, and alizarin crimson for the warm areas. Raw sienna, burnt umber, ivory black, and titanium white will be used for toning. As I steadily build up the painting with these colors, I'll vary the type of brushstroke I use.

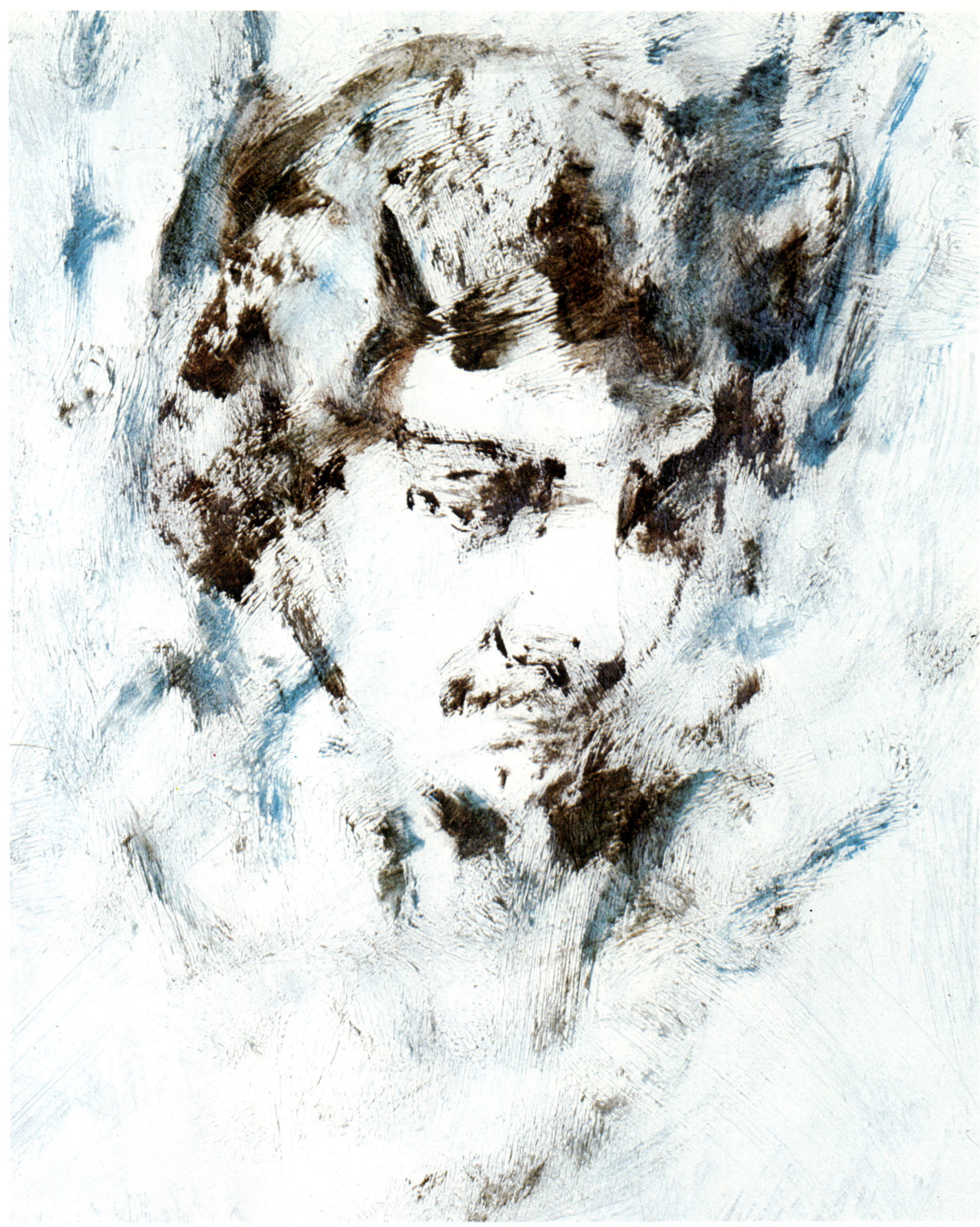

Step 1. For the preliminary sketch I've picked a Japanese watercolor brush by J.B.A. Langnickel with a 7″ (18 cm) long bamboo handle. This brush is modestly priced and yet holds up surprisingly well when used with oil.

The brush has the virtue of flexibility. It makes wide, uneven, or narrow, linear strokes, depending on the way it's held. I even lay it on its side and drag it for a varied effect. It's fun to use. I love to experiment and I'm not a creature of habit, so this painting—like much of my work—is an adventure.

Using cobalt blue, phthalo green, and raw sienna, I draw in the face. On the left eye, left eyebrow, nose, cheek, and mustache you can see the fine lines of brushwork. The light source in this painting is from the left.

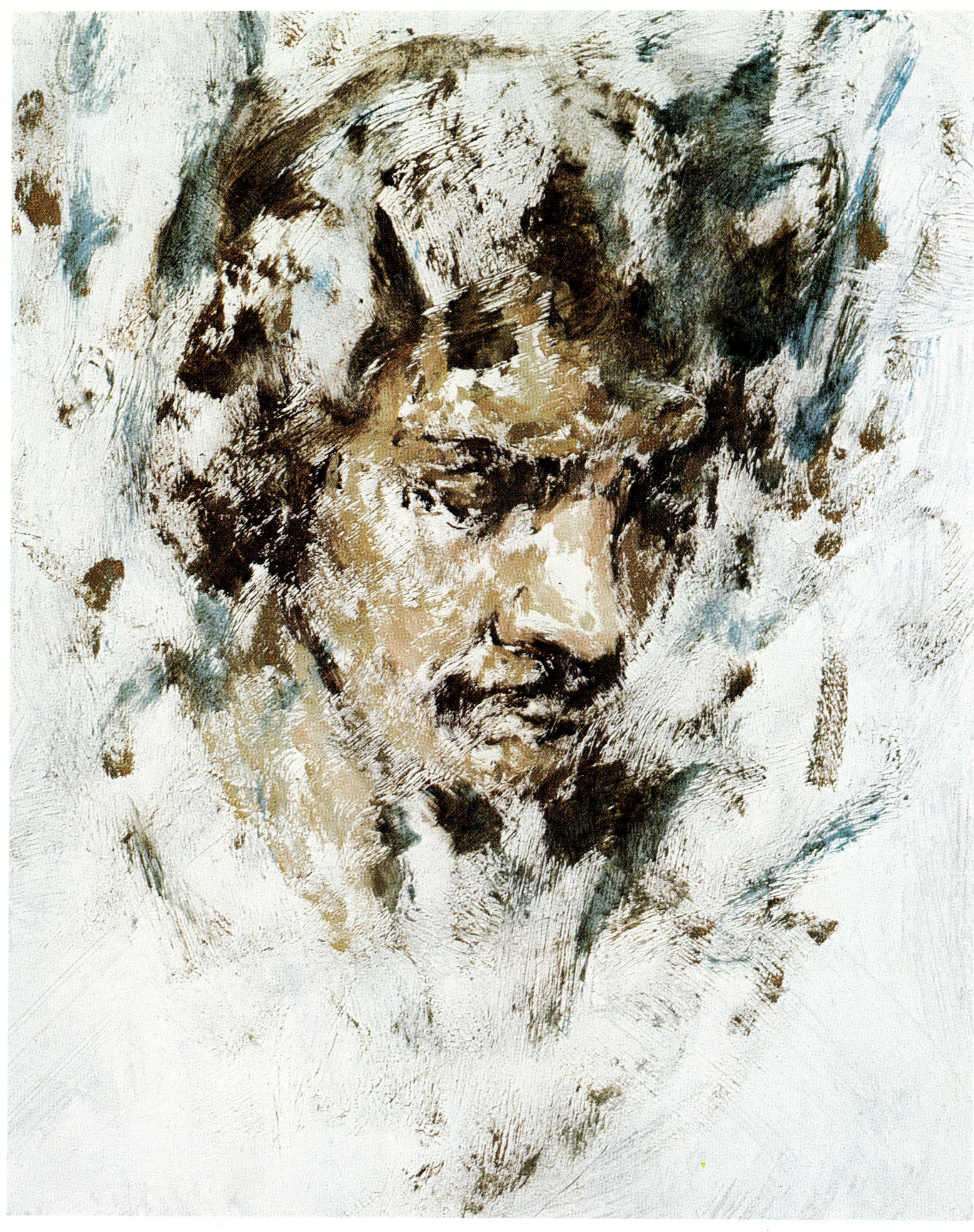

Step 2. With a number 4 filbert, I add cool color to the face in small strokes. I'm using phthalo green, cadmium yellow, and a little alizarin crimson toned down with a touch of burnt umber. I work around the forehead, left cheek, mustache, and chin with its stubble of beard. On the left cheek and chin I add more phthalo green and alizarin crimson, and then bring in warm flesh tones of cadmium scarlet, alizarin crimson, with a little white, on the bridge of the nose, bottom of the left nostril, under the eye, and on the left cheek.

This is not a large painting, but I want it to have a strong impact. So I scumble strokes of the same flesh tones onto the right side of the face and on the background around the head. I'm being as bold and direct as possible here while I'm still laying in and adjusting the placement. At this stage, it's a mistake to put in a lot of work on a single feature. You have to concentrate on the placement first because it's still easy to change it at this point.

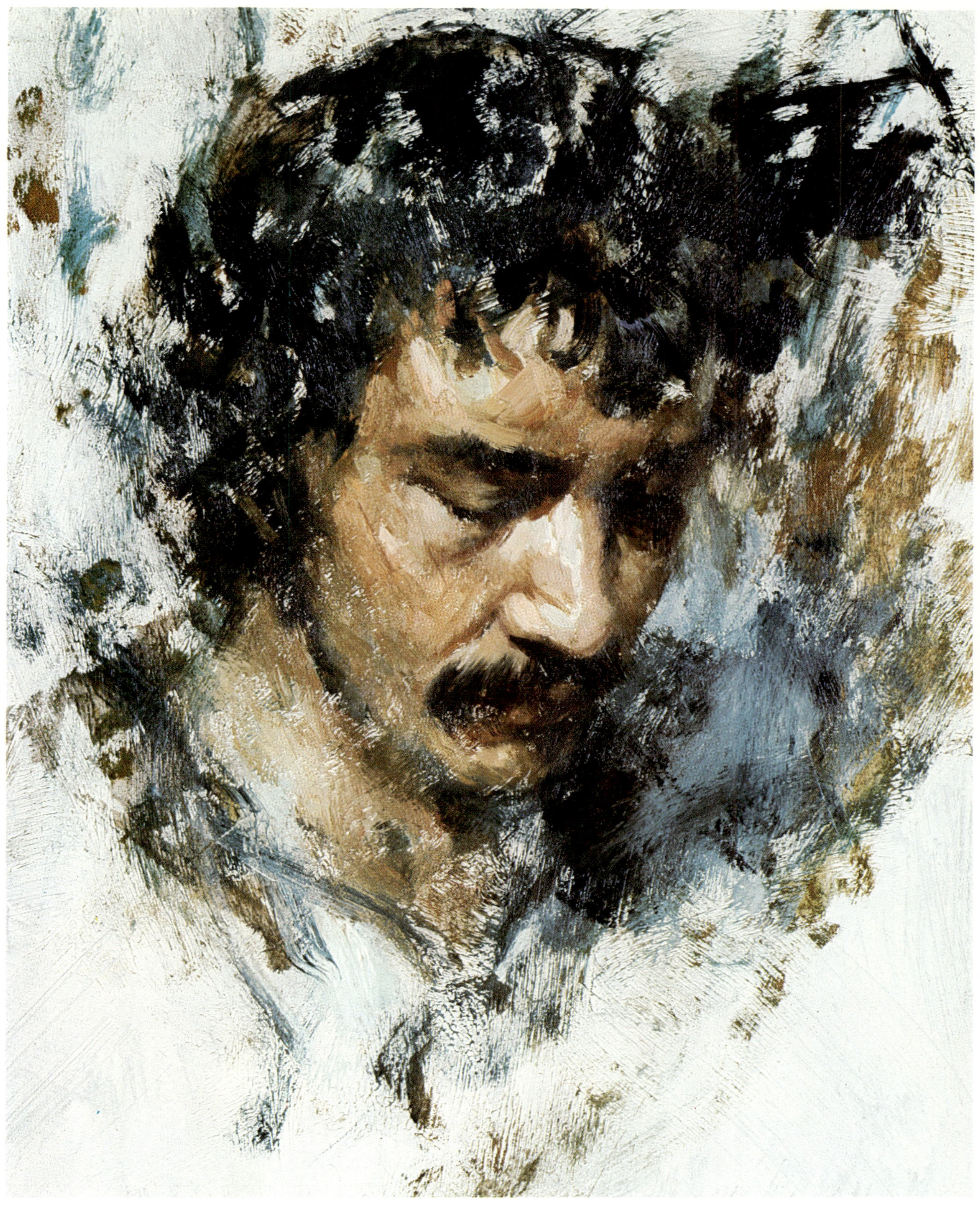

Step 3. My first effort is to get the shape of the hair. Ernie has black hair, but painting it all black would create too much of a contrast between the hair and the face. So instead I use cobalt blue and phthalo green with raw sienna, in addition to black. I put some cool highlights on the curls here and there. Under the curl over the center forehead, I add warm color. On the far left, I cool the hair with phthalo green.

I'm also creating a contrast between the warm flesh and the cool stubble of the beard. From the left cheekbone down to the chin, there's a nice cool effect now. Because this is a male subject, I cool the lips by adding cobalt violet and phthalo green to cadmium scarlet and alizarin crimson.

This is a crucial stage in modeling the head. I warm the edges between the light and shadow areas on the forehead, the cheekbone near the right eye, and on the neck. The neck goes from the cool, lighted side to warmer tones in the shadow and down below in the open shirt area.

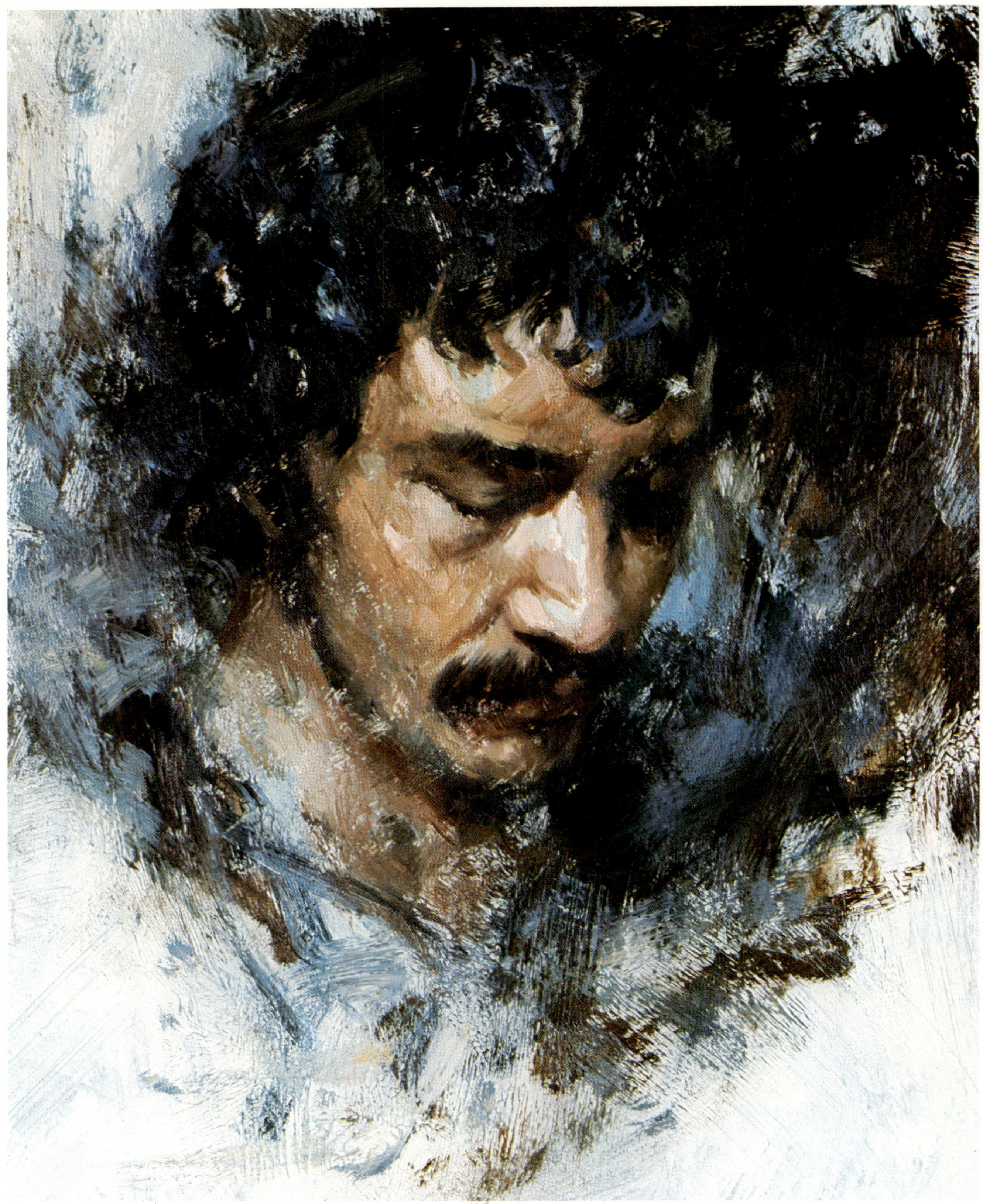

Step 4. I want Ernie's head to emerge from the background, which is to be dark on the right side and light on the left. The problem now is to figure out how to make it work.

I decide to vary the values of the hair and background to create a three-dimensional effect. Notice here that the contrast is sharpest at the top left where the background is nearly white and the hair is very dark. The shadowed background on the right pulls away dramatically from the shadowed cheek because there are subtle variations in the values of the background against the face.

The tone under the chin is warm now in contrast with the stubble of the beard and mustache. There is a warm crease by the left nostril that suggests where the cheek starts to roll. I spend some time searching for reflections of light on the forehead—and for the highlights on projecting areas of the forehead, bridge and tip of the nose, the lip, and on the neck. Light catches the upper lip near the mustache.

Little, open, unpainted areas still must be covered or the painting will appear to be flaking. I use the Japanese brush again to lay on generous amounts of paint in the background, especially on the top center and right side, and under the chin of the model. There's brushwork visible on the left side now, too.

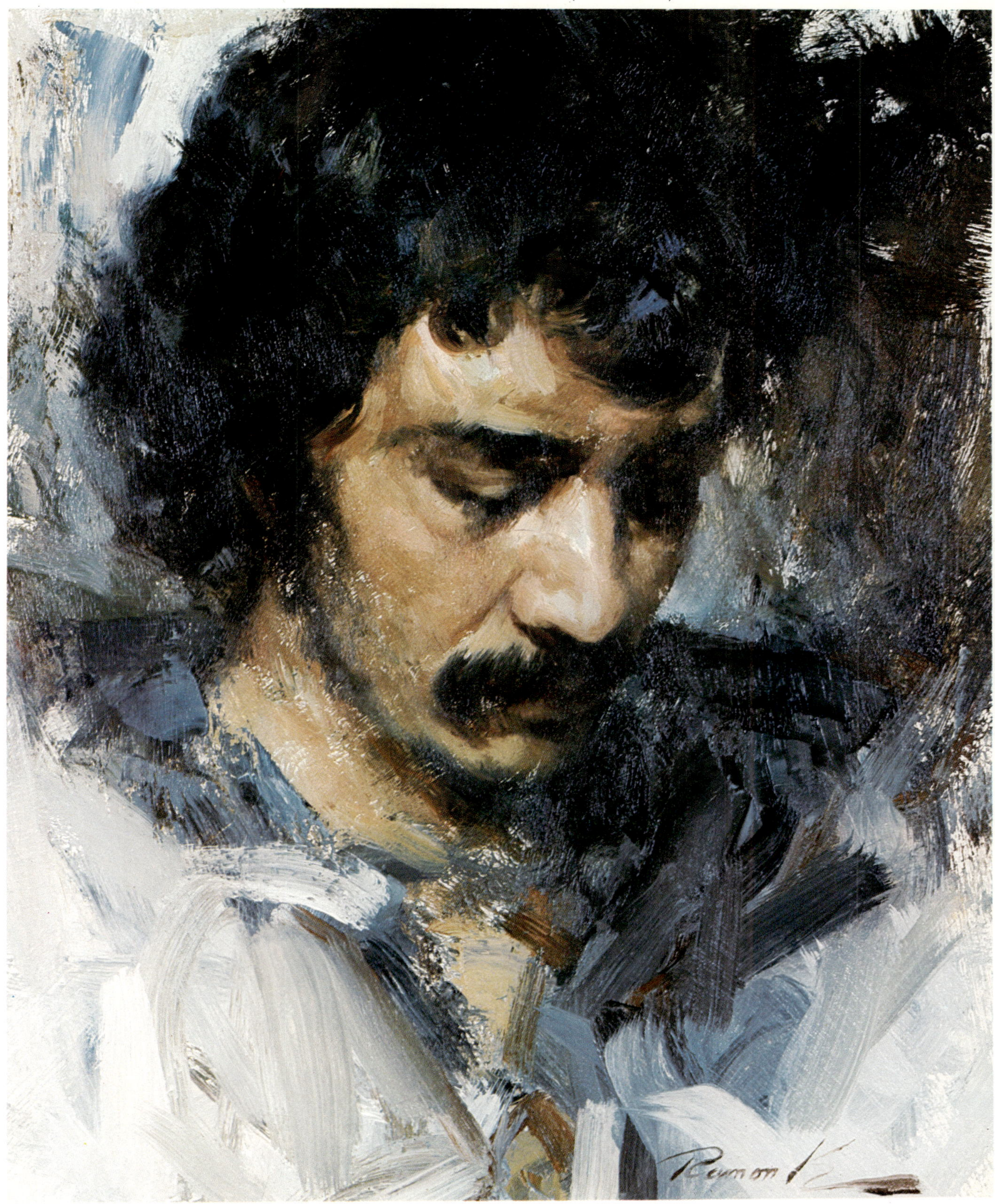

Step 5. I could have left the painting as it was at the end of the last step—bold, artistic, and spontaneous—but I decide to work on it more. I'm an impressionistic-style painter and I like brushwork, scumbling, and palette knife effects to play their part in the final painting.

I work more on the shadow and reflections under the chin. I define the shirt further and then add palette knife work to both shoulders.

If you study the pattern of warm colors in the painting, you'll see it makes almost an *S* shape coming around the forehead from the right and then down and under the chin. The placement of skin tones on the open shirt balances well with the tones of the face.

I put in palette knife strokes of cool color in the left and right foreground—nice, buttery paint as opposed to the drybrush effect on the shirt and neck. By now, almost all of the white spots on the board are well covered except in the mustache, where they work well.

I do some final defining of the eyelids and cheek, the mustache, and the bottom lip. I then strengthen the high-key, warm edge of the nose and put a warm highlight in the hair on the left as if it were reflected off the white background there.

I could carry this painting even further toward a refined finish, but I prefer to leave it like this—still bold and not overly finished.

THE FIGURE IN OIL

Stephanie is a chubby little two-year-old child. I want to bring out her cherubic quality in this three-quarter figure painting, but I have another goal besides just capturing her likeness. The warm colors of her flesh tones and the decorative costume she's wearing are the kind of elements that excite me in painting.

This will be an exercise in color. My concern is to use contrasting warms and cools to separate Stephanie from the background—to give her roundness and life and to create a moving pattern of color that is beautiful in itself.

My palette is raw sienna, burnt umber, cadmium yellow, cadmium orange, cadmium scarlet, alizarin crimson, cobalt blue, cobalt violet, phthalo green, ivory black, and titanium white. I am working on 24" x 18" (61 x 45.5 cm) Masonite.

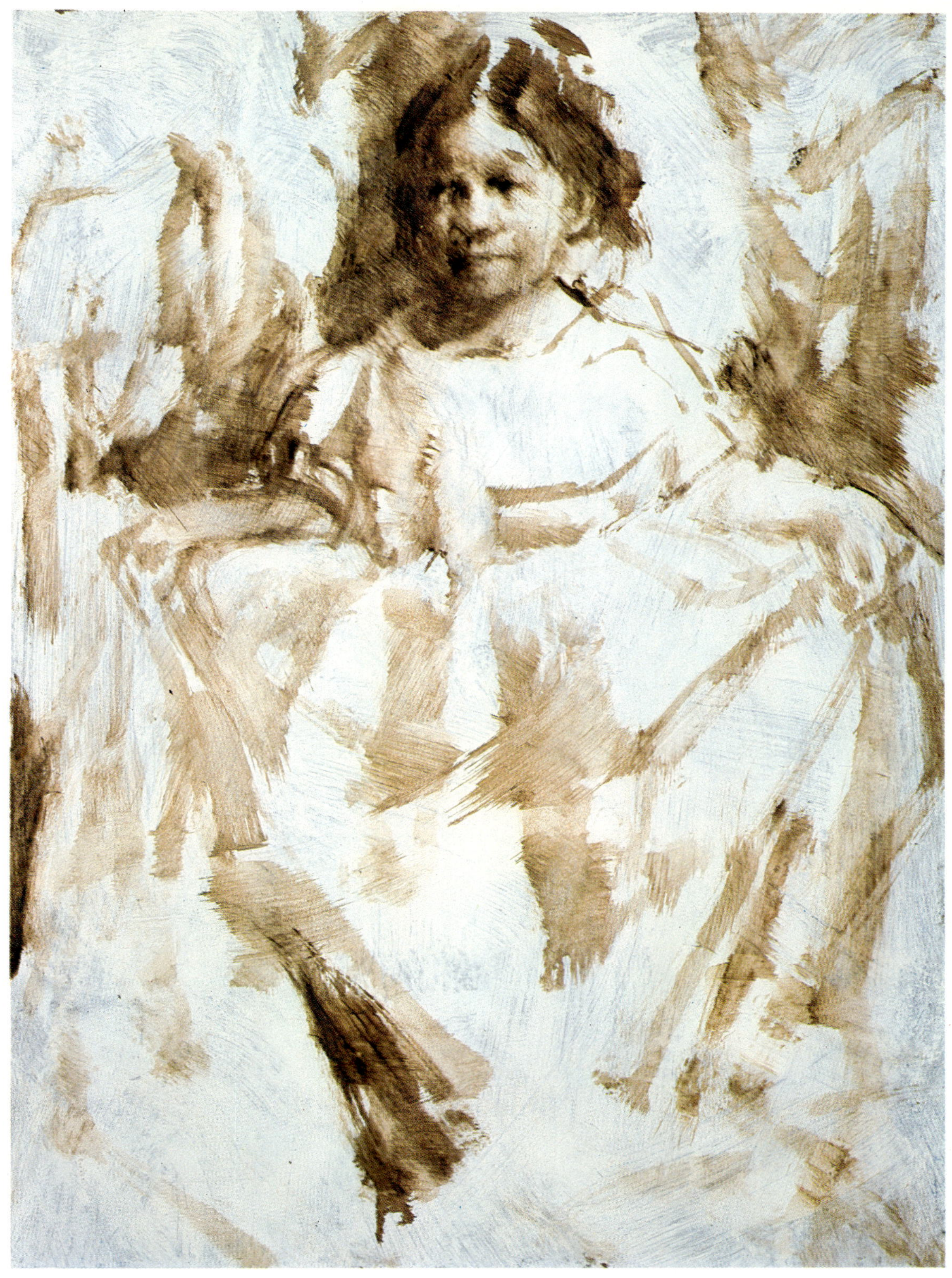

Step 1. With washes of ivory black and raw sienna diluted with turpentine, I lay in the darks boldly using a number 12 filbert. My darkest darks, where I've used less turpentine and more pigment, are concentrated on the hair, on the left and right sides of the background, and on the center bottom of the panel. I make big broad strokes here at first.

Switching to a number 4 egbert, I draw in the features of the face, the right side of the neck, the right shoulder, the blouse, and the hands with finer lines. At this stage the painting is still rather rough. I'm searching for placement and the general character of the model.

I try not to use too much turpentine because when I lay on heavier color in the next step, I don't want the paint to ride or skid over the turpentine. I'm hoping the underpainted washes will be dry enough by then so that the pigment will catch into the texture of the board and stay put, allowing me to scumble or paint a stroke without sliding.

My line and wash drawing is now complete and I'm ready for the first strokes of color.

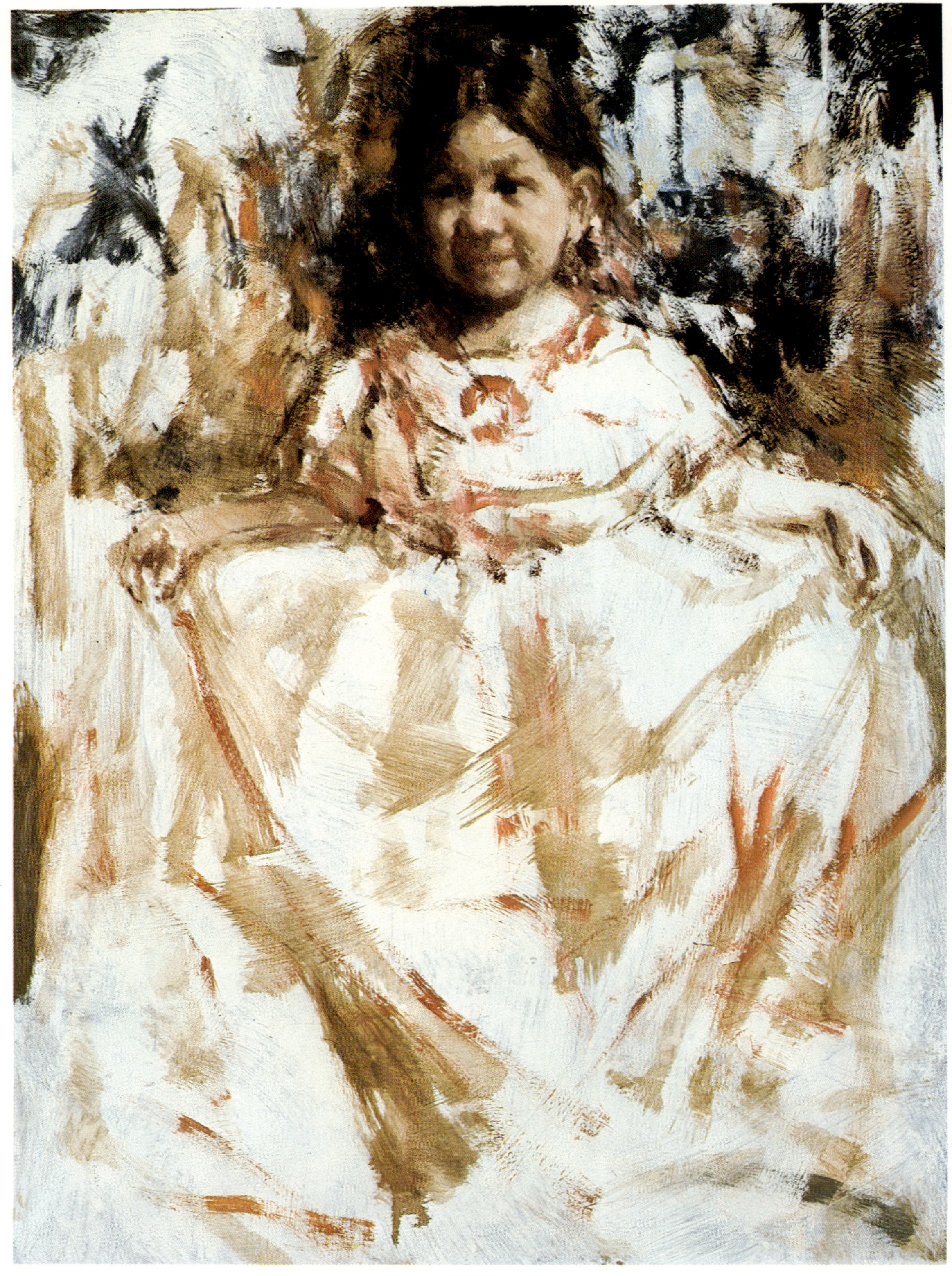

Step 2. The face will serve as a color guide for the rest of the painting, so I begin work on it first. For flesh tones, I use raw sienna, cadmium yellow, cadmium scarlet, and titanium white. For these strokes I use medium filberts, some small egberts, and round sables.

After blocking in the face, I immediately lay some strokes of these flesh colors in the background for harmony. On the lips and at the top of the right ear, my mixture is raw sienna, alizarin crimson, and a touch of cobalt violet. I block in the hair with raw sienna and ivory black, and I give the hands just a bit of definition with the flesh tones.

In the background, the scumbled strokes are dark values of cobalt blue, ivory black, and a touch of phthalo green. I also add cadmium orange and a touch of ivory black to tone it down in value. The blouse gets a few strokes of black and alizarin crimson—just a beginning of the floral design of the cloth. I make a few scumbled strokes on the skirt at the bottom right and left. This is the most enjoyable part of the painting, where everything is still free and nothing is finished.

I go pretty dark on the hair, eyes, bottom of the nose, bottom of the lips, and under the chin. These deep tones indicate shadow areas. Later I'll go back into them with color. My light source is from the right, so I make a definite shadow on the left side of the face and blouse. This shadow lightens toward the bottom of the painting. The underpainting still shows through at this stage.

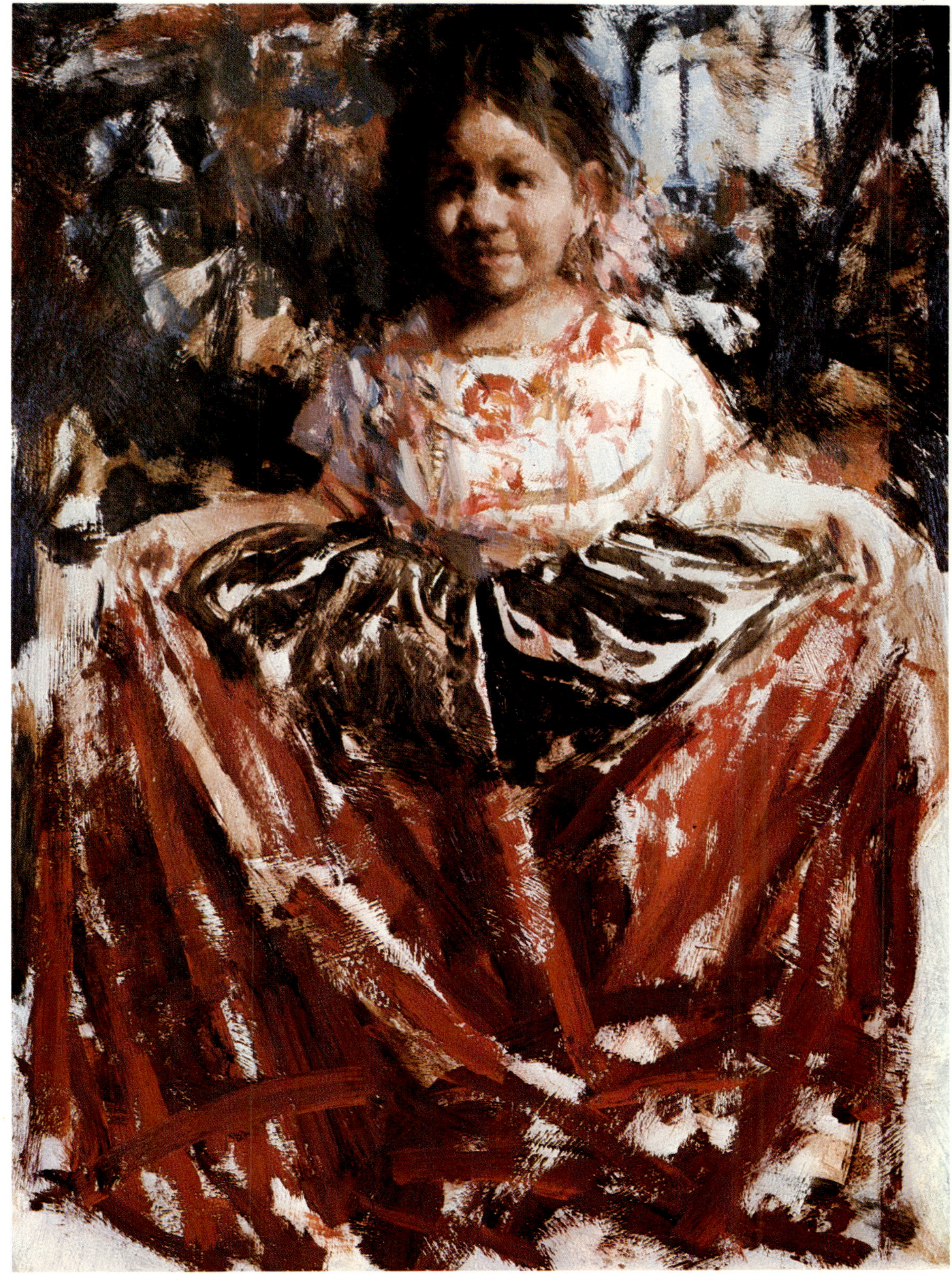

Step 3. I'm working now on the darks of the blouse with cobalt blue, ivory black, and cobalt violet. The left sleeve is darker than the right, but I add strokes of cadmium scarlet, alizarin crimson, and titanium white on that sleeve so there's color in the shadow.

On the face and neck, where the light is most concentrated, I keep the color cool; but as it moves toward the shadow, I use warmer color. I work both cool and warm touches into the hair and blouse.

In the background at the left there's a shadow. Into it, I throw a few broad strokes of cobalt blue and ivory black with a touch of phthalo green. In the background at the upper right, my strokes are a cool blue, made mostly with cobalt violet and ivory black.

My next area of interest is the skirt, with its strong colors, patterns, and shapes. I apply powerful vertical brushstrokes of ivory black, raw sienna, and a touch of cobalt violet in order to set off the dark folds of the cloth as they come out from the waist. I then add two or three almost horizontal strokes for a contrast in direction.

There are still many areas I still haven't touched with paint, but at this middle stage, I'm happy with what's happening. From here on, I'll be adding details and searching for interesting patterns until the painting is finished.

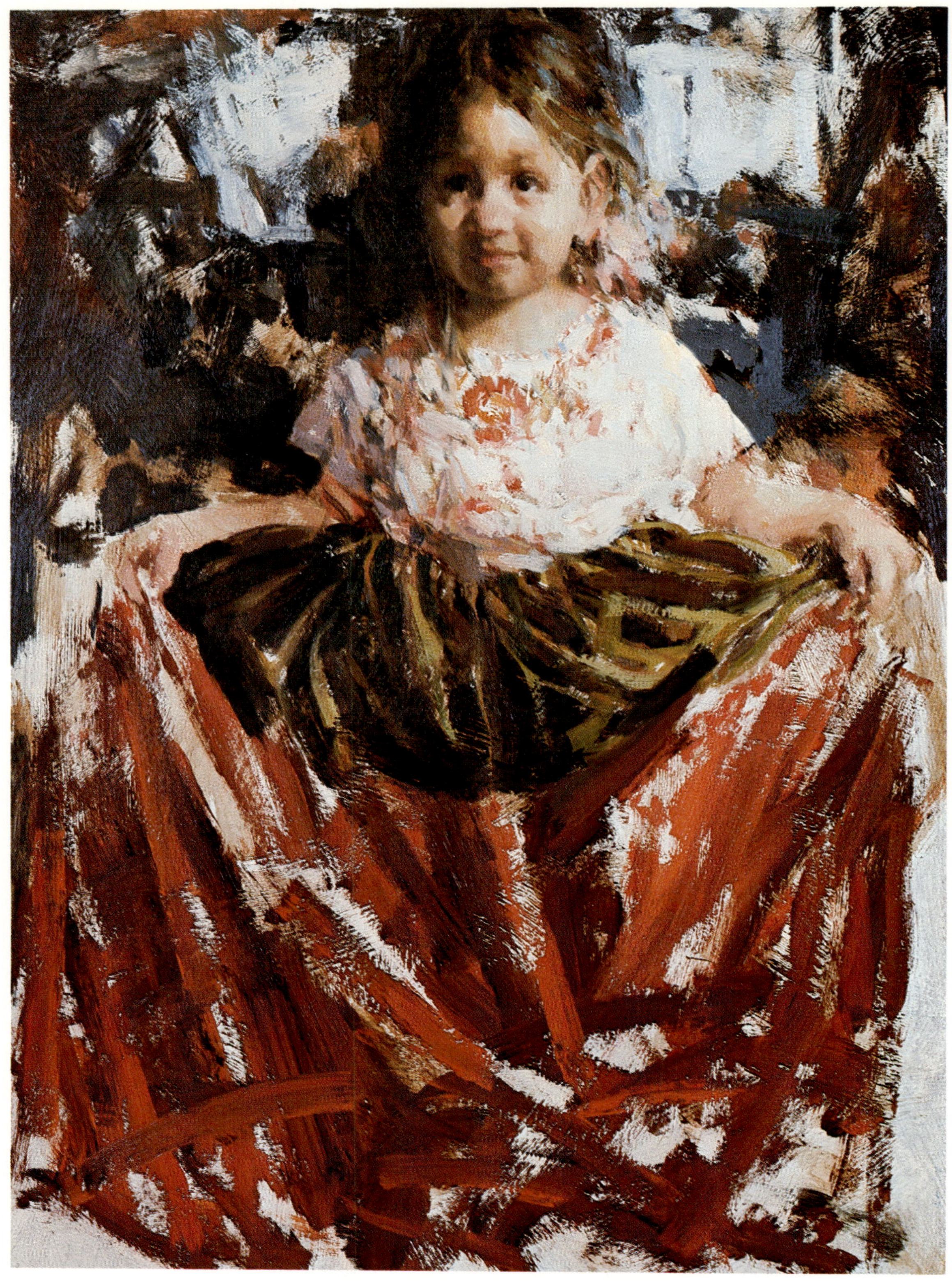

Step 4. I'm covering up more of the underpainting now, working all over the board. I add white with a bit of cobalt blue and cadmium yellow to the background at the left. Both hands are beginning to take on more form with the cadmium yellow, cadmium scarlet, and cobalt violet strokes I place there. Because there's so much light on the face, the hair needs to be lighter also. On the hair near the light source, I build up the highlight with cobalt blue, phthalo green, and cadmium yellow.

I add cadmium yellow and a little raw sienna to the light on the skirt folds. Now there's a clear color change from the waist to the reds at the bottom of the skirt.

The effect I'm after—a figure separated by air and space from the background—is starting to work for me. The face and blouse are beginning to have three-dimensional form. I'm gradually pulling the figure away from the background by emphasizing light and dark contrasts. The position of the arms and hands adds a feeling of projection to the work.

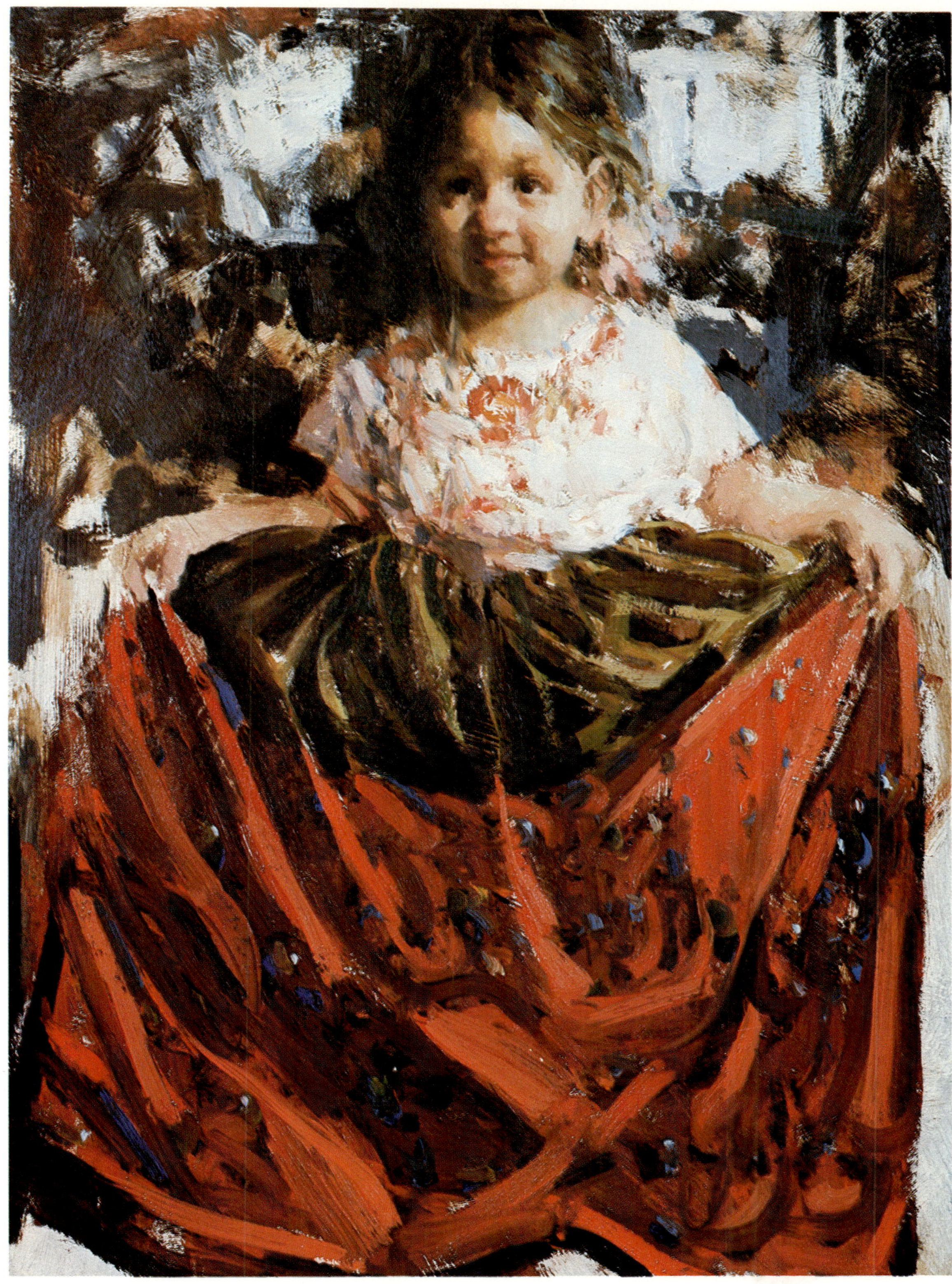

Step 5. Because so much space will be covered by the skirt, I must be bold in painting it. I exaggerate the dark folds with cobalt violet and black and then hit the lighter areas with the reds, using cadmium yellow, cadmium scarlet, alizarin crimson, and white. You can almost count the big brushstrokes where light catches the folds. This is another part of the painting that I find fun—where I'm really enjoying it.

I notice that there's a concentration of red in the lower skirt. I want to incorporate that area into the painting more, so I add touches of cool blue in little dabs. Then with mixtures of cadmium yellow and white I make warm, bright dabs. It gives the glittery effect of embroidery on a Mexican skirt and I like it, so I don't change it.

On the blouse I have warm colors playing in cool shadows on the left and cool colors playing in warm light on the right. The left arm and hand are almost finished now. I'm still trying to decide if I should leave some underpainting visible or cover it up completely.

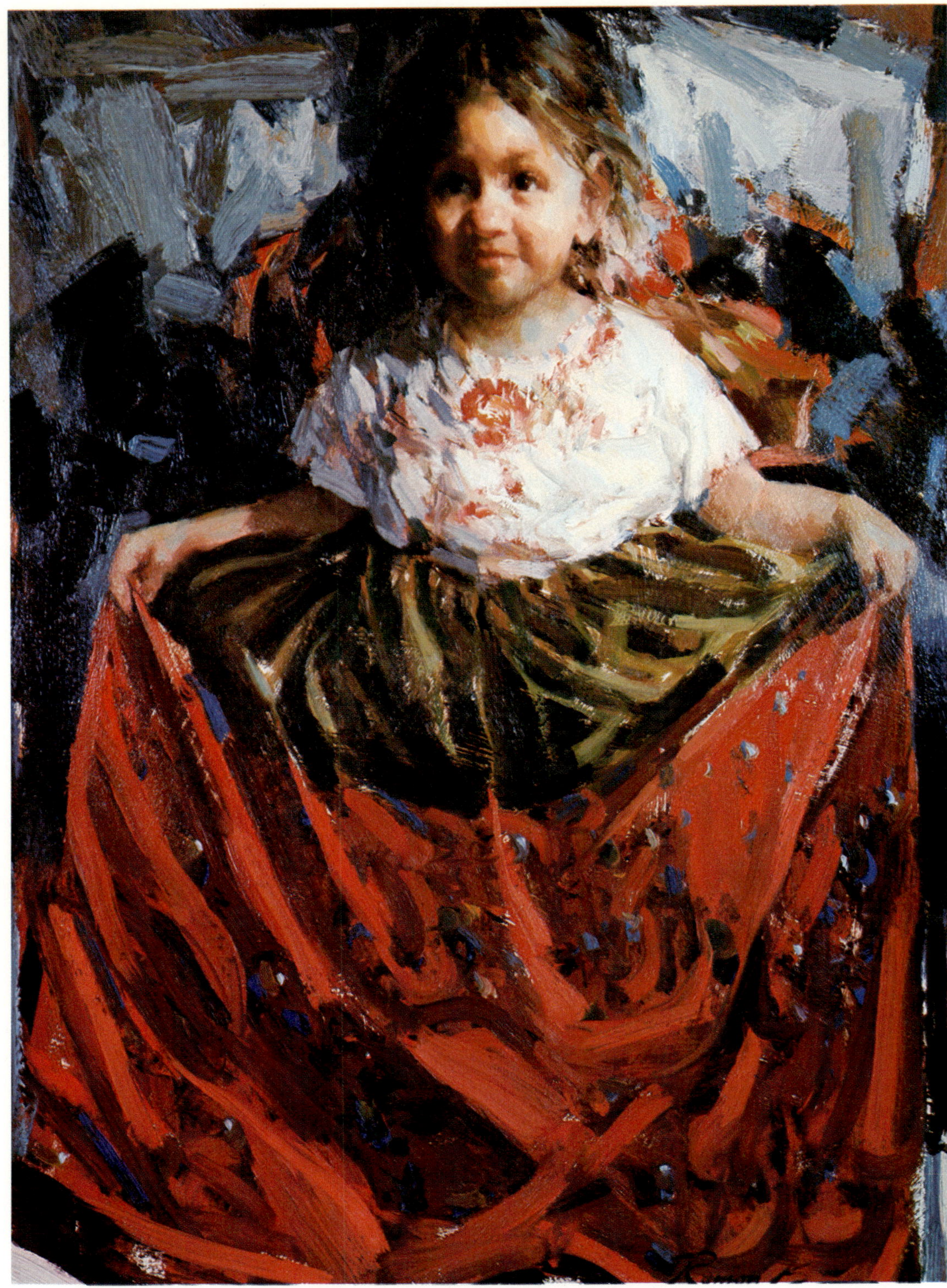

Step 6. I am covering up the background after all. There's almost nothing of the underpainting visible.

With boldly painted, broad strokes of black, cobalt blue, and phthalo green, I make a very dark ground and then go lighter on top around the blouse and arms. You can feel the space behind Stephanie now, just the way I wanted it to be.

The little model has a bright scarf tied in the back of her hair. I'm using that to give me an excuse for placing warm touches of cadmium scarlet, cadmium orange, alizarin crimson, and white on both sides of her hair—lighter on the right and darker on the left. This is an arbitrary decision on my part, but I'm doing it for better balance and color flow.

Degas said something like, "If it feels right to you, then paint it that way"—and that's how I paint. A good example of what feels right is the way I'm coloring the shadow on the left arm. Because that arm is really flesh, I make the shadow on it warm— and it reads right to me.

In the hands, I use my warm mix for the flesh of fingers and thumb, but on the left hand, for the knuckles of the thumb and first finger I go cool with a mix of white, cobalt blue, and phthalo green, lightened toward white. This is also used on the right hand and arm where I use the warmer tones for the shadows.

Finishing off the painting, I make three or four cool strokes on the warm, light side. The colors playing in the face and clothes are found now in the background all the way up the right side. I darken the background more at the bottom to push out the skirt.

You can see that I've refined the features, warming the skin, adding a glint to the eye, and so forth —all this is second nature to me. But the real effort here is to make a harmonious and colorful painting with generous use of pigment, where every area plays its part in a vivid portrait. I believe it's now finished.

THE FIGURE IN WATERCOLOR

When Toni, the model for this watercolor nude, took a reclining pose quite unconsciously, I felt inspired to paint it with a somewhat different approach than usual. Toni is lying in a twisted pose with pronounced torsion between her upper and lower body.

On 140 lb Arches paper, 12″ x 16″ (30.5 x 40.5 cm), I will paint directly, beginning with suggestions of a background setting. The location of the model will be barely indicated with a broad wash in the simplest way, using flesh tones to indicate only where the figure is to be placed in the composition.

This is chancy—to put in background areas before making sure of the pose and placement—and I wouldn't recommend it for a beginner: but at this stage of my career, I try to present myself with new challenges to keep up my excitement in painting. The results of such varied technical approaches are often as satisfying as those from my more practiced methods.

My palette is yellow ochre, burnt sienna, raw umber, burnt umber, cadmium red light, alizarin crimson, light purple, phthalo purple, cobalt blue, Winsor green, viridian, and ivory black. I use ivory black in my watercolor palette rather than lamp black because it dries with a luster I like.

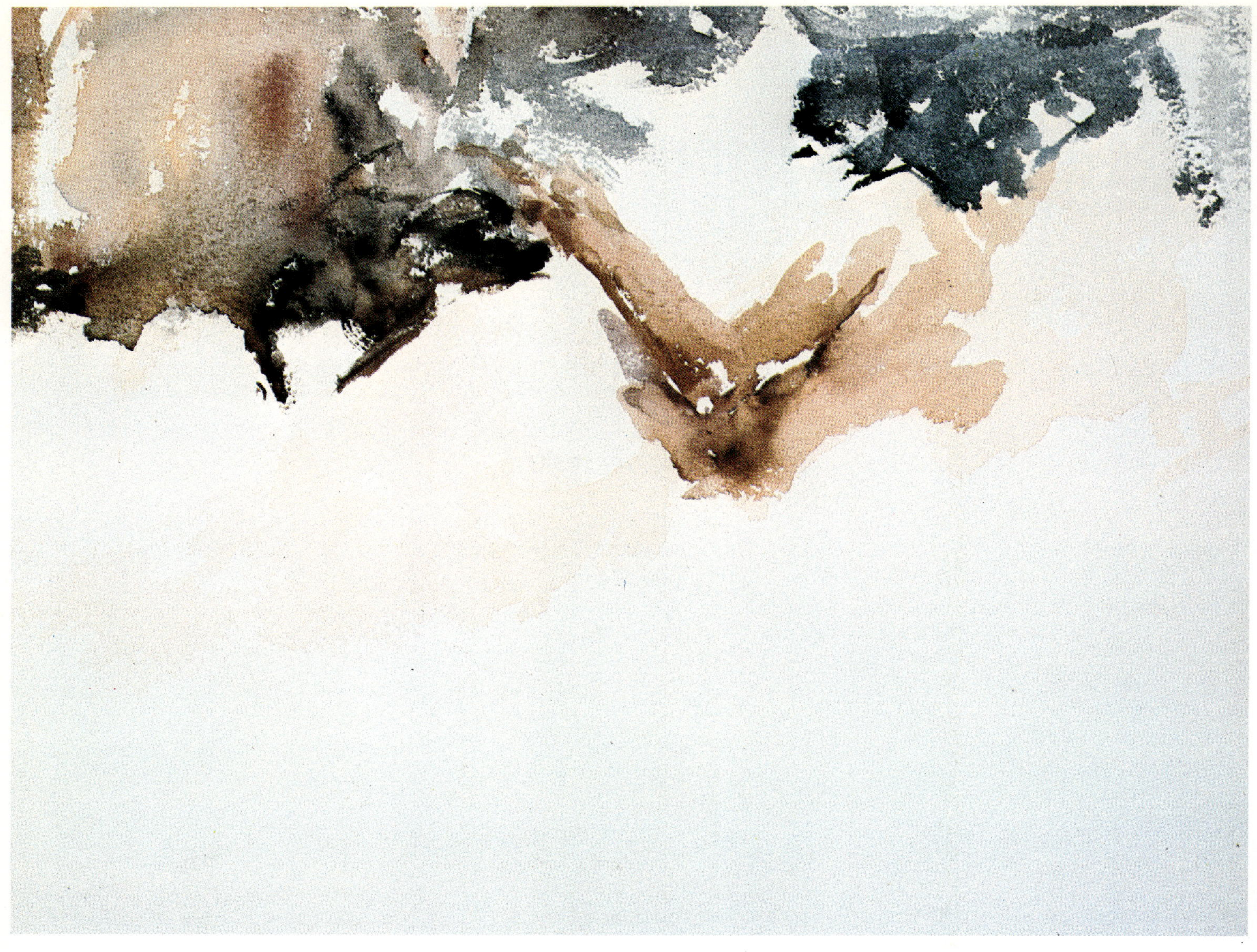

Step 1. Using a number 18 round sable brush, I go right to work on the dry paper, laying a broad, light, flesh-colored wash across the paper to establish the placement of the figure in a very general way. The flesh colors I'm using are cadmium red, light purple (an opaque mixture of white, alizarin crimson, and cobalt blue), and burnt sienna. I plan to keep the figure on the cool side.

With yellow ochre, a touch of cobalt blue, and white, I paint in the suggestions of a background. I lay another wash in this area with alizarin crimson and the light purple mixture.

Moving to the center-right background, I lay washes of cobalt blue, ivory black, and Winsor green mixtures. Directly above the area that will be the model's hip, I place strokes of concentrated ivory black and burnt umber. This acts almost as a guideline, indicating where the left hip will be. It's just beside the raised hand on the left.

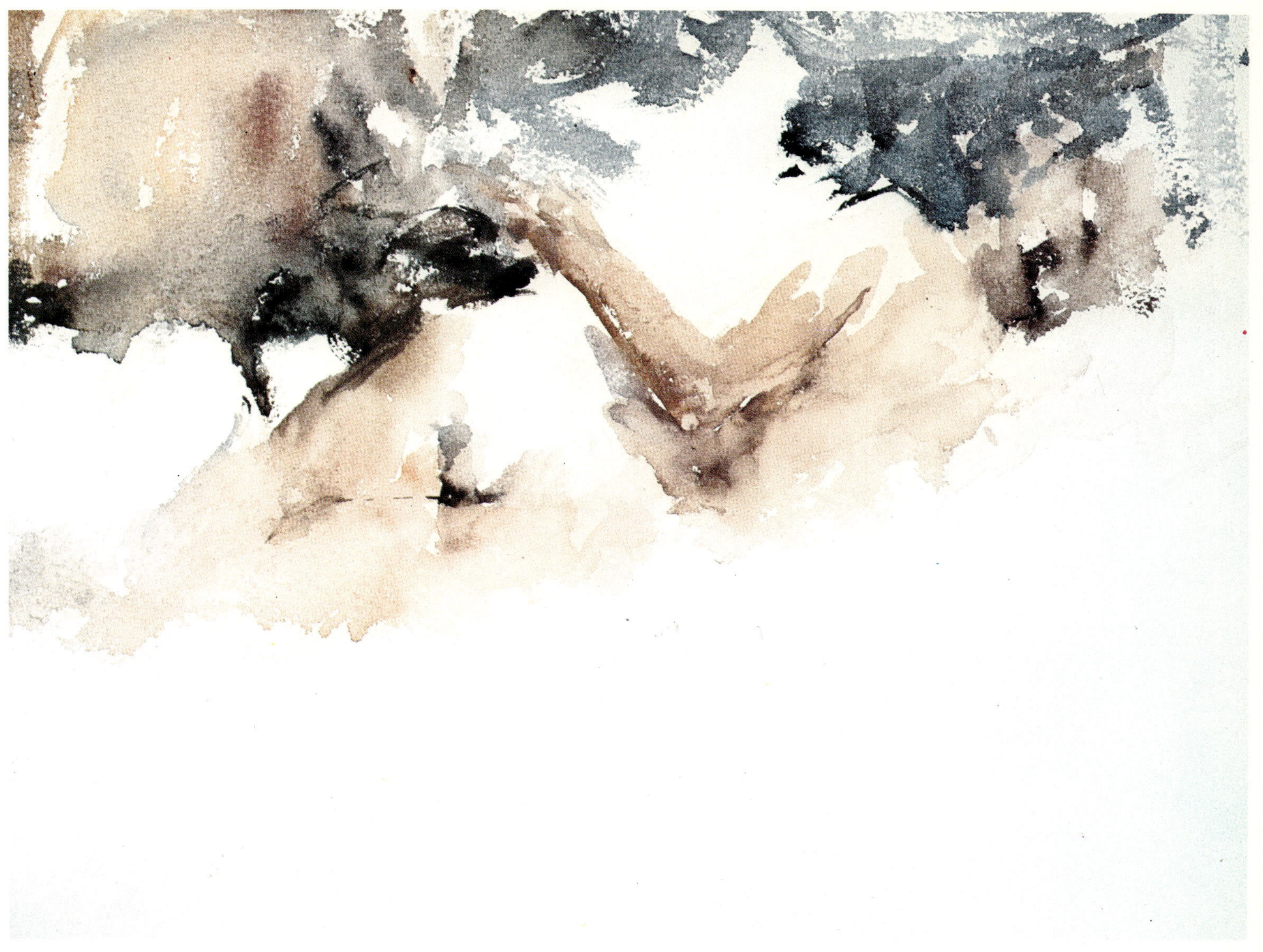

Step 2. I leave areas open in places that are to be light in the final painting. For example, the area in the background above the model's waist could become a draped sheet.

With number 2 and 4 egberts, I stroke in the background on the upper right-hand side, and scumble in the center and left side of the background using alizarin crimson, the light purple mixture (of white, alizarin crimson, and cobalt blue), and yellow ochre—all on the cool side.

I lay in guidelines to indicate the various areas of the figure. One line runs down between the buttocks and legs. The left hip is developing a three-dimensional feeling, with a warm stroke at the top and cooler ones below on the lower leg and buttock. With mixtures of cobalt blue, the light purple mixture, and alizarin crimson, I add shadows below the left raised elbow. Now, with the sable brush, I paint a dark wash of phthalo purple and cobalt blue, shadowing over the left arm with a pointed stroke. I use ivory black with the light purple mixture, viridian, and raw umber in the hair. As yet, no work has been done in the foreground.

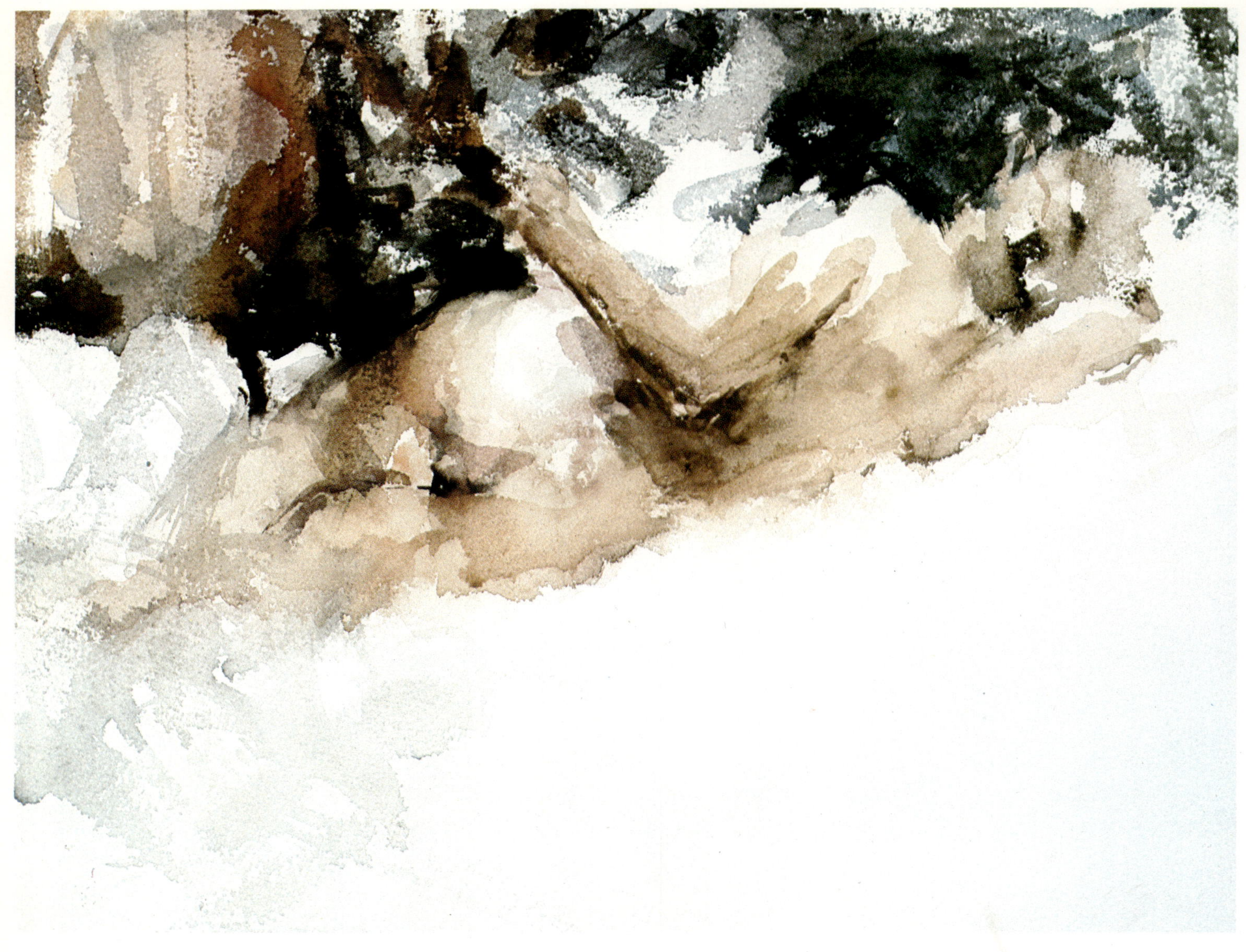

Step 3. Although the background has an interesting mix of wet and scumbled strokes, the figure has been only roughly indicated. So, I'll work now on the figure.

Using a wash of cobalt blue, alizarin crimson, and light purple, with a touch of black to tone it down, I darken the shadow under the left elbow that seems to be projecting toward the viewer. The left hip is warm and the buttocks, creases, and left leg are cooler. With a number 5 filbert, I stroke on ivory black, Winsor green, and raw umber in the background over the model's raised hip.

With the number 18 sable brush, I lay on strokes of alizarin crimson, cadmium red, and burnt sienna mixtures and make the upper section of the background hot. Darker areas, cooled with cobalt blue, are placed over the model's shoulder, neck, and hair. I vary the strokes from wet to drybrush. The brushstrokes are beginning to suggest drapery in the background and the figure is slowly emerging from the background.

Remember, dark strokes made with a loaded brush will dry two values lighter. I make a single, deliberate stroke of dark, cool colors on the bottom of the right buttock; I will strengthen it later.

I want to lay a light, cool wash around the top of the back and around the neck and arm; to do it, I use cobalt blue, alizarin crimson, and the light purple mixture with a lot of water. In oil, I could only get this light a value by adding white, but in watercolor, all I need to do is add water. The more water, the less pigment there is to stain the paper, and so the lighter the values.

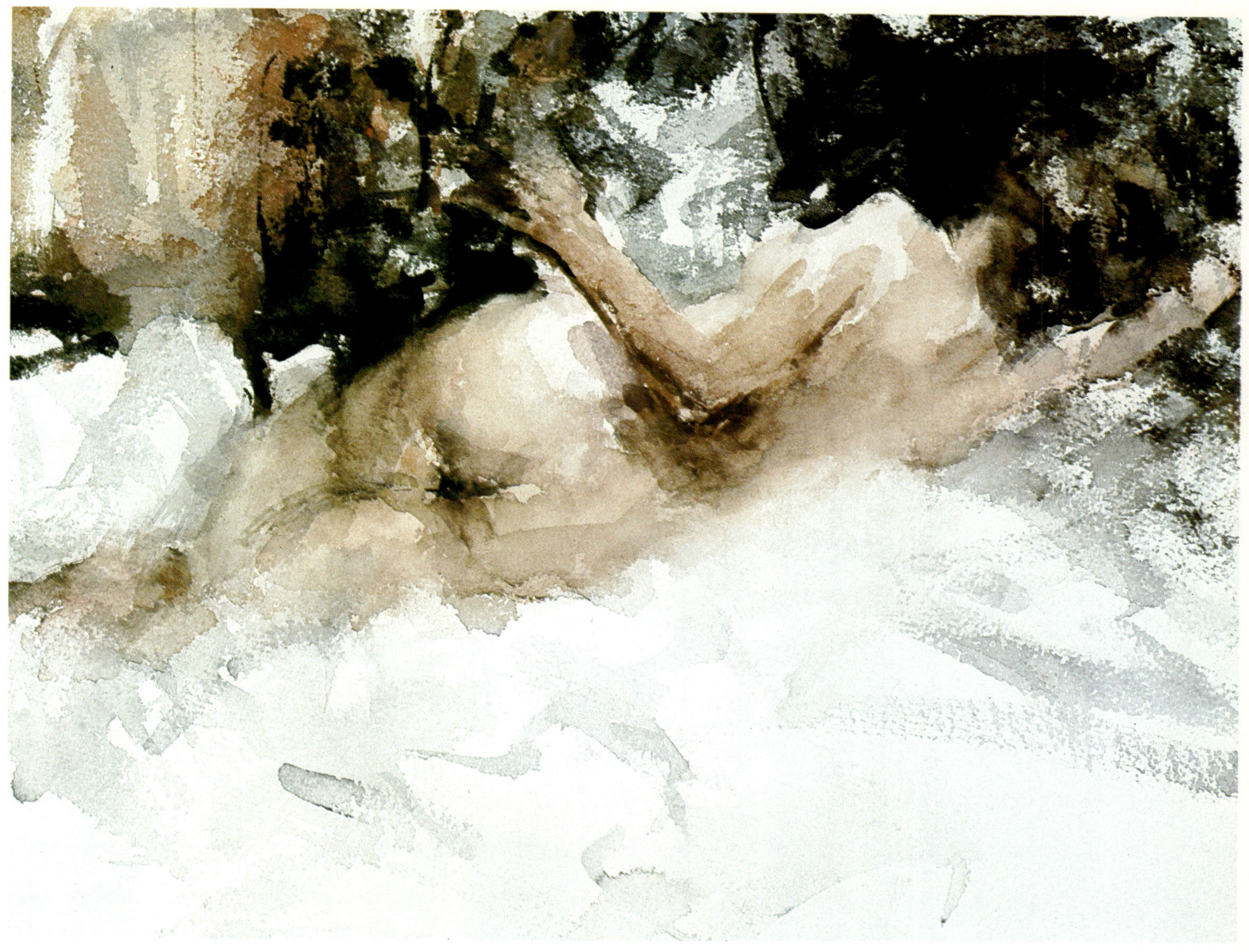

Step 4. There is now a good separation between the dark background and the high key of the figure. A shadowed, mysterious area is in the upper right area. The head will be lost in this darkness.

With cool washes of cobalt blue, ivory black, and the opaque light purple mixture, I develop the form of the bent arm on which the model's head is resting. Notice that my strokes start off wet and gradually get more like drybrush.

There's more definition now in the left, raised hand. Because the hand is in front of a warm background, I make it cooler than usual, since hands are normally warm areas. I indicate fingers and show that the hand is lighted from behind.

There are good design elements in the contrasting lines of the figure. Though the back is horizontal, the legs and arm are almost vertical in their direction. I will play with these lines later.

The light drapery above the model's waist gives me a chance to soften and fade the edge there. The line of the hip is more definite, but the edge of the figure at the right grows more fused with the background and then becomes defined again at the shoulder and hair.

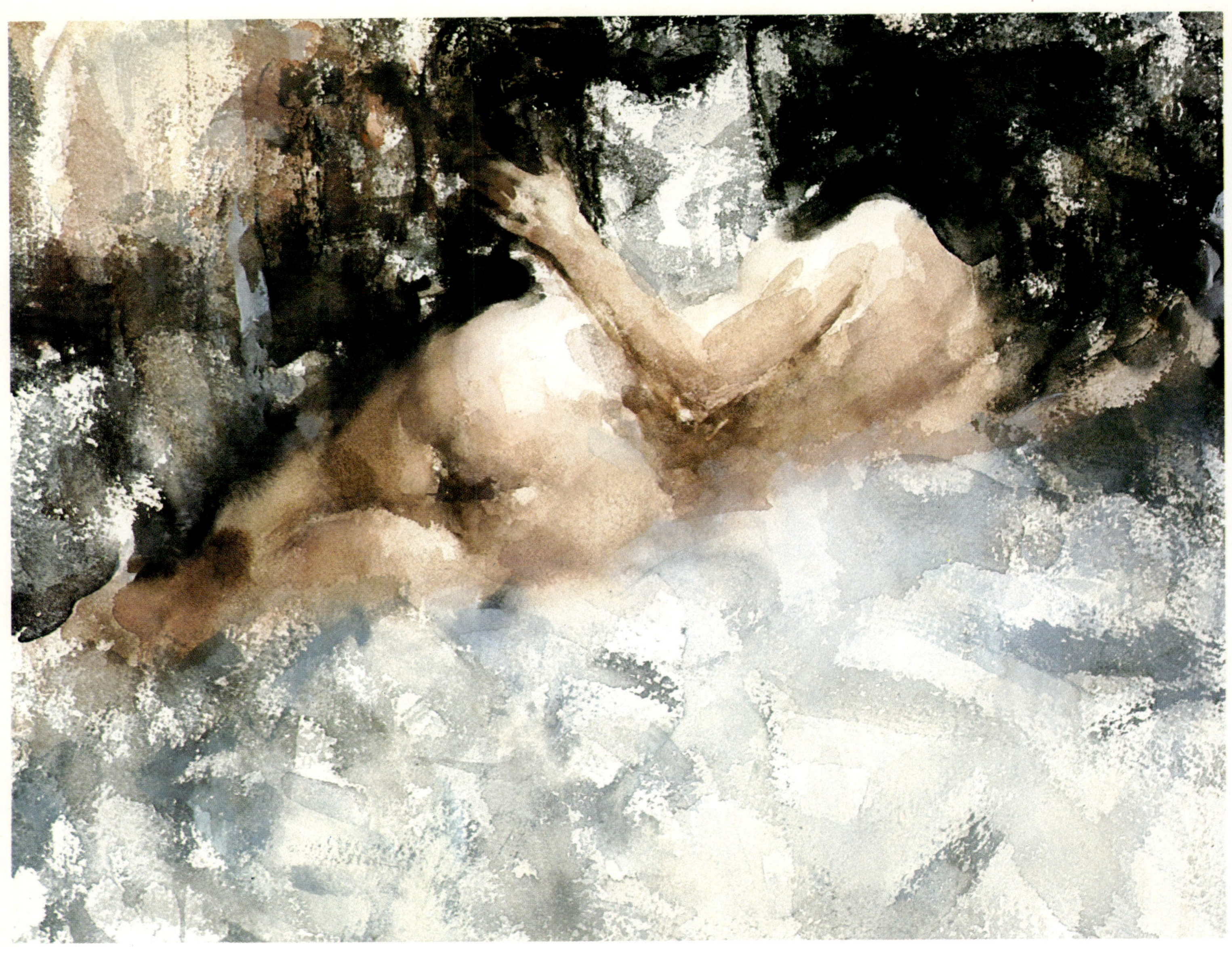

Step 5. The illusion of an edge on a figure creates a strong visual impression—of course, in reality, edges don't exist on the figure. However, I find it exciting to give the illusion of boundaries by using a variety of edges. For instance, along the top edge of the figure you can find an interplay of both lost and found—hard and soft—edges.

I develop the darks in the left background—the hand, and the hip—with cool colors. I bring the dark from under the arm on the right-hand side of the painting down to the bottom of the painting with drybrush strokes.

As I work all around the painting, especially on the shape of the hair, I realize that the neck isn't right. With a dark wash from the left shoulder, I lengthen and lower the neck. I'm essentially drawing in this brushwork—continually refining the proportions of the figure. They satisfy me now.

With the sable brush, I lay some cooler opaque washes over the hot background colors; I also work in drybrush strokes. In the foreground and hair I've used filberts and egberts. These brushes make direct, broad strokes.

The painting has a bold feeling: I want to leave it that way and not pick it to death, but there are still a few areas that require work.

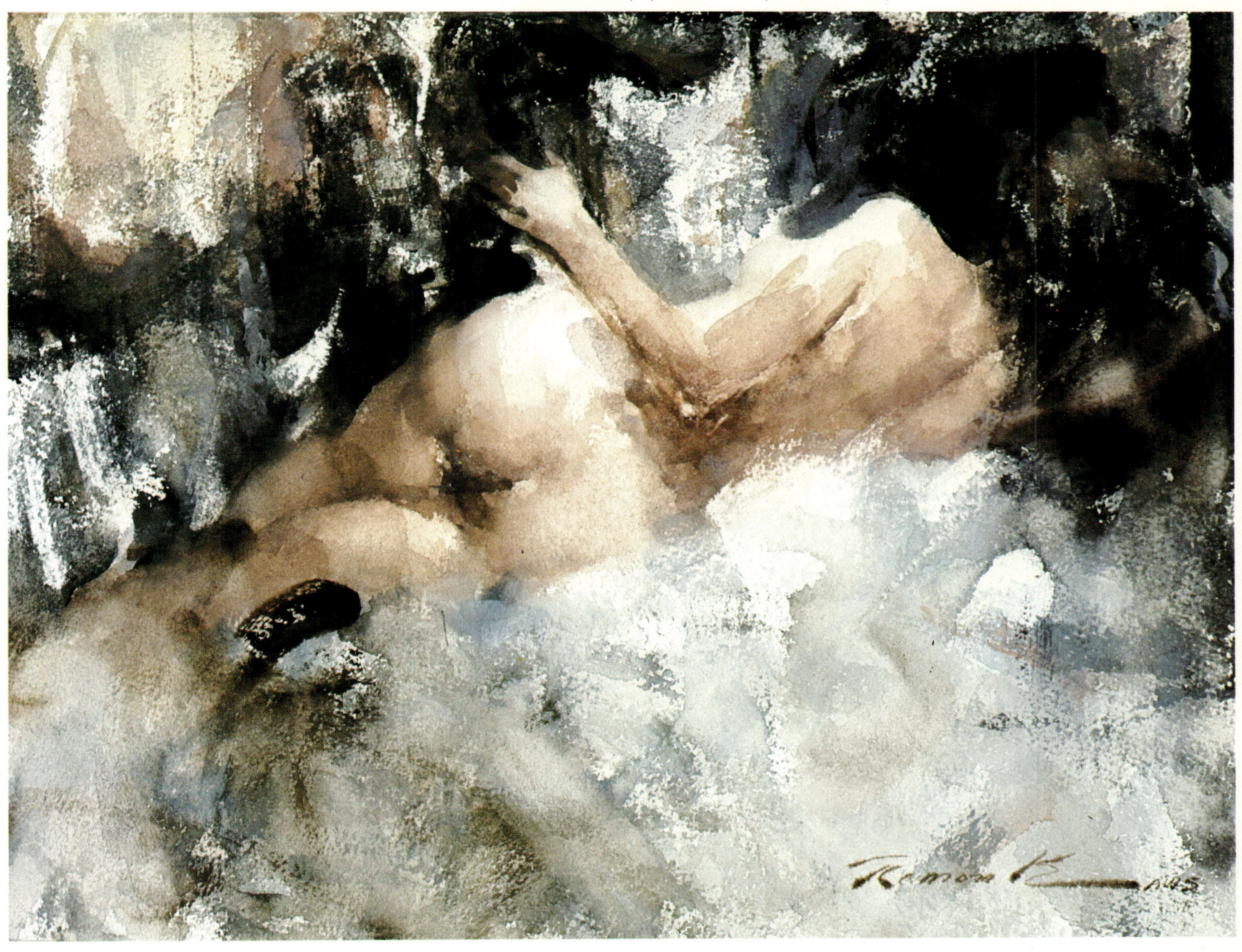

Step 6. This is the final step. There are many places where the first washes are untouched and are now adding to the final effect of the painting. One such area is on the left arm below the shoulder.

Strokes that are easy to read and follow are adding to the strength of the painting. The line of the backbone crease up to the shoulder blade is a prominent stroke; another such stroke is around the left elbow.

I feel that some areas are too dark, so I use a razor blade to scrape them away. This scraping gives a linear effect from the left knee down to the left foot. In the background near that foot, I scrape up and down, making a vertical pattern that contrasts with the pose of the model and enlivens that area. I also scrape a few highlights into the hair.

I lay some cool opaque washes of cobalt blue, light purple, and white over the warm colors on the left background. These are the same cool colors I used on the flesh; the interplay is effective. If I wanted to, I could stop here—the painting is basically complete now. But I still have more to do.

With a big, heavily charged stroke under the right knee, I add the reflected warmth of the drapery to the cooler tones of the body. This isn't absolutely necessary, but it does relate the tones in the painting. It picks up the dark background colors and carries the eye from the model's hair to the dark of the left hip and elbow, then back into the background again. This strengthens the stroke I made earlier in Step 3 that dried lighter than I wanted it to.

At the top of the hair, I scrub out an area to give the effect of light hitting the head. My method is as follows: with a clean bristle brush charged with water, I scrub the area. I then wipe it with a clean cloth, removing the color. In the center of the bottom foreground, I lighten a shape in a direction opposite to the pose to balance it.

My goal here was to focus on the flesh of the back, shoulders, hips, and buttocks, fading the head and feet into the background. I like to stimulate the viewer's imagination by leaving out details, as I've done here.

THE PORTRAIT IN WATERCOLOR

Ike was shoveling snow outside one day when I did my original color sketch of him in watercolor. I'm doing this portrait on 300 lb 12″ x 16″ (30.5 x 40.5 cm) Arches paper with a rough texture because I like the crispness that comes from dragging the brush over raised texture.

This is a portrait of a thirty-year-old Black, and I want to stress the warmth of color in his face and his distinctive racial features. Yet, I'll be doing a painting that is more restrained in color than my usual vivid ones because I plan to capture the coldness of the day when I saw him.

My palette is raw sienna, yellow ochre, alizarin crimson, cobalt blue, phthalo green, Hooker's green, and ivory black.

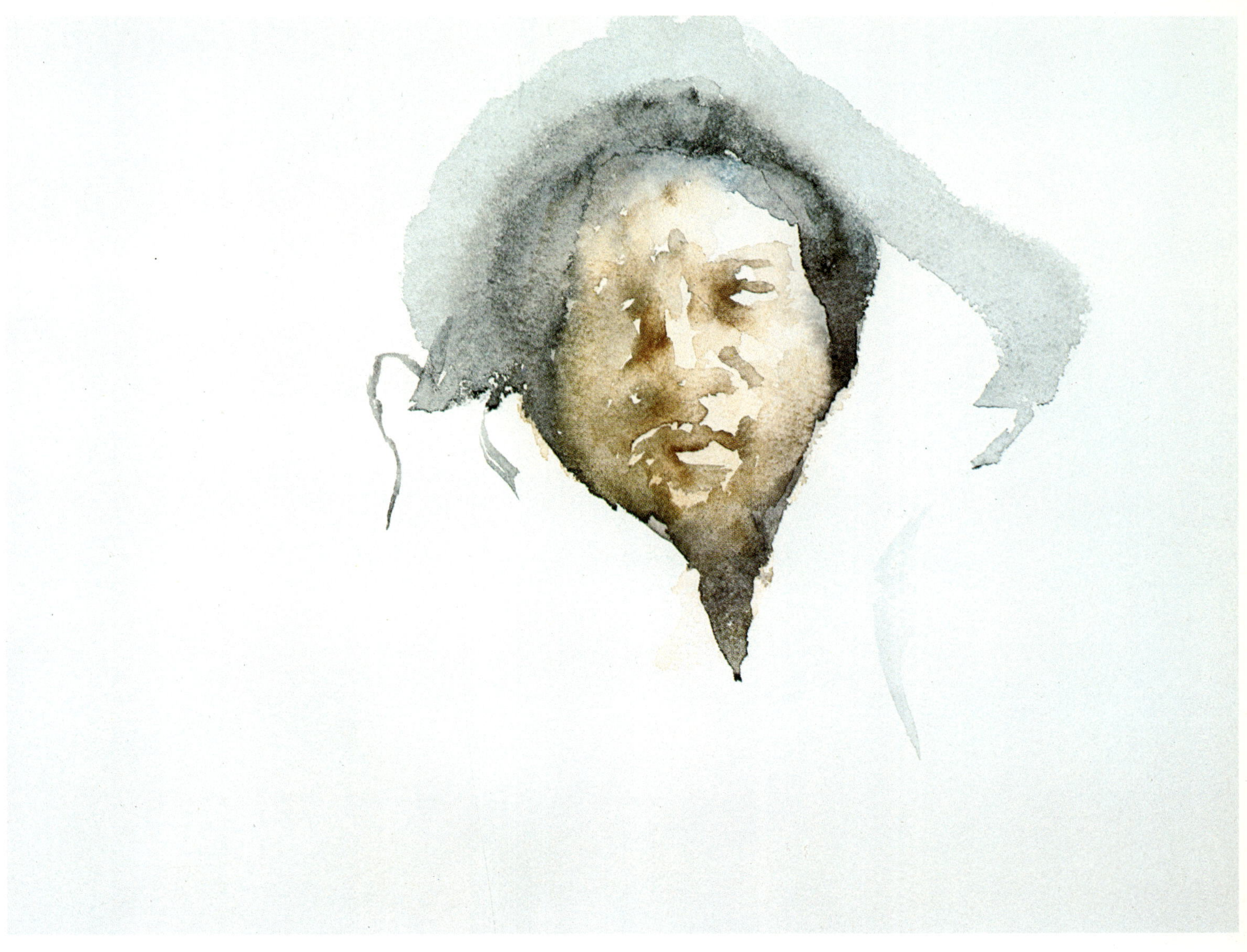

Step 1. I use a number 18 round sable brush throughout this painting. First I just suggest Ike's face and the hood of the parka around his head. I leave open an area under the heavy coat that will be his hooded sweatshirt.

His head is slightly to the right of center and near the top of the paper. I work wet so color flows down the face. A dark shadow is breaking under the chin. The light source is from the right.

I use yellow ochre with a touch of alizarin crimson on the features; cobalt blue over ivory black for the top right of the hair; and then ivory black, Hooker's green, and cobalt blue on the rest of the hair. I use cobalt blue and a touch of Hooker's green to make the large squarish wash of the jacket.

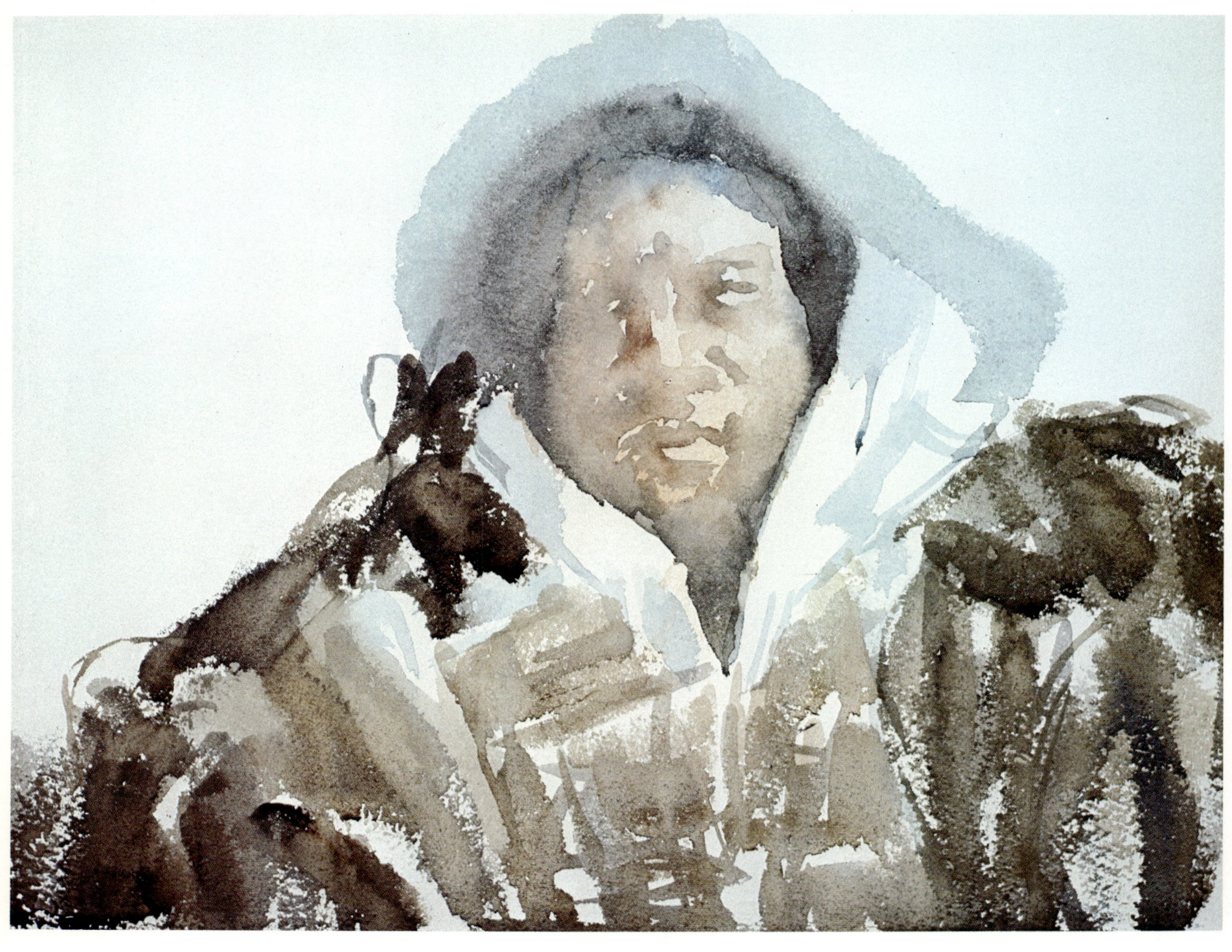

Step 2. With raw sienna, cobalt blue, and Hooker's green, in a wash that is neither warm nor cool, I work on the jacket. You could almost count the strokes I make with the large sable. Over the area of white I saved where the sweatshirt is to be, I flow on a cool, cobalt blue shadow.

The background is unworked. I don't work on the face in this step. I enjoy the variation of strokes on the jacket made with the sable brush—fine lines, washes, wide bold strokes, wet, and drybrush.

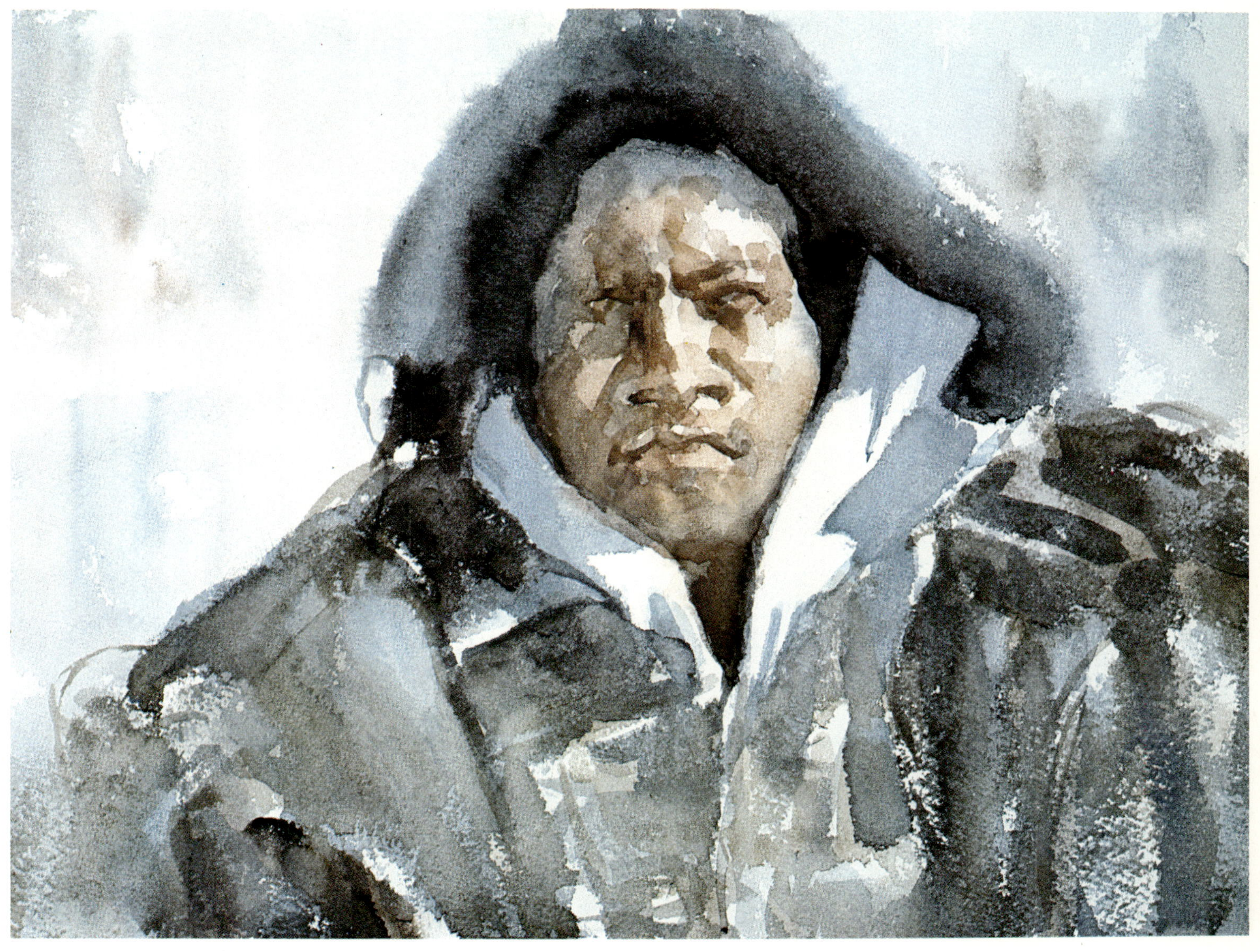

Step 3. Now I concentrate on the face and clarify the features. Careful drawing is very important to bring out the wide, full bottom lip and the wide, flat nose.

The oval shadow around Ike's head inside the hood is the key to the darks in this painting. The values on the face are dark enough to go well with the value of that dark shadow. The facial shadow moves down the side of Ike's head on the left.

The colors of his face are light purple (alizarin crimson and cobalt blue), alizarin crimson, and raw sienna. For the chin, I'm using light washes of cobalt blue, phthalo green, and raw sienna. The top of the forehead is blue near the hood; the center of the head is warm; and the stubble on the chin is cool. There's a very dark V-shape below the neck.

In watercolor, a shape and value may sometimes occur by accident. But somehow that accidental shape will work well in the final painting. A shape like this has developed on the right shoulder.

I'm darkening an area under the left collar to indicate that the arm is coming out there. I scrub out the bottom left of the painting. I paint a cool wet wash into the background at the right but on the left I add alizarin crimson also.

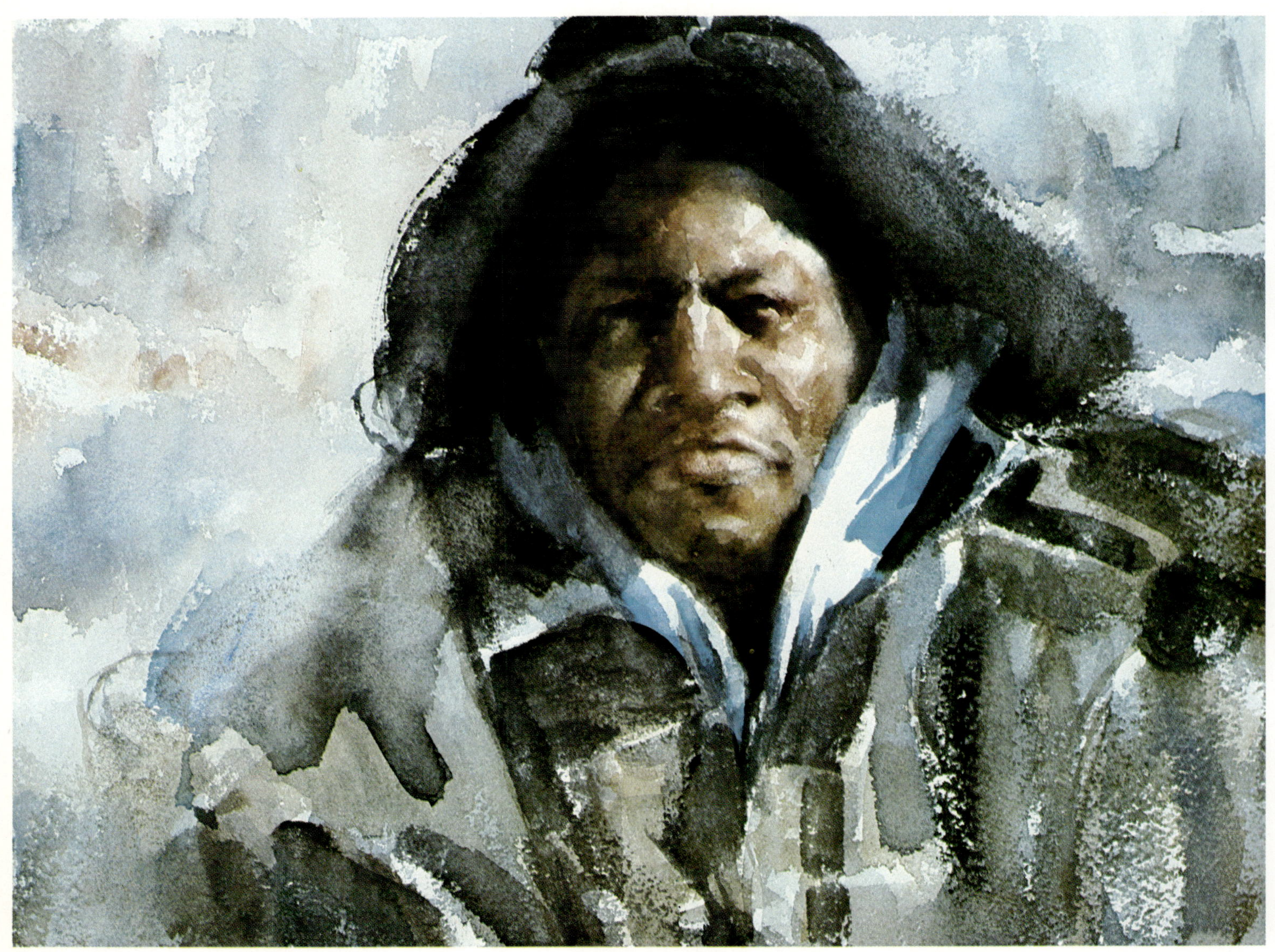

Step 4. I now enrich the dark under the hood again with ivory black, cobalt blue, and Hooker's green. Then I harmonize it with the values in the face by adding darker darks around the eyes and down the face. The face is now shaded like an egg, warm on the shadow side, and cool on the lighted side. On the shadowed side there are some reflected highlights. The cheekbones, bridge and tip of the nose, and the forehead all catch light. The nostril and lips also project into the light.

The left shoulder seems high, so I scrub it out; but I postpone working on it. Instead I work on the background. The background around the hood needs to be darker so I add a dark wash of cobalt blue and Hooker's green. To soften the edges I brush around the stroke with water and let it bleed and fade out. Further up, icy colors of cobalt blue and Hooker's green fade toward the top of the hood.

I add some drybrush strokes to the background with alizarin crimson and cobalt blue. This distributes the warmer facial colors better over other areas of the painting.

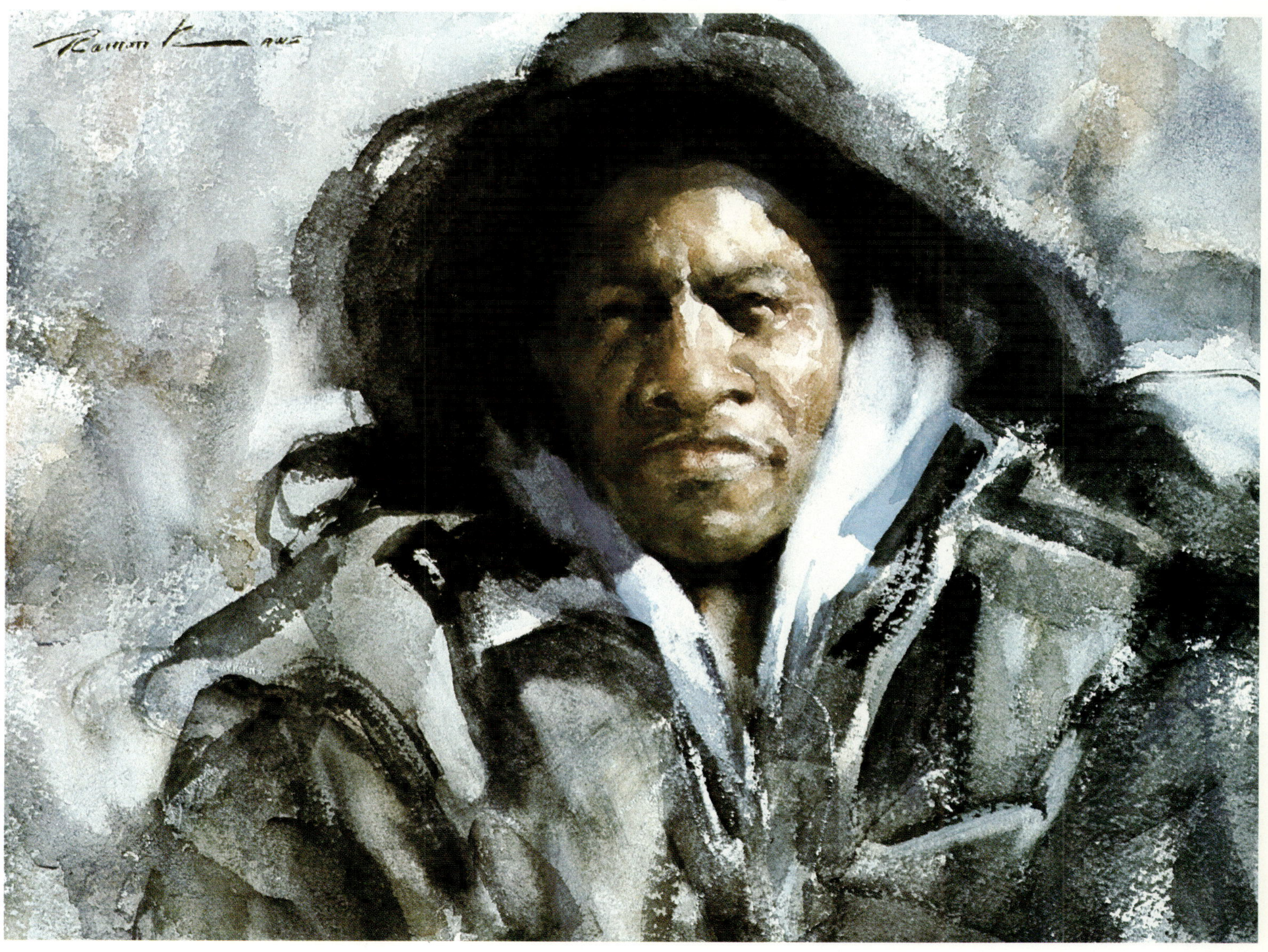

Ike. Watercolor on 300 lb Arches paper, 12" x 16" (30.5 x 40.5 cm)

Step 5. In this final step, I recheck my darks. The darkest areas are under the hood, under the chin, and under the collar. If I were setting up a value scale, the lightest value would be on the forehead, by the light cobalt blue wash. Next would be the lighted cheek. Third would be the tip of the nose. The bottoms of both eyes are catching the light before breaking into the cheeks.

The V-shaped dark below the neck seems too dark, so I scrub some of it out in the center, let it dry, and then lay a warm color wash over it; now it looks more fleshlike. I correct the right shoulder, mostly by darkening the values of strokes already there. I add warm licks of color to the background on the right and center.

I use calligraphic strokes for the fine lines of the ties of the hood. They make a counterpoint to the broad brushwork on the face and jacket of this transparent watercolor.

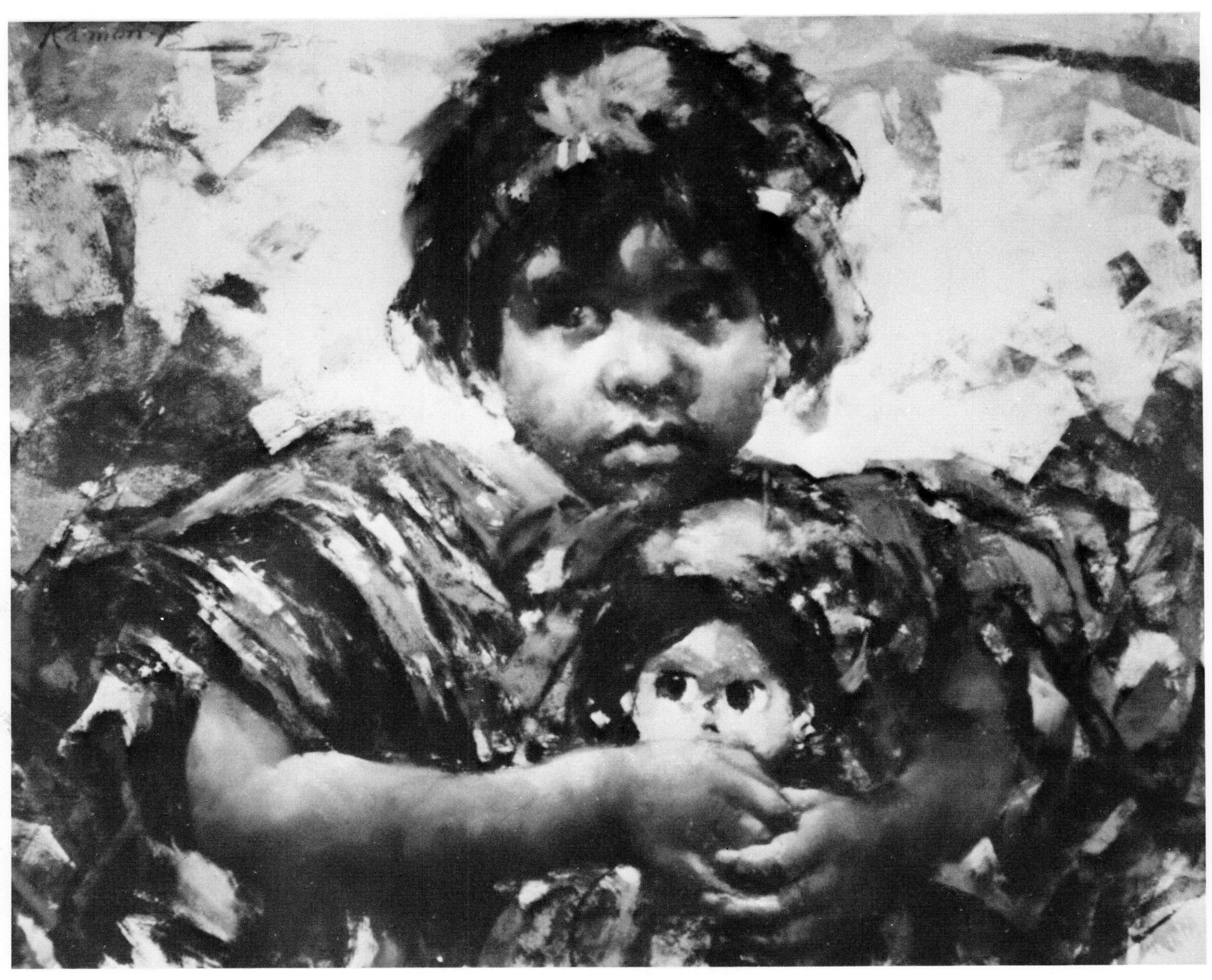

Fiesta Costume. Pastel over watercolor on rough sanded board, 11″ x 14″ (28 x 35.5 cm). Over an underwashed tone, done with watercolor, I went into the painting directly with strong wide strokes of pastel. A record of the energy and boldness of the alla prima approach can be seen in the pastel strokes themselves, many of which remain unchanged by any ensuing ones. Although there's more layering on the face than elsewhere, it was done with speed, and I worked all over the board. Despite my alla prima style, the softness of the skin textures, the smoothness of the doll's face, and the roughness of the clothes are well realized against the impasto background.

ONE-MAN SHOW

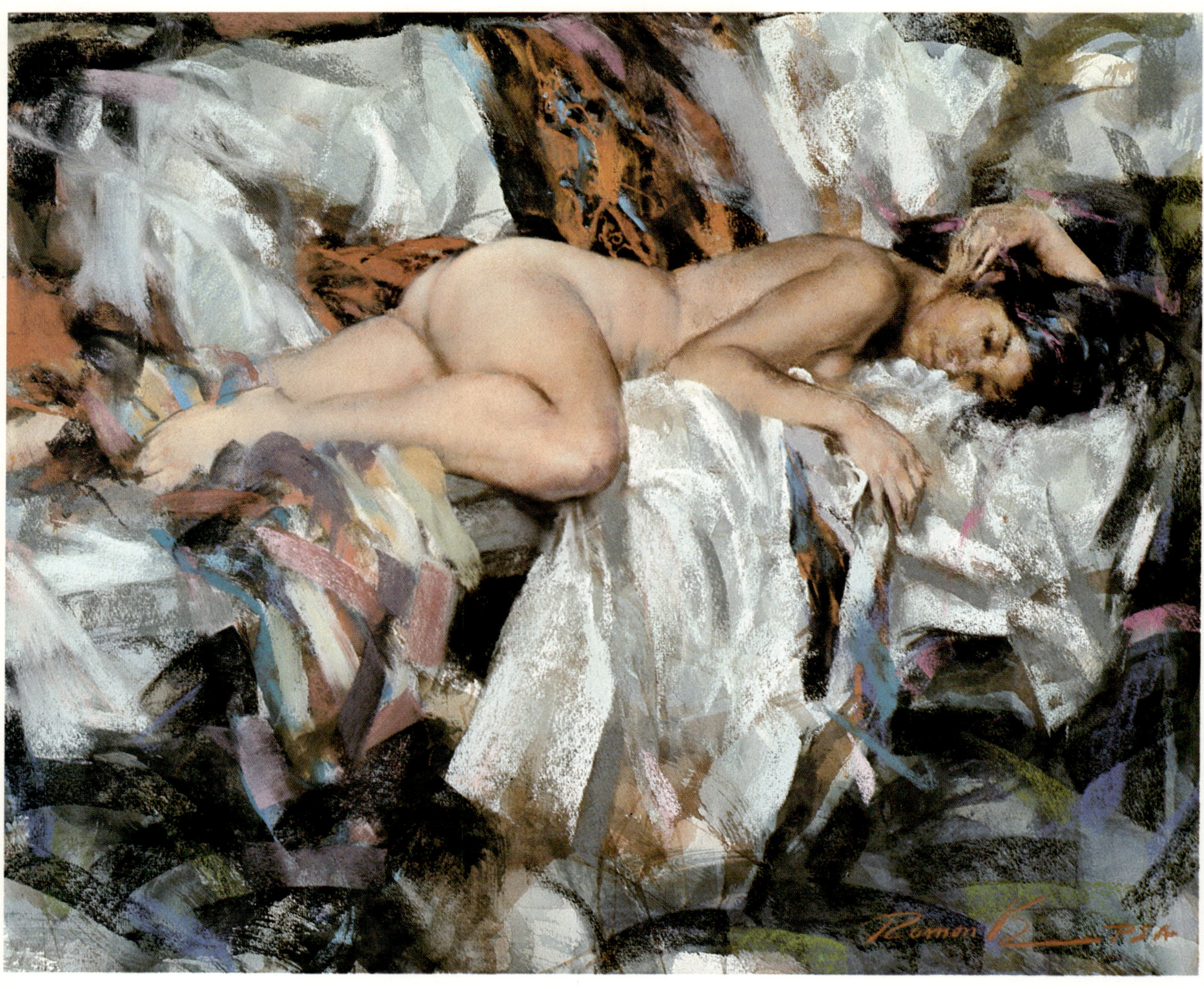

Bernadette (above). Pastel over watercolor on
paper, 16″ x 20″ (40.5 x 51 cm). I used the draperies
to make a bold composition, and inserted the
model into it, which created a contrast of warm
flesh tones and smooth skin textures against rum-
pled, broadly painted drapery areas. I draped a
piece of colorful cloth over the back of the couch as
a focal point, to draw the eye to the figure. A pattern of brushstrokes in pink, cobalt violet, cadmium red, cadmium orange, cadmium yellow, and
phthalo green forms a circular pathway around the
model. Underpainted watercolor washes are visible
at both the top and bottom of the painting. White
is reflected from the sheet on the left onto the
model's pink buttocks, so that they're related in
hue; but the model's face and shoulder are sun-
tanned and so differ in color.

Kristina (right). Oil on canvas, 14″ x 11″ (35.5 x
28 cm). I like experimenting with different types of
surfaces and textures. This one is an English pre-
primed linen canvas called Herga that comes in a
roll. It has a medium texture, smoother than Belsize (which I used for *Gina* on page 101). When I
painted the flesh I worked in smooth, thin layers,
which is appropriate for this canvas. Then I began
to work on the more heavily impastoed area of the
robe and I found that the canvas lacked sufficient
tooth to hold my usual alla prima strokes. In frustration, I picked up my palette knife and laid down
a heavy scoop of pigment. To my surprise and
pleasure, the stroke that it made was something
new—not a scumbled, rough drag but a creamy
slather that really excited me. I finished the foreground with knifework. I painted the area behind
the model with a brush. The delicacy of the hair
against the breast results from the quality of the
canvas. To feather the edge of the hair, I worked
upward with a clean brush and gently fused the
juncture of skin and hair.

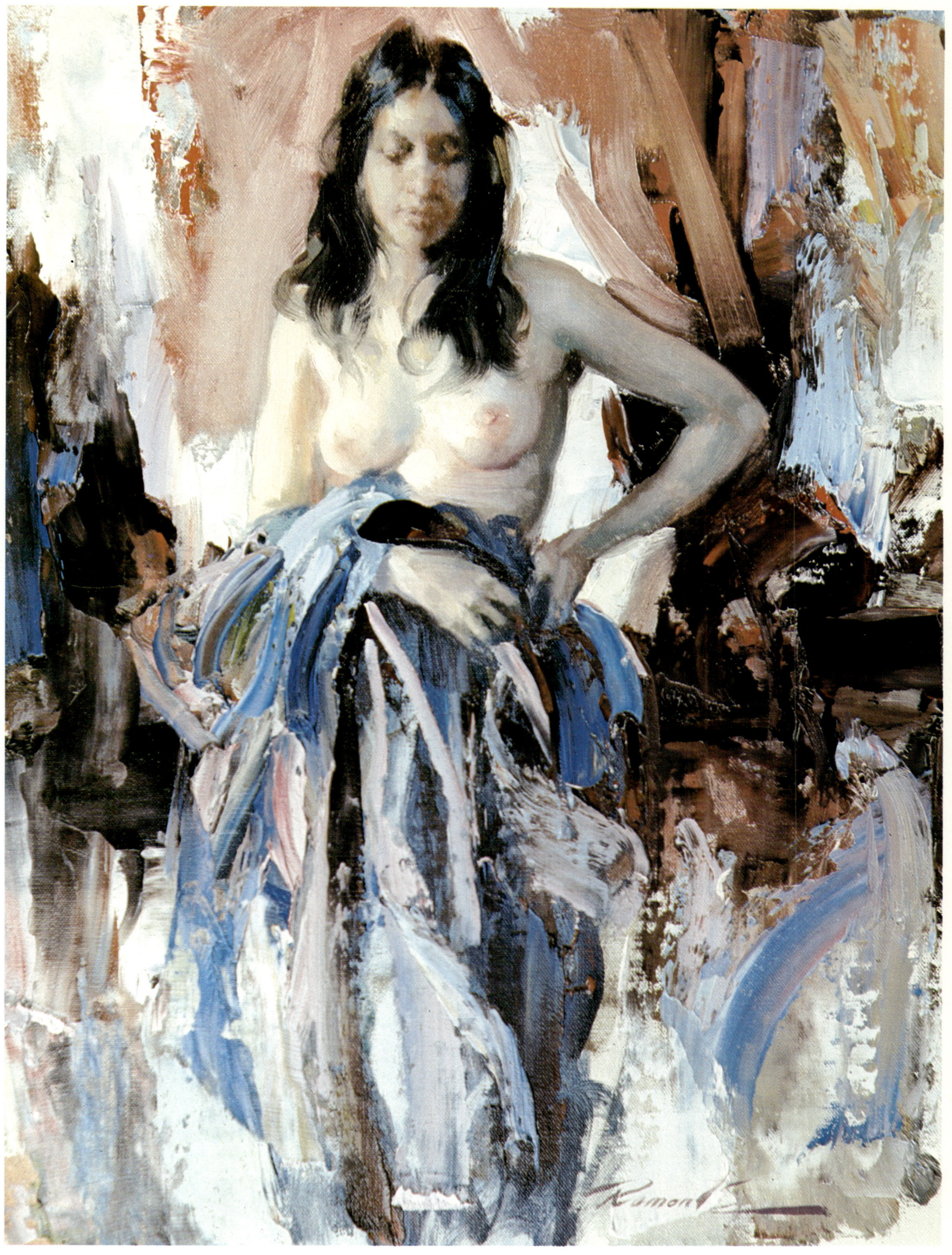

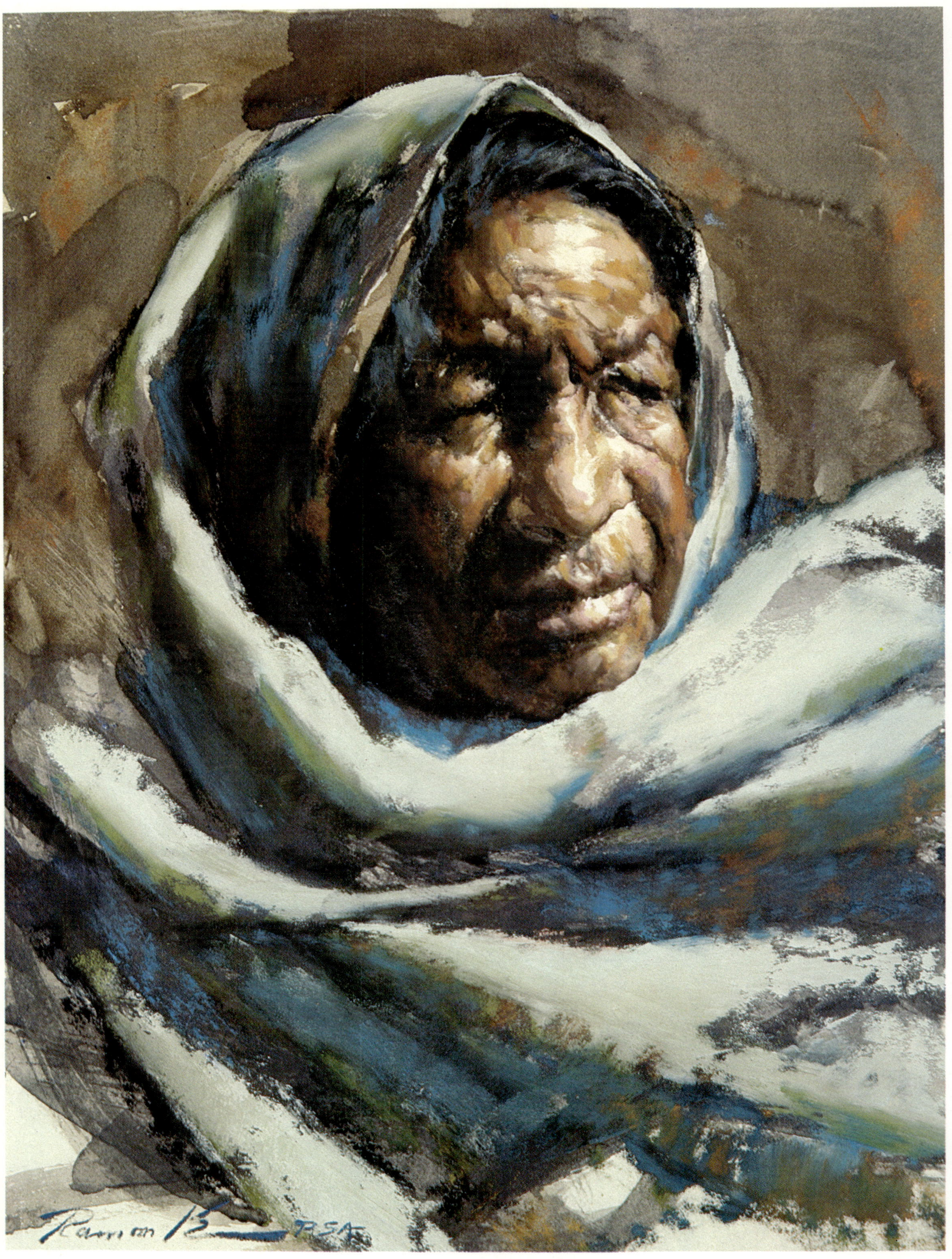

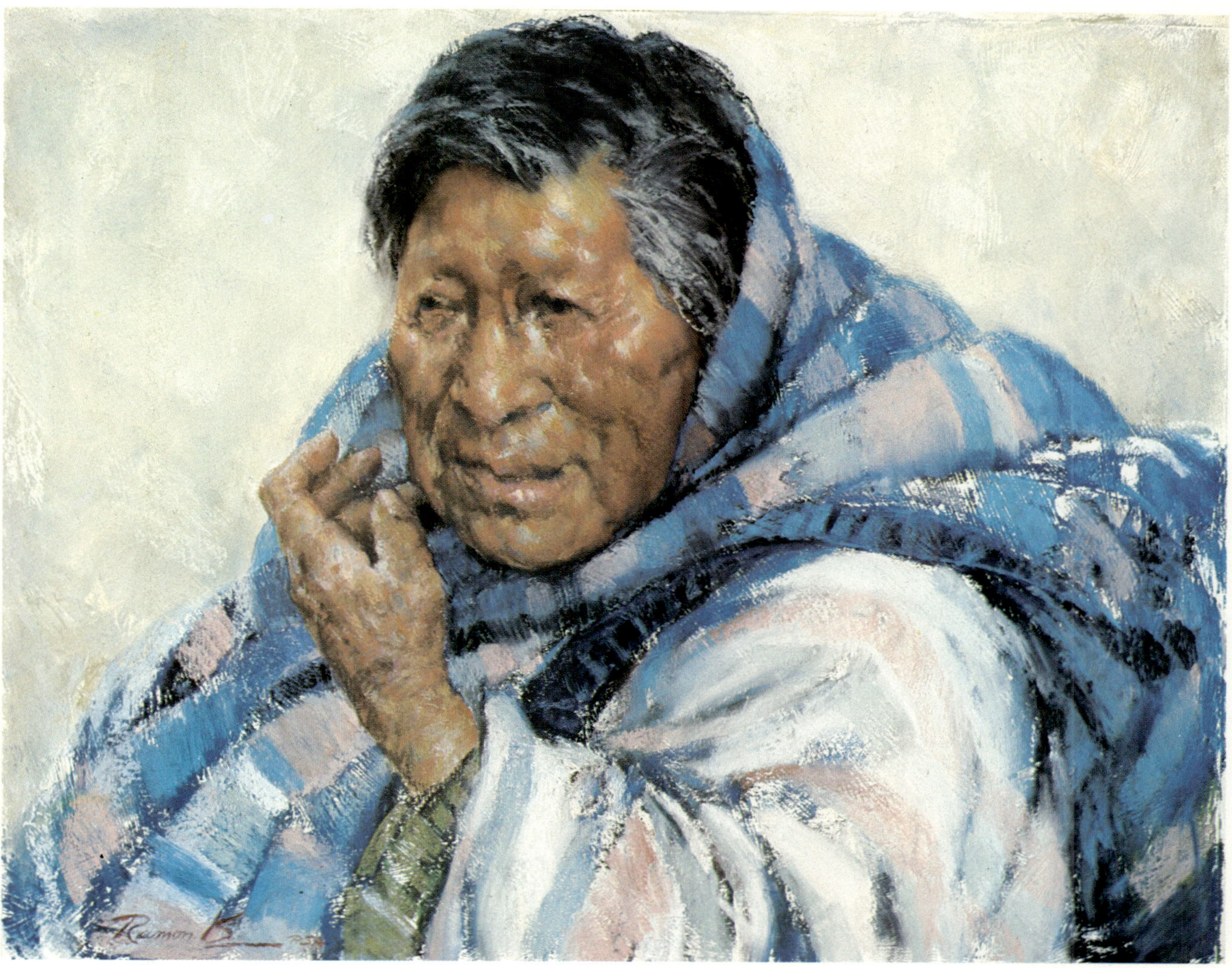

Prairie Wolf (left). Pastel over watercolor on rough sanded board, 12″ x 9″ (30.5 x 23 cm). In this small painting, I aimed for a strong sculptural effect. A feeling of monumentality can be achieved, even in a small format. The powerful sense of three-dimensions in this work results from the play of light and shade on the subject. Both the face and the blanket project toward the viewer in a compelling way. The model and blanket are richly painted in pastel and they emerge from the flat background, which is simply stated in several watercolor washes. Notice that the model's nose is broken, which causes it to look flat and twisted. Some of the characteristic colors of the Pueblo Indian are: cadmium orange, cadmium yellow, cool highlights of cobalt blue and white, and cobalt violet. I used black on the hair, to which I added cool blue highlights.

Indian Grandmother (above). Pastel on rough sanded board, 16″ x 20″ (40.5 x 51 cm). Clear New Mexican light is reflected in the simple, understated background of this painting. I use a strong modeling technique to emphasize the facial features, the hand, and the shawl wrapped around the model's head and shoulders. I carried the structural definition of the face further than usual and created a portrait that describes the model's anatomy as well as her expression. Cool pastel blues and pinks encircle her vividly colored face and hand. Other cool touches can be seen in the skin itself. Edges are crisply drawn everywhere except on the far left where the shawl is close in value to the background.

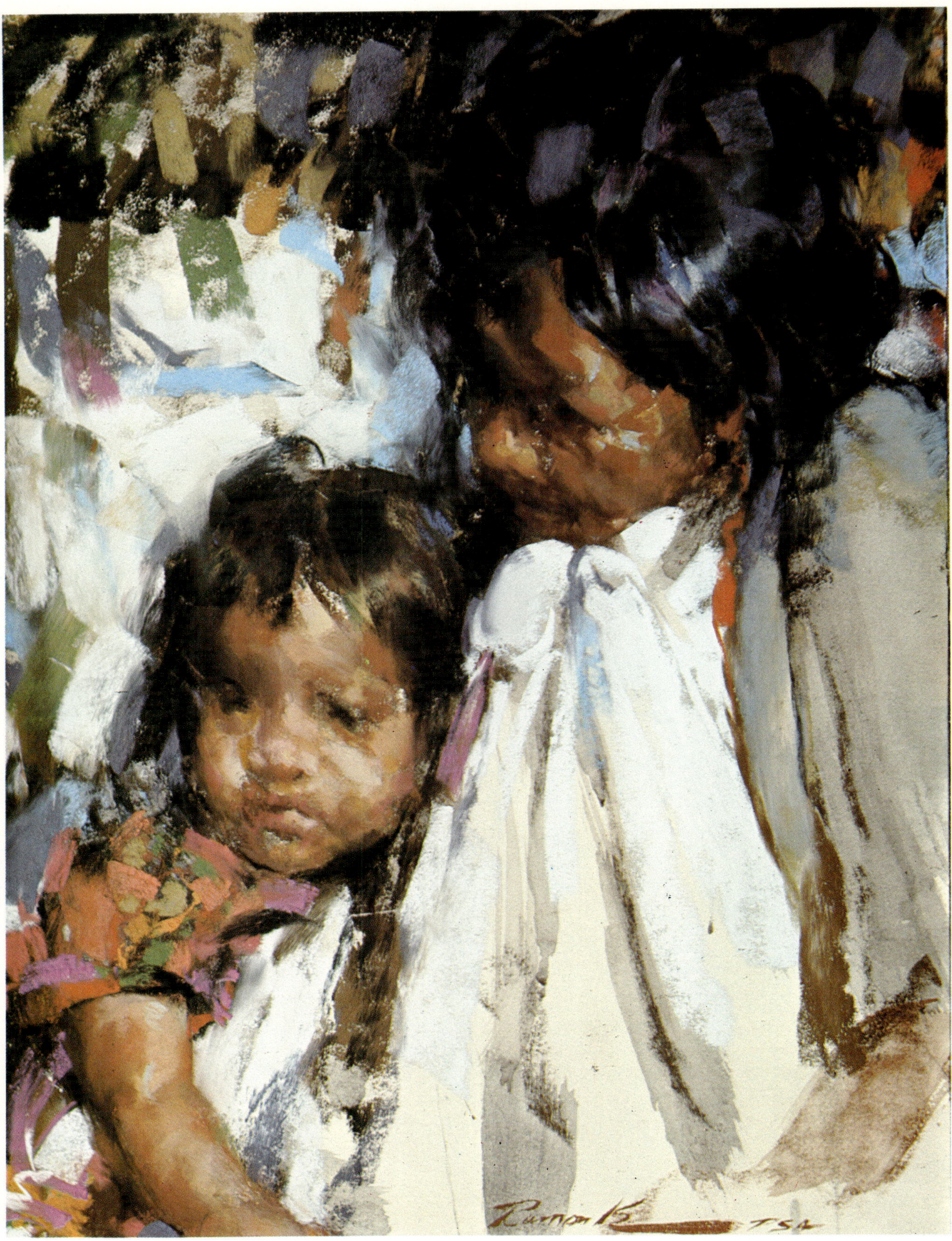

Indian Madonna. Pastel over watercolor on rough sanded board, 14″ x 11″ (35.5 x 28 cm). This pastel was begun on location in Mexico. My two appealing models sat for me for about twenty minutes, giving me time to block in the painting and to take several photos of it. When I returned to Denver I finished the pastel from memory using the photographs for reference. The strength of the composition lies in the diagonal from the mother to the child. I concentrated warm colors on both the flesh tones and the child's dress. On either side I painted broad shapes in neutral tones. At the top of the painting I made squarish strokes in a medley of colors to suggest the roof of the cabaña and to harmonize all the colors in the painting. I wanted to convey the excitement with which I began this painting, so I used bold, prominent strokes on the hair and on the drapery. There's just a bare suggestion of the mother's arm. Cobalt blue and cobalt violet played against cadmium yellow, cadmium orange, and vermilion give zing to the color scheme. An ice-cold reflected blue light right beside the mother's nose makes a sharp contrast of temperature.

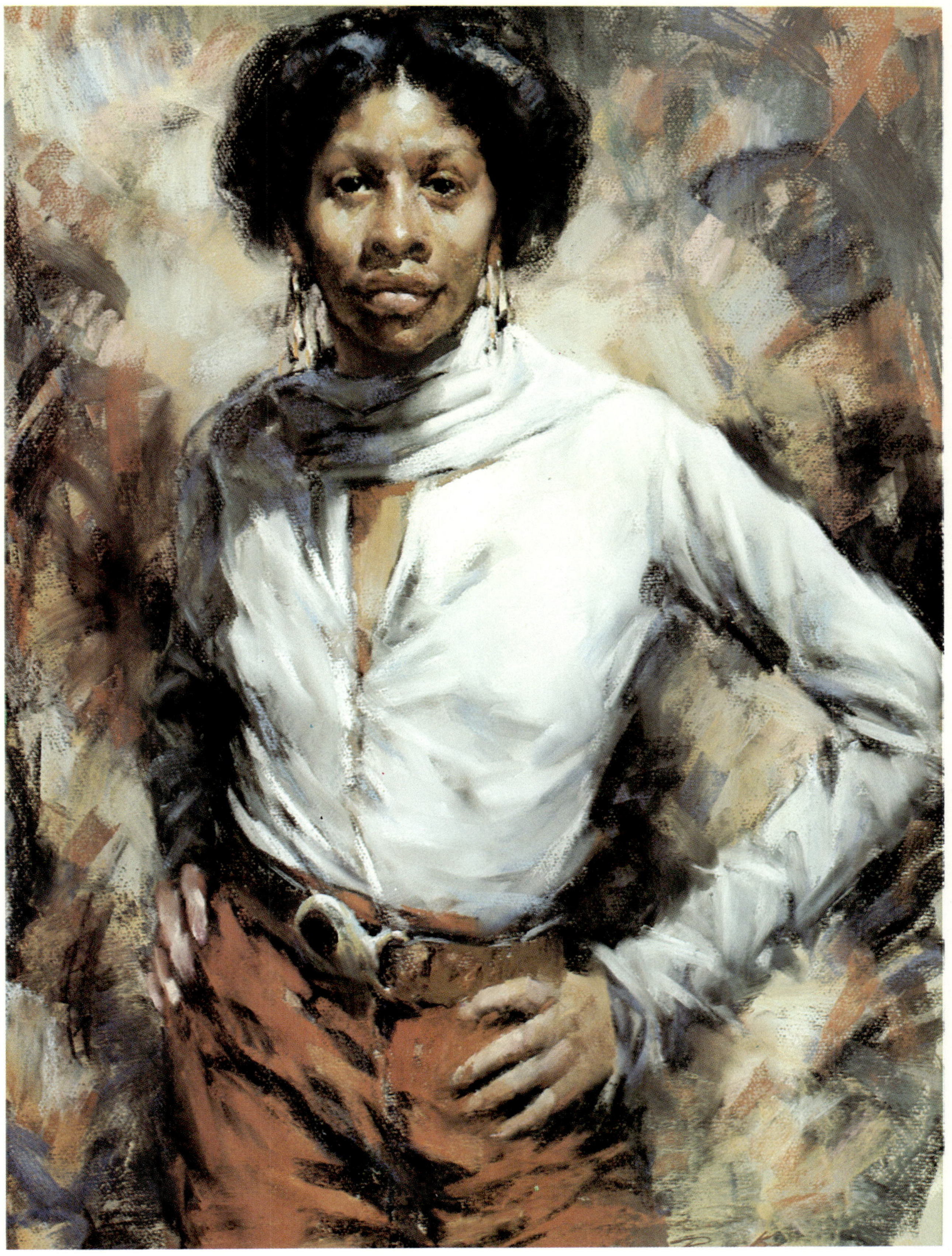

Nadine. Pastel over watercolor on pastel paper, 24" x 18" (61 x 45.5 cm). Nadine has the grace and poise of a fashion model and she carries clothes with flair. Therefore, in painting her, I emphasized her clothes and elegant pose. All colors used on the figure and in the costume are melded into the freely painted background. Nadine's head dominates the painting. Her dark hair and strongly modeled face attract the eye first, and lead the eye to the warm flesh of her chest, from there to her arm, then to the curve of her trousers, and from there up her right arm and back along her shoulder to the head again. This circular path is echoed by a faint oval aura around the figure. Though this painting appears to be highly finished, no single area is brought too far—not even the face. The nice, cool shadow cast by her warm face adds a crisp diagonal to the painting, which is prolonged by the warm shadow on the skin below the scarf. I add the final details of her gold earrings and metal belt buckle to the painting.

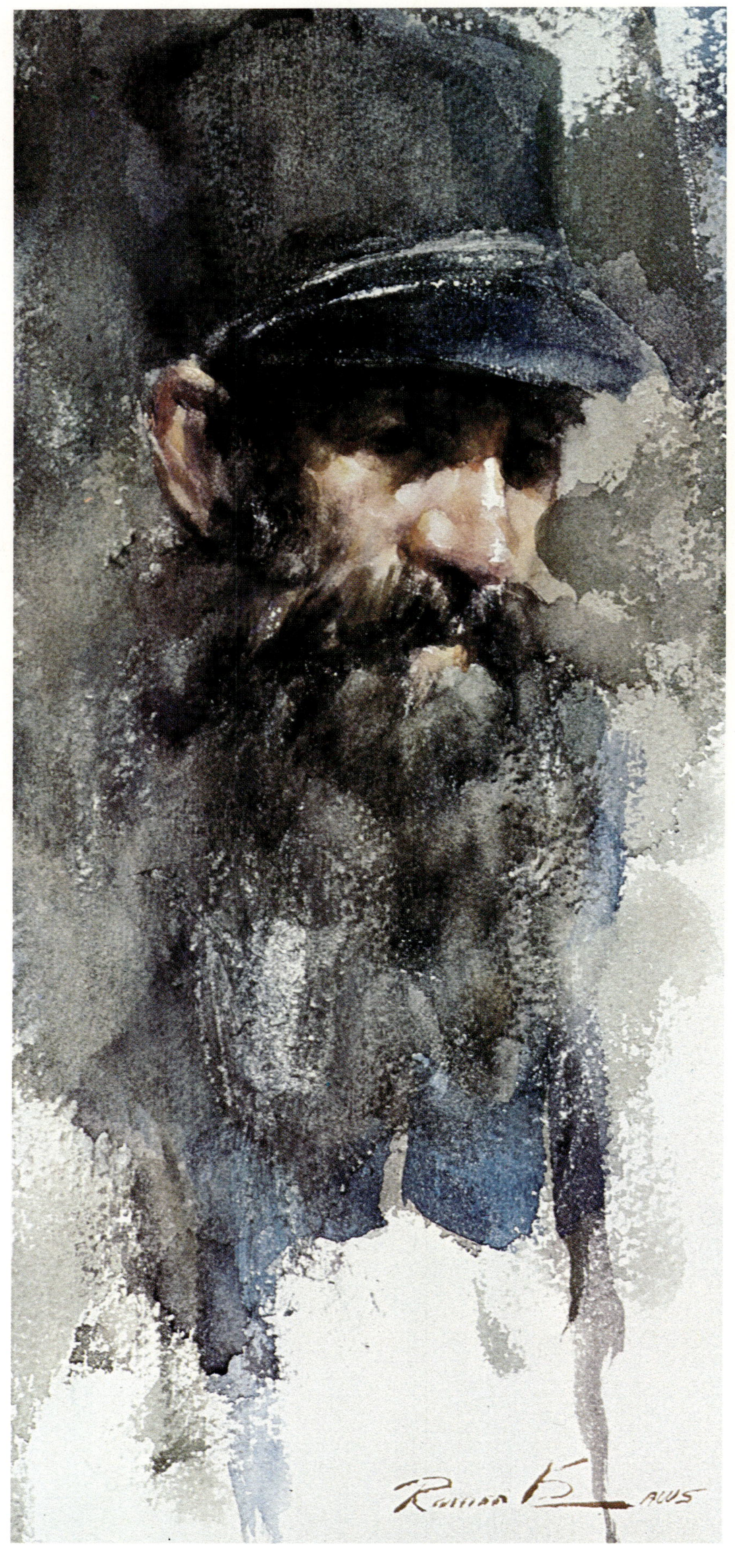

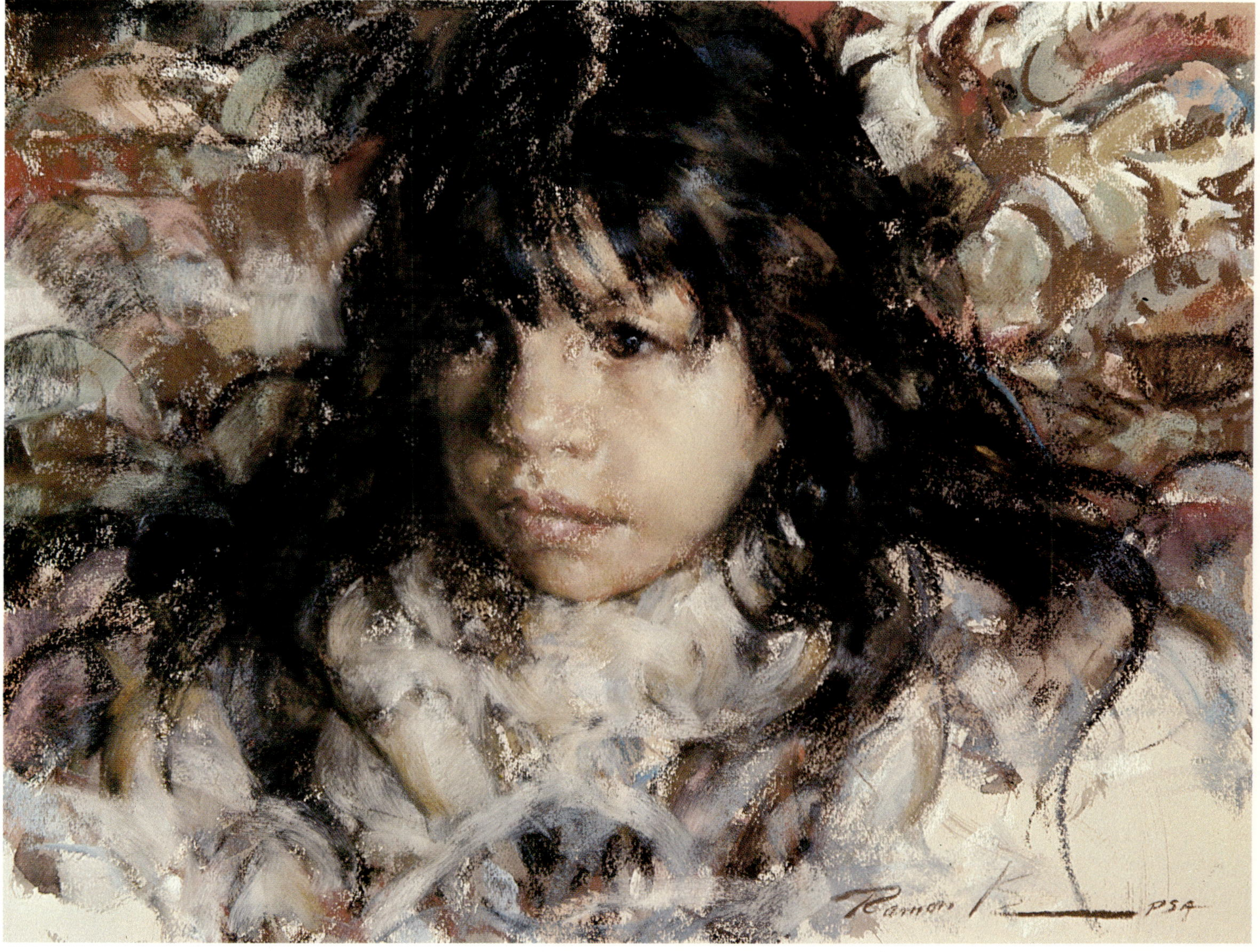

Slim (left). Transparent watercolor on 300 lb
Arches paper, 11″ x 6″ (28 x 15 cm). When I
cut off a piece of an expensive sheet of 300 lb
Arches, I had this interesting narrow shape left
over and was inspired to paint this portrait within
the limits of the format. The paper's rough texture
lent itself to a drybrush effect in the beard which
appears even bolder here than it would seem in a
larger painting. I used a number 18 watercolor
sable brush. The little cracks of light around Slim's
hat are saved areas of the white paper. However, I
did scrape out the lightened area on the upper
right and the light on the left side of the beard.

Gina (above). Pastel on French sanded board, 14″ x
18″ (35.5 x 45.5 cm). I painted this pastel portrait in
my studio under north light, concentrating on the
values of the face. When painting by natural light
on a clear day, the lighted side of the model's face
appears lighter than it would under artificial light.
On a value scale where number 1 is white and
number 10 is black, the light side of Gina's face
would be numbers 2 and 3. Had I painted under
artificial light, I would have used a number 4 value.
Practicing control of values by painting still lifes
has been of great help to me in my portrait work.

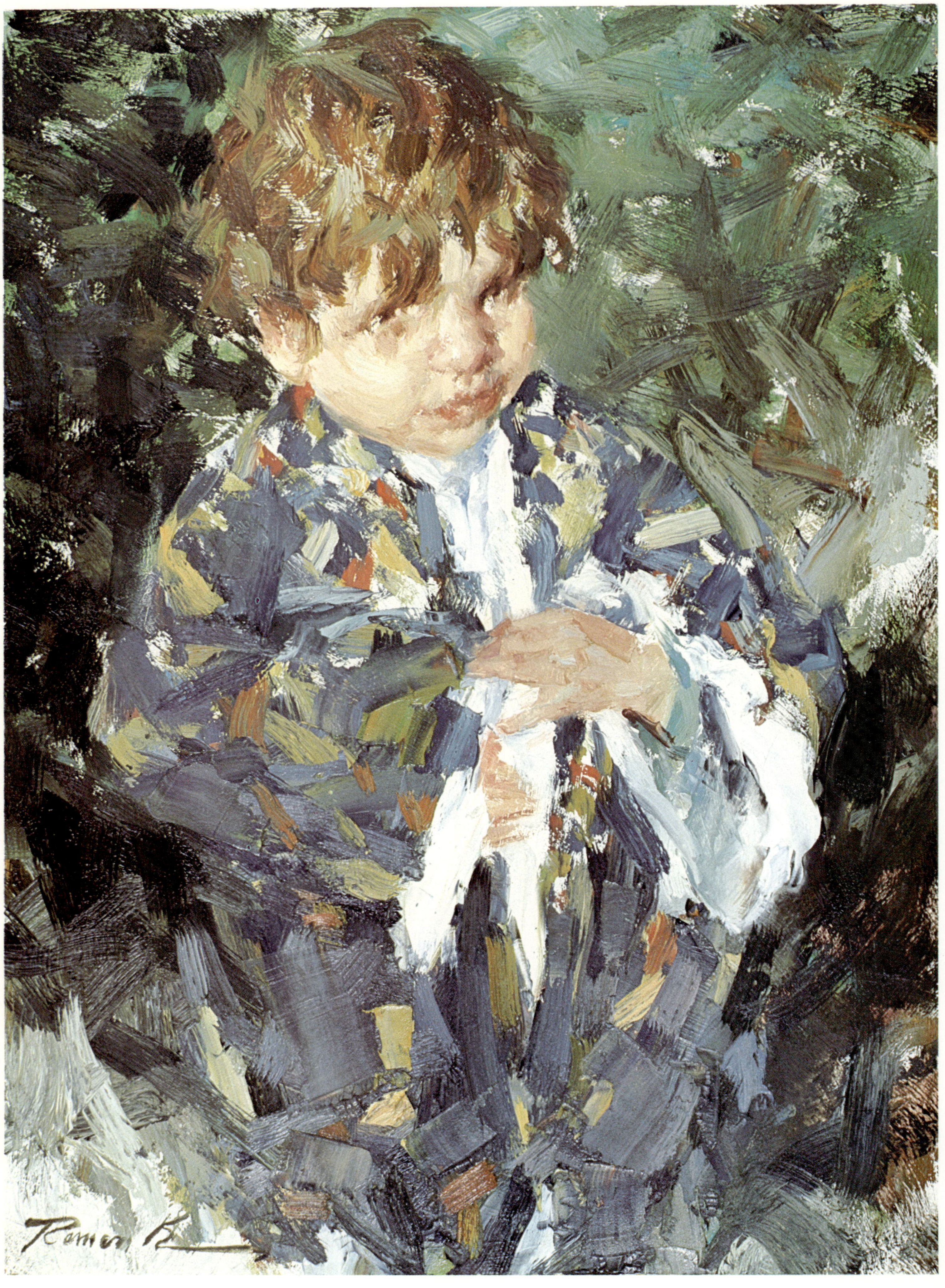

Ramon K

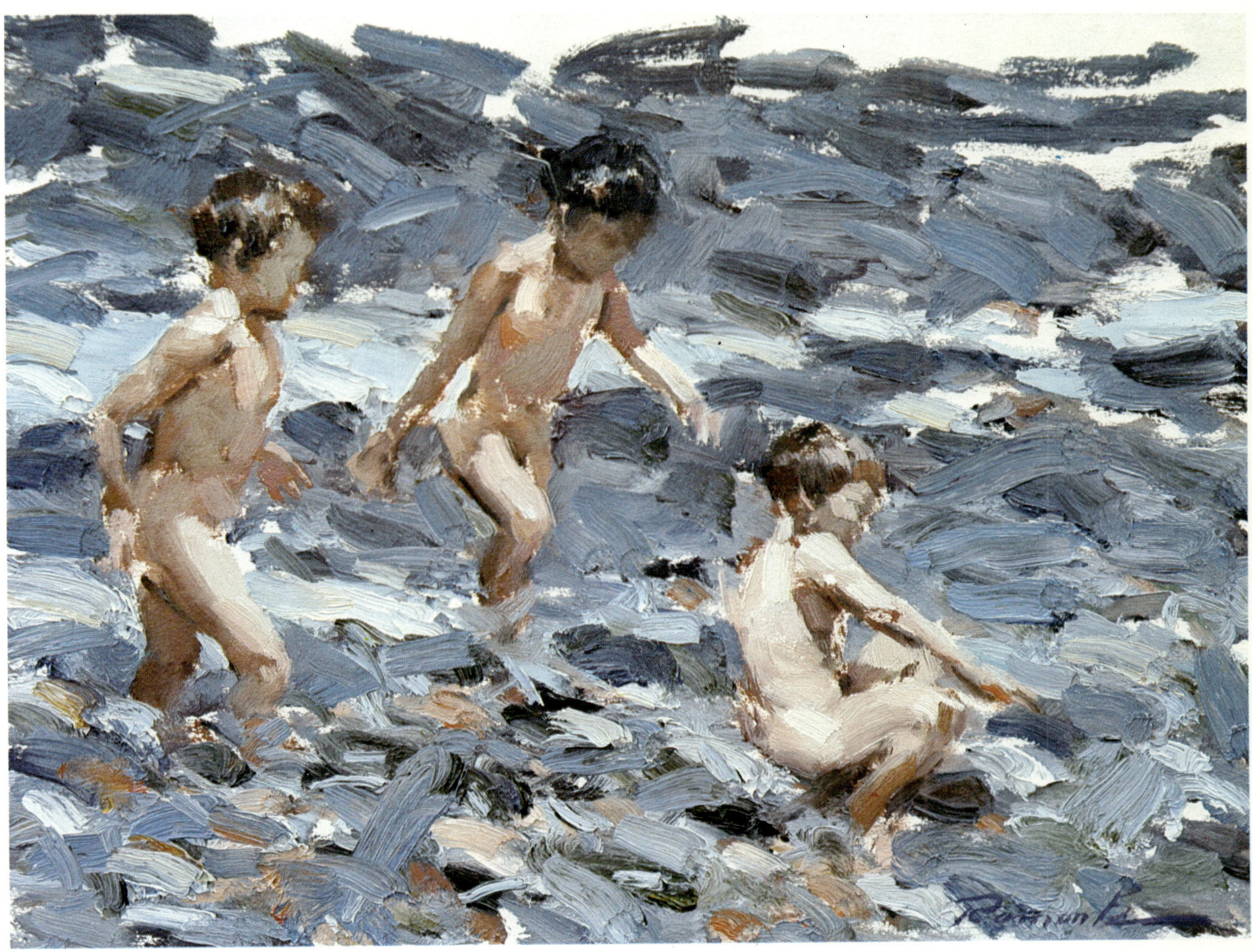

Baby Girl (left). Oil on Masonite, 12″ x 9″ (30.5 x 23 cm). This painting is done so directly, it almost reveals the process I used while painting it. I began by blocking in the colors on the head, working on it a bit, and moving on to the greenery of the background and the blue patterned robe. My little model was in daylight and I painted this with a fresh outdoor color scheme. My brushstrokes were mostly short, blunt ones and they make a pattern all over the surface.

Boys Playing in the Surf (above). Oil on illustration board, 9″ x 12″ (23 x 30.5 cm). I was inspired to paint this after seeing my children playing on the beach in Mazatlán, Mexico, one summer. On primed illustration board, I indicated the figures in flesh tones and then made a strong suggestion of water with alla prima strokes of cobalt blue, cobalt violet, cadmium yellow, and white mixtures. Reflections of the flesh tones can be seen in the foreground water.

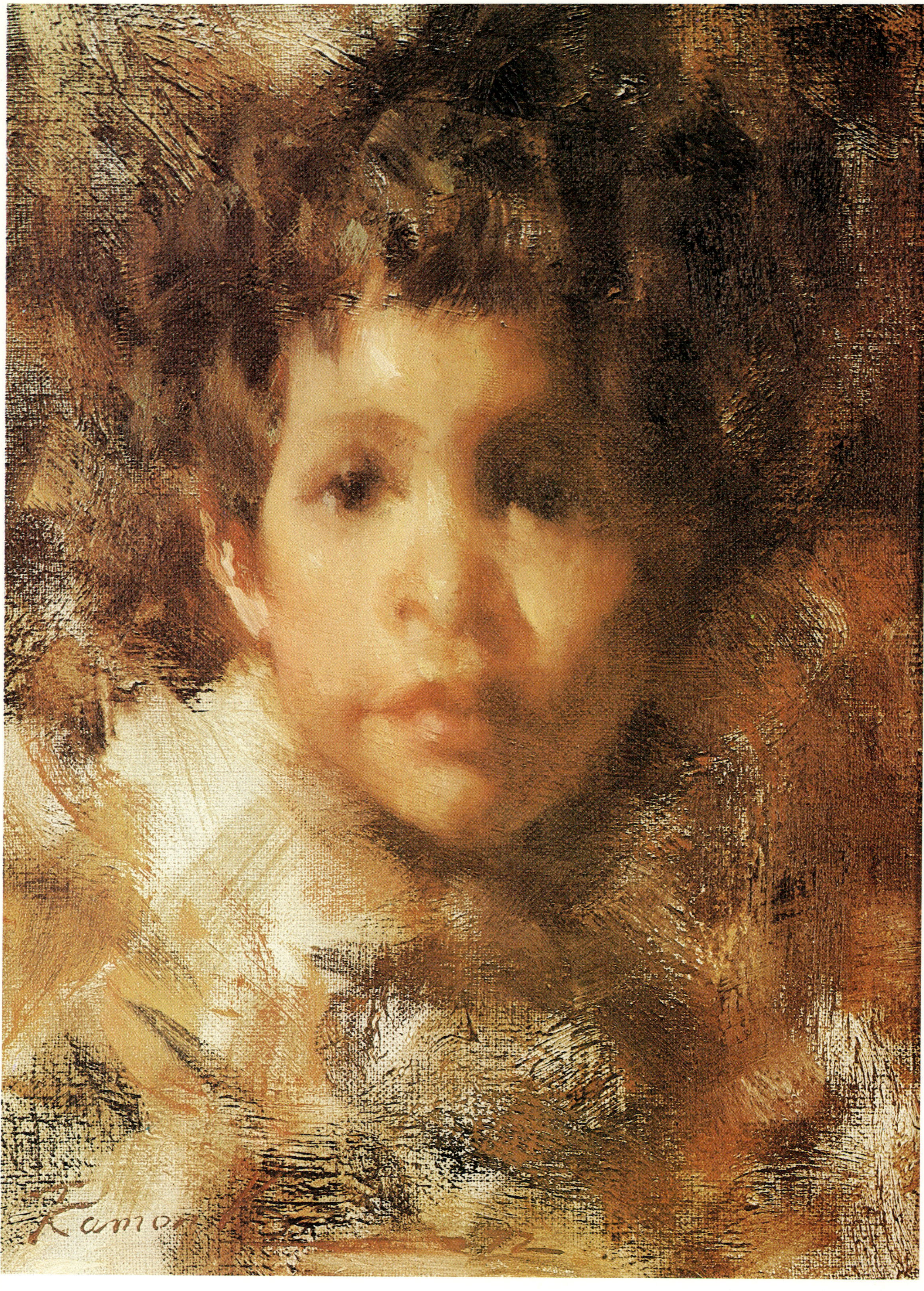

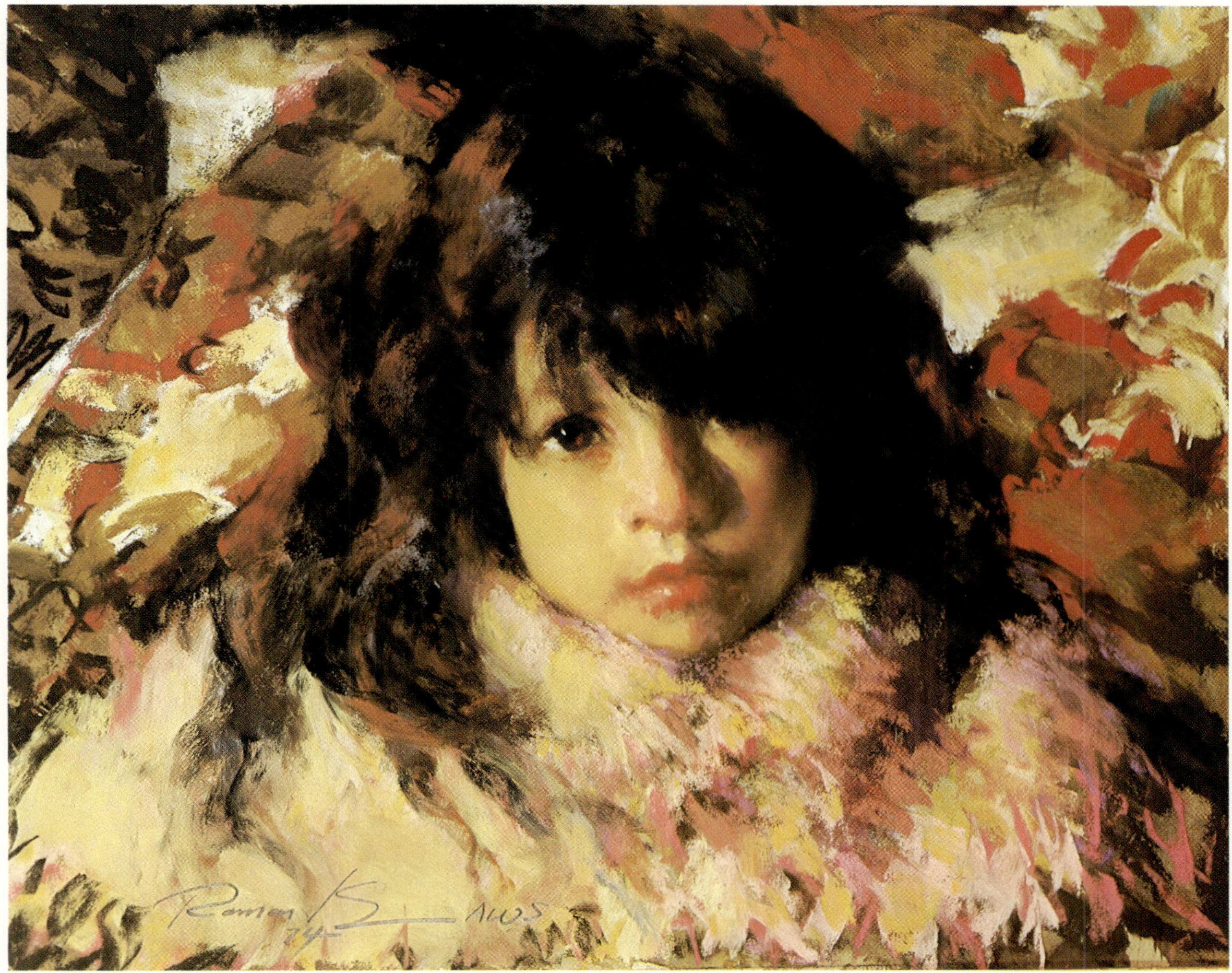

Lea (left). Oil on canvas, 12″ x 9″ (30.5 x 23 cm).
I painted this chromatic study of my little
daughter Lea with yellow ochre, cadmium red, a
little alizarin crimson, and cadmium orange. Burnt
sienna mixed with black is the dominant color of
the background and shadowed side, but I worked
some of the flesh tones over it. I focused on the
shape of the head and her modeled features lit
from the left by a warm light. I allowed the canvas
to show through on the left collar and elsewhere in
a pleasantly random manner.

Little Girl in Shawl (above). Pastel on rough
sanded board, 12″ x 16″ (30.5 x 40.5 cm). Against
the strongly patterned background in this painting,
I modeled the child's face in a warm, bright
sidelight that cast deep shadows on the face and
hair. The modeling on the lighted side was mini-
mal, but the face, where the shadows begin, projects well. On the right side of the nose, notice that
there are a number of changes, both in value and
temperature, which serve to interpret the form of
the nose and cheek. On the far right of the cheek is
a reflected light that softly distinguishes the con-
tour. Edges are softly blended, with two excep-
tions: there are harder edges on the left-hand side
of the cheek and on the top right-hand side of the
hair. The effect is feminine and textures are soft,
especially the knit shawl the model is wearing. The
coolest color in the painting is the cobalt blue I
used to accent the hair. The cadmium yellow on
the left side of the face and the cadmium reds with
alizarin crimson on the right side of the face form
the basis of my palette for this painting.

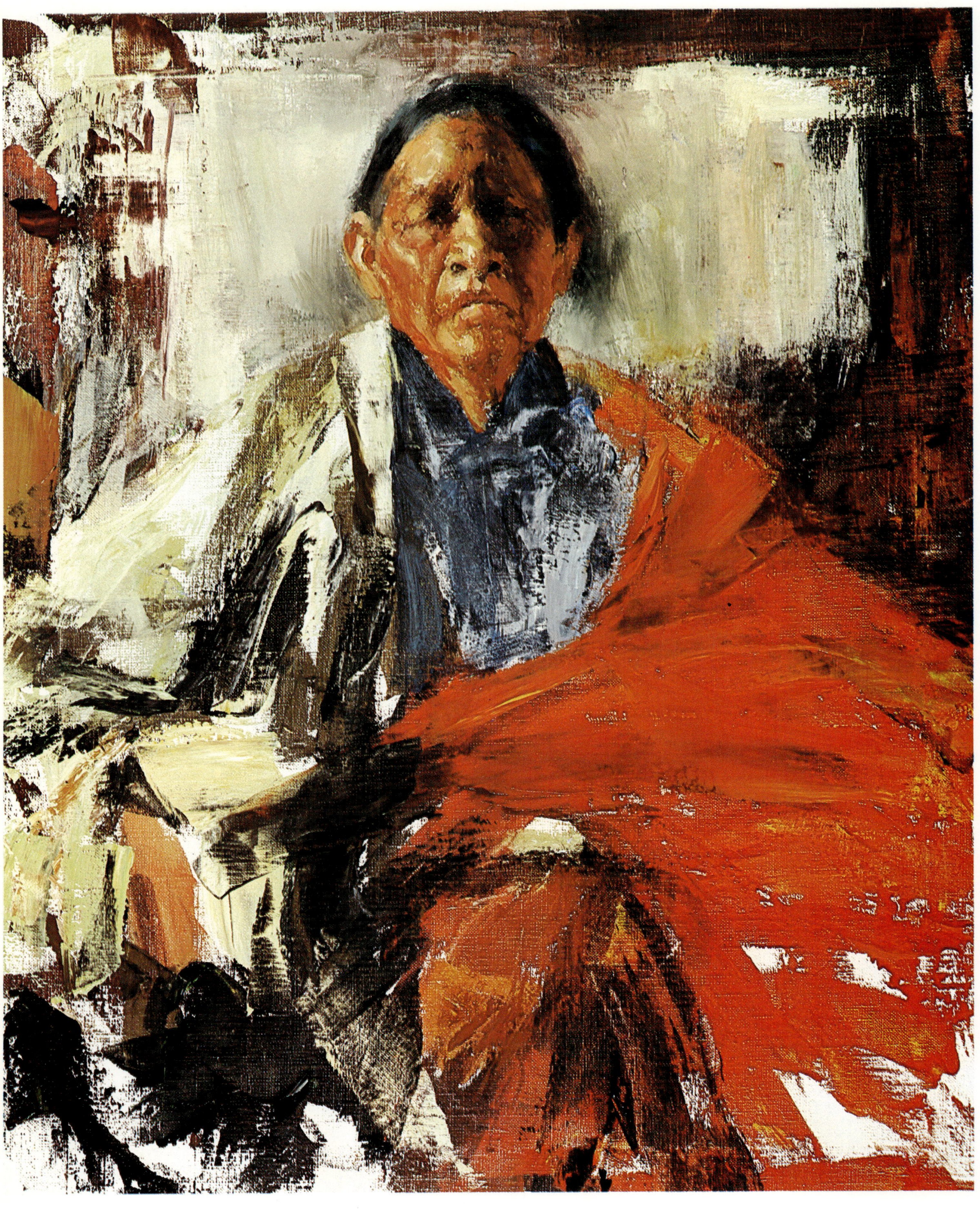

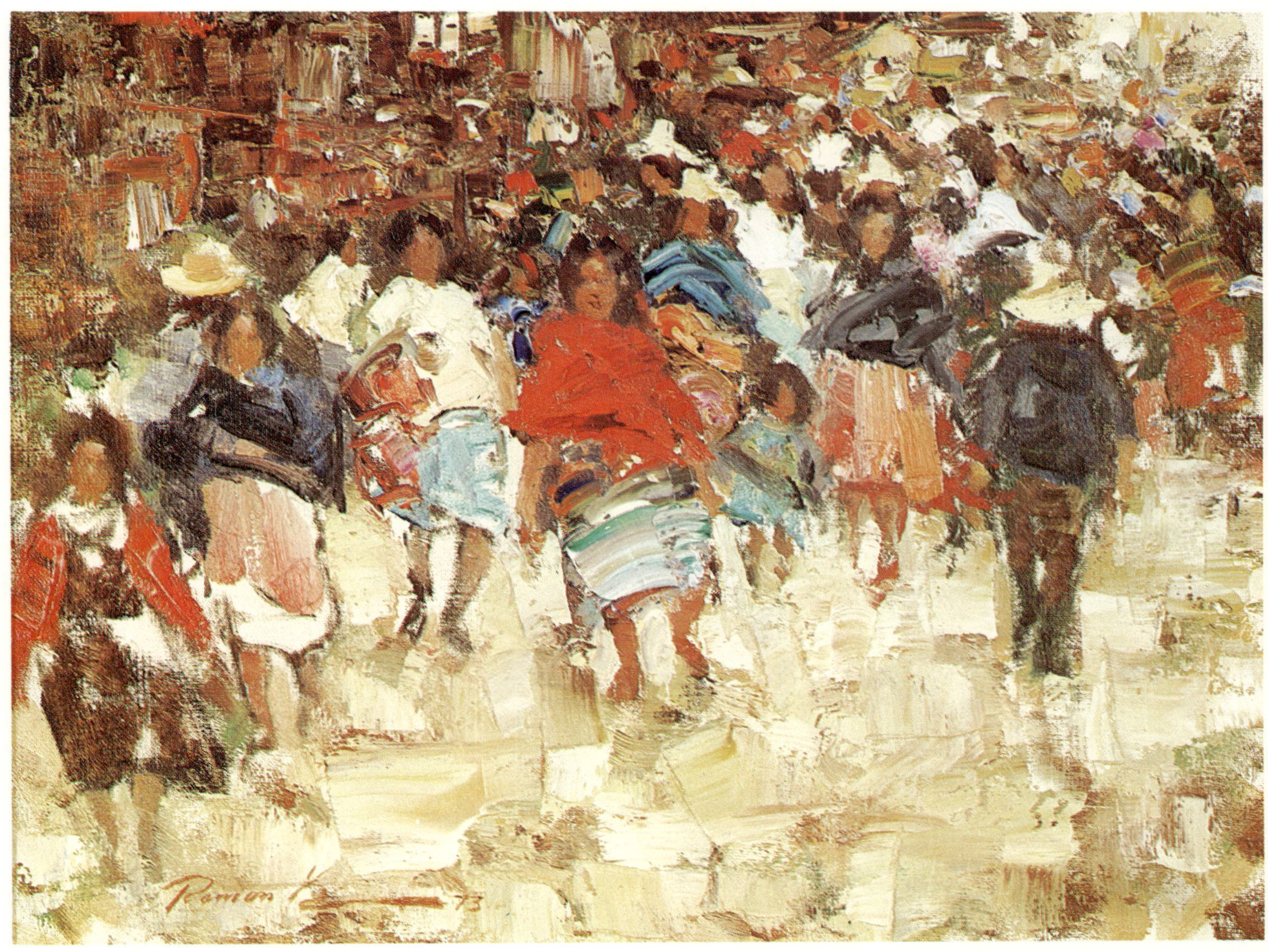

Taos Indian (left). Acrylic on canvas, 24″ x 20″ (61 x 51 cm). Every once in a while, with almost no effort, a painting just happens—it's complete immediately at the blocking in stage. This is one of those paintings. The only area I worked on after the initial layer was the face, hair, and around the head, where I used a brush. The rest of the painting was done with a palette knife.

Market Day, Mexico (above). Oil on canvas, 11″ x 14″ (28 x 35.5 cm). I made the big dominant shape on this canvas by painting people in a myriad of colors and with the barest definition possible. I was painting a crowd in motion and I let the flicker of colors set up this movement throughout the scene. To see how this works, notice that the eye is attracted to the red of the rebozo on the woman in the center. As the eye seeks out all the other reds in the painting, an impression of a moving crowd is strongly felt.

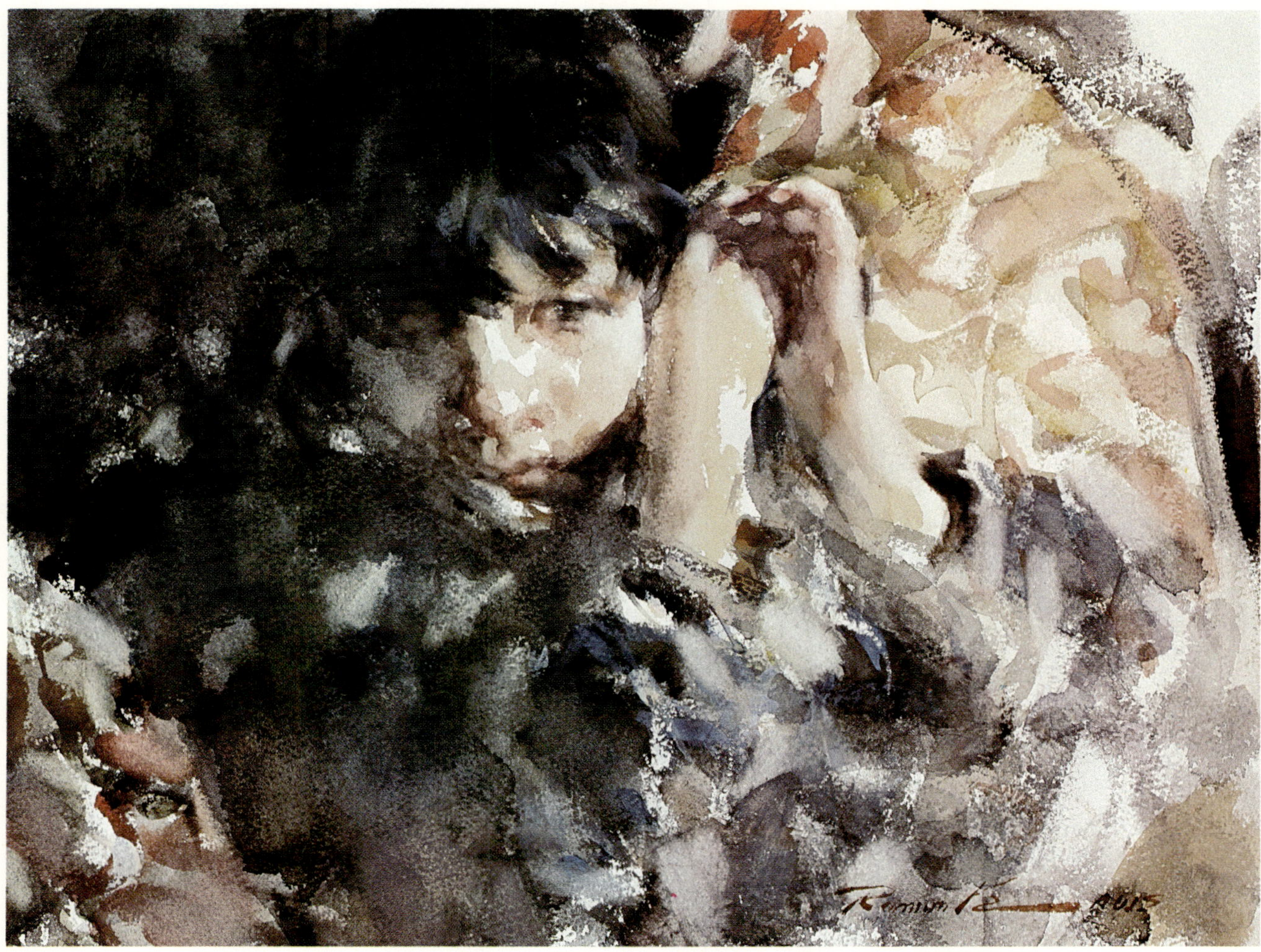

Primping (above). Watercolor on 300 lb Arches paper, 12″ x 16″ (30.5 x 40.5 cm). I painted this transparent watercolor rapidly, without a preliminary drawing, using a number 18 sable brush. First I indicated the gesture of the hands, the lighted side of the face, and the patterned area of the chair on the right. I never reworked these areas; the immediacy of the brushwork there carries the painting. These areas are lit by an intense, natural light coming from the upper right, casting a rich, dark shadow on the left that includes the child's hair. With strong brushstrokes of pure black, I separated the hair from the background. This may seem like too bold a thing to do, but it can be effective when the washes are laid down freshly and left untouched, and when subtle value distinctions are made. I used yellow ochre and cadmium red very lightly on the face. To emphasize the nose and lips, I added alizarin crimson, deepening the value of the mixture. Under the cupped hand, the shadow is a combination of alizarin crimson and cobalt violet. The sharp line of shadow under the right cheek is black with alizarin crimson and a touch of cadmium red placed against the flesh.

Silver Bracelet (right). Pastel over watercolor on rough sanded board, 16″ x 12″ (40.5 x 30.5 cm). Watercolor plays a prominent role in this painting. I use it to form a dark shape that surrounds the model. Within this dark area, the wash is enlivened with the blooms and waterspots characteristic of watercolor. On this underpainting I used pastel in a simple way, doing the least possible to bring out the form. There's little color in the figure. The background is warm and the figure, cool. I spent more time on the hands than on the face. As a result, the face is more suggestive. The child's shawl is made with strokes of white mixed with alizarin crimson, cobalt violet dark, and cobalt blue to form an active pattern, especially on the fringe. As the child posed, she was intent on the bracelet in her hands (another larger bangle was on her arm) and she seemed to have forgotten that she was posing. With a limited palette I feel I've created a strong image in lights and darks.

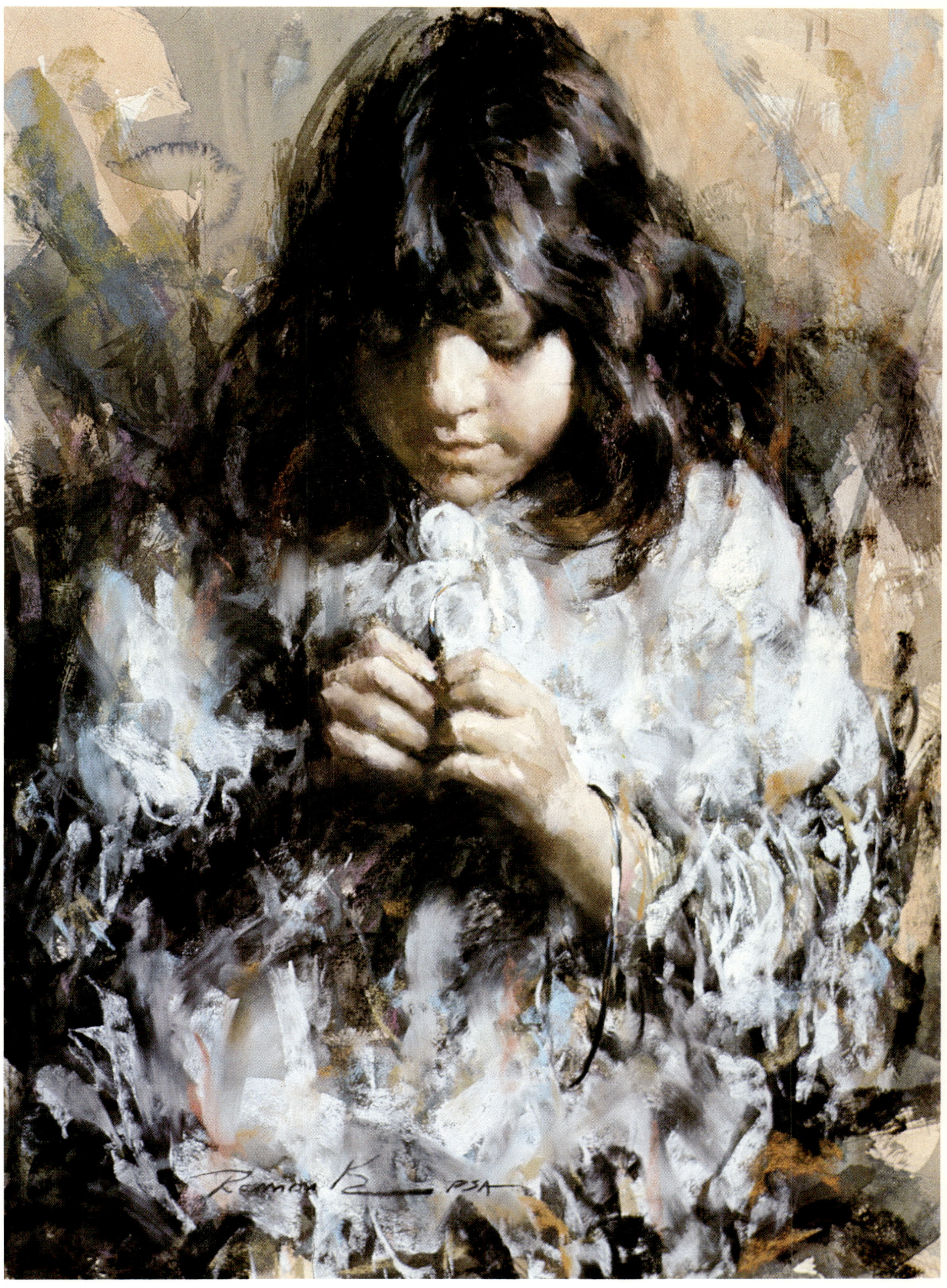

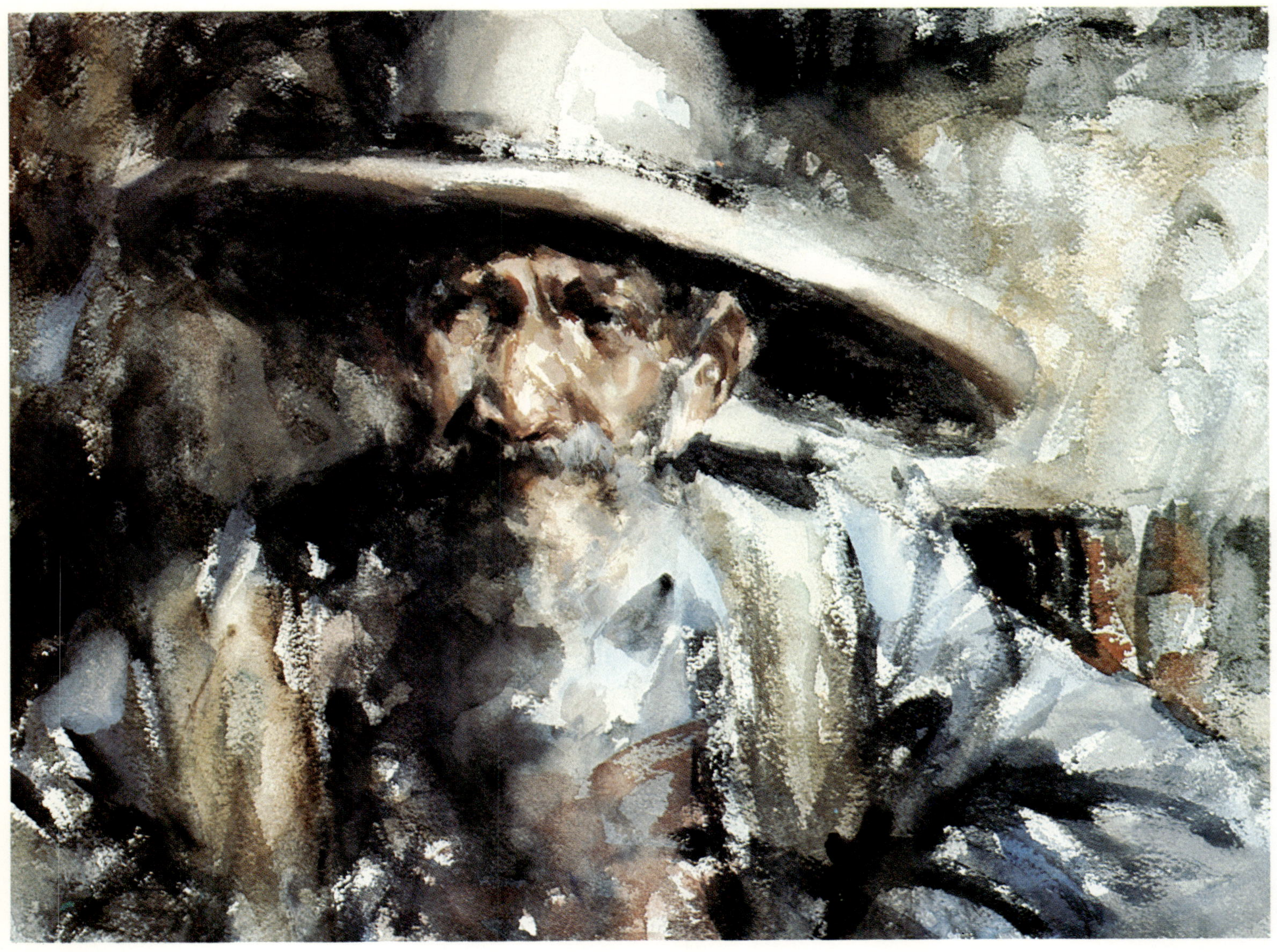

Grampo (above). Watercolor on 300 lb Arches paper, 12″ x 16″ (30.5 x 40.5 cm). When I painted this, I deliberately restricted my range of values and limited my palette. I kept the painting delicate and high keyed, with a dappled effect of cool light from beard to shirt to background to hat. Where it was necessary to set one form off against another, I placed a range of medium-dark values made with Hooker's green, cobalt blue, and black. I used both a number 18 round sable and a number 6 filbert bristle to paint the picture. The variety of brushstrokes adds textural interest to the surface.

A Crow Chief (right). Watercolor and gouache on illustration board, 12″ x 10″ (30.5 x 25.5 cm). Here I incorporated both transparent and opaque passages into the painting. The light coming from the upper left almost washes out the detail of the feathers of the war bonnet and casts a shadow on the upper part of the face. Prominent highlights can be seen on the left cheek, nose, chin, and on the fullness of the right cheek. For the lightest areas on the left cheek and to the right of the shadow under the nose, I let the board show through. The patterned area at the lower right is a mixture of underwash, scumble, and some of the still uncovered board. The ribbons and skins hanging from the headband are painted with a bristle brush and opaque paint. I use the red of the feathers to draw the eye toward the face.

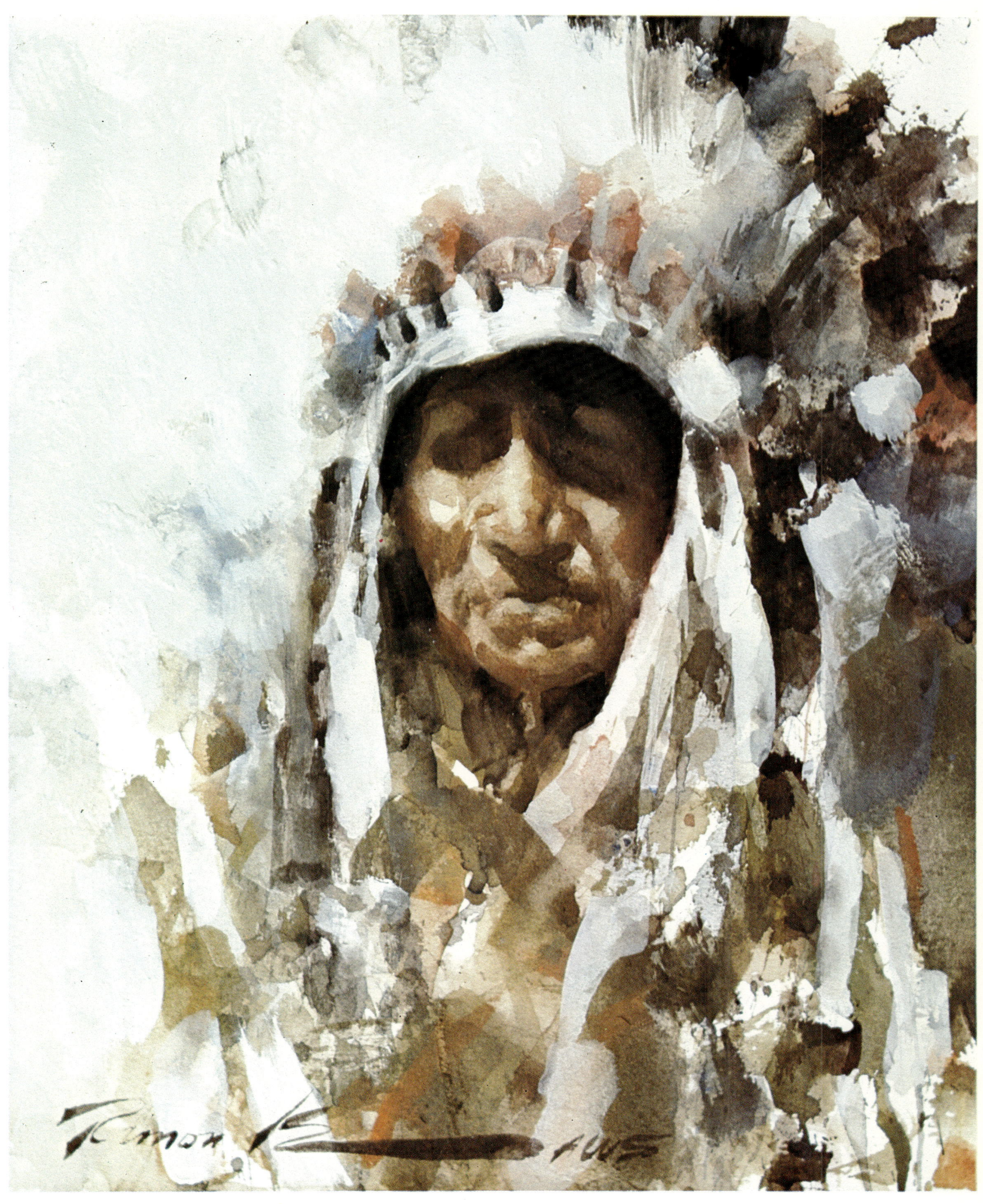

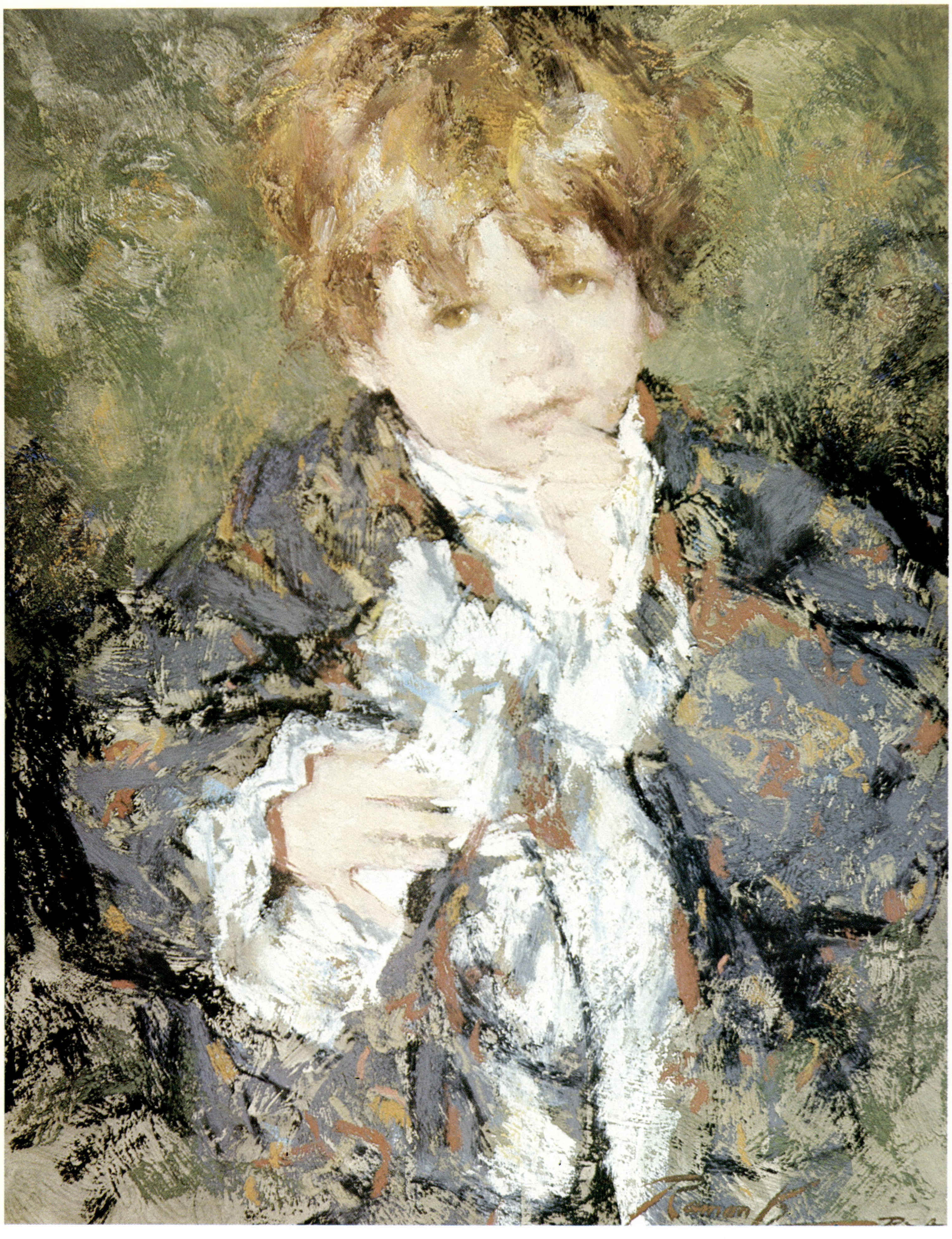

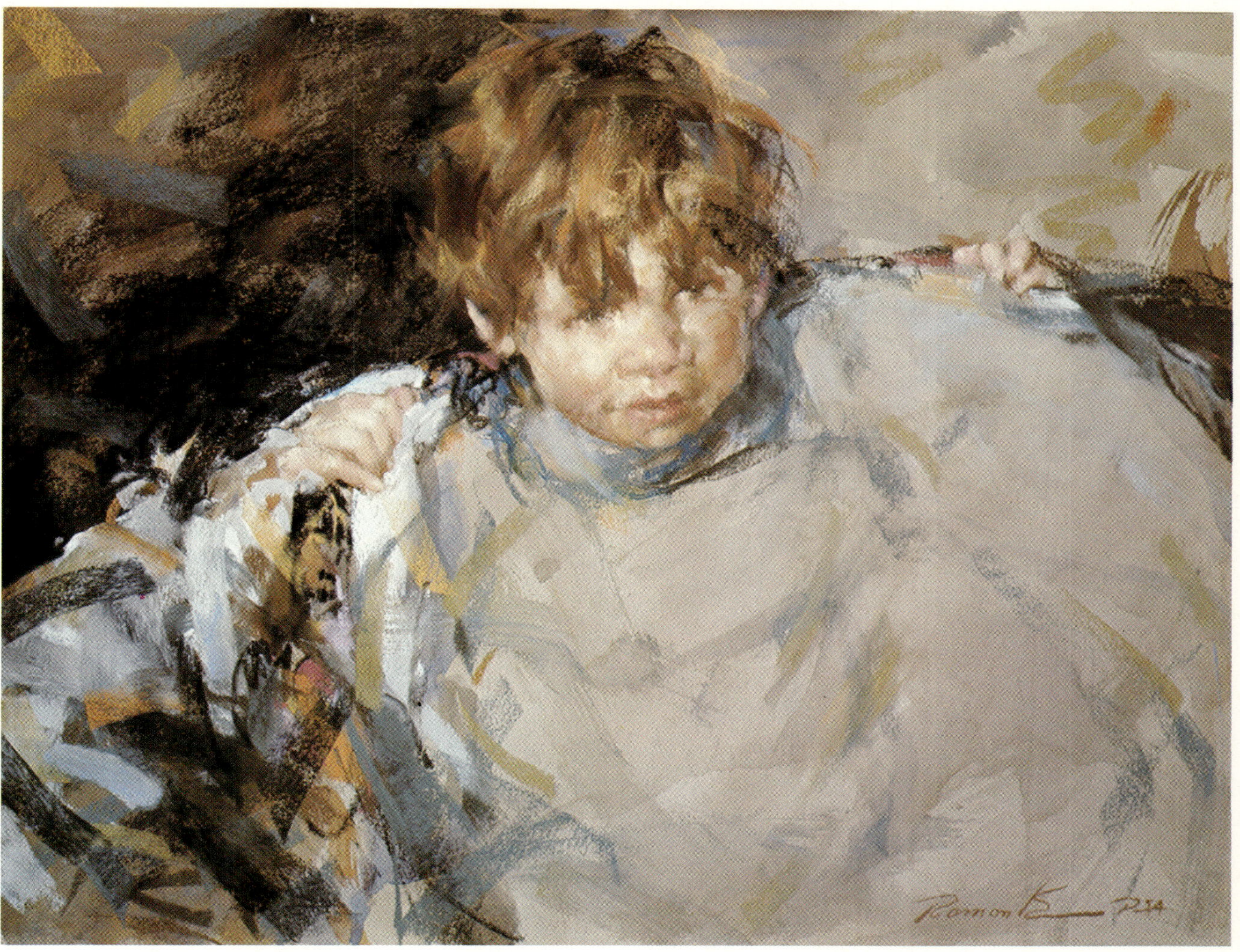

Baby Dasha (left). Pastel over watercolor on rough sanded board, 14″ x 11″ (35.5 x 28 cm). I used tinted water to loosen the sand grains somewhat on the board for increased texture. I then let it dry. The baby is posed outdoors, as suggested by the vegetation in the background. Strong natural light cools and bleaches the color of this high-key painting. The very light skin and reddish brown hair have cool highlights. There's little detail in the modeling of the face and hands because of the subtle value changes. Colors used in the hair are picked up throughout the painting for a harmonious effect. I used Indian red and burnt umber with cadmium yellow and orange for the warm colors. Cool blue-gray and green earth with black make a contrast with them. I defined the shape of the robe with dark accent lines in a simple way so as not to distract from the delicacy of the face and hands.

Ashley's Robe (above). Pastel over watercolor on rough sanded board, 12″ x 16″ (30.5 x 40.5 cm). I took liberties with the design of this painting. The child's head is almost centered in a space that's nearly empty. A finished likeness of the face and hair with the hands forms the positive area—and all the rest is negative; that is, undefined. Underpainted washes make a subtle pattern on the child's nightgown and robe. A bold patchwork of blue and gray strokes provides the dark on the left that contrasts with the light values of the other two-thirds of the space. Though unusual, the design satisfies me and I think it has a distinctive quality. I made a conscious effort to vary the pastel strokes so that there's an underlying rhythm to the work.

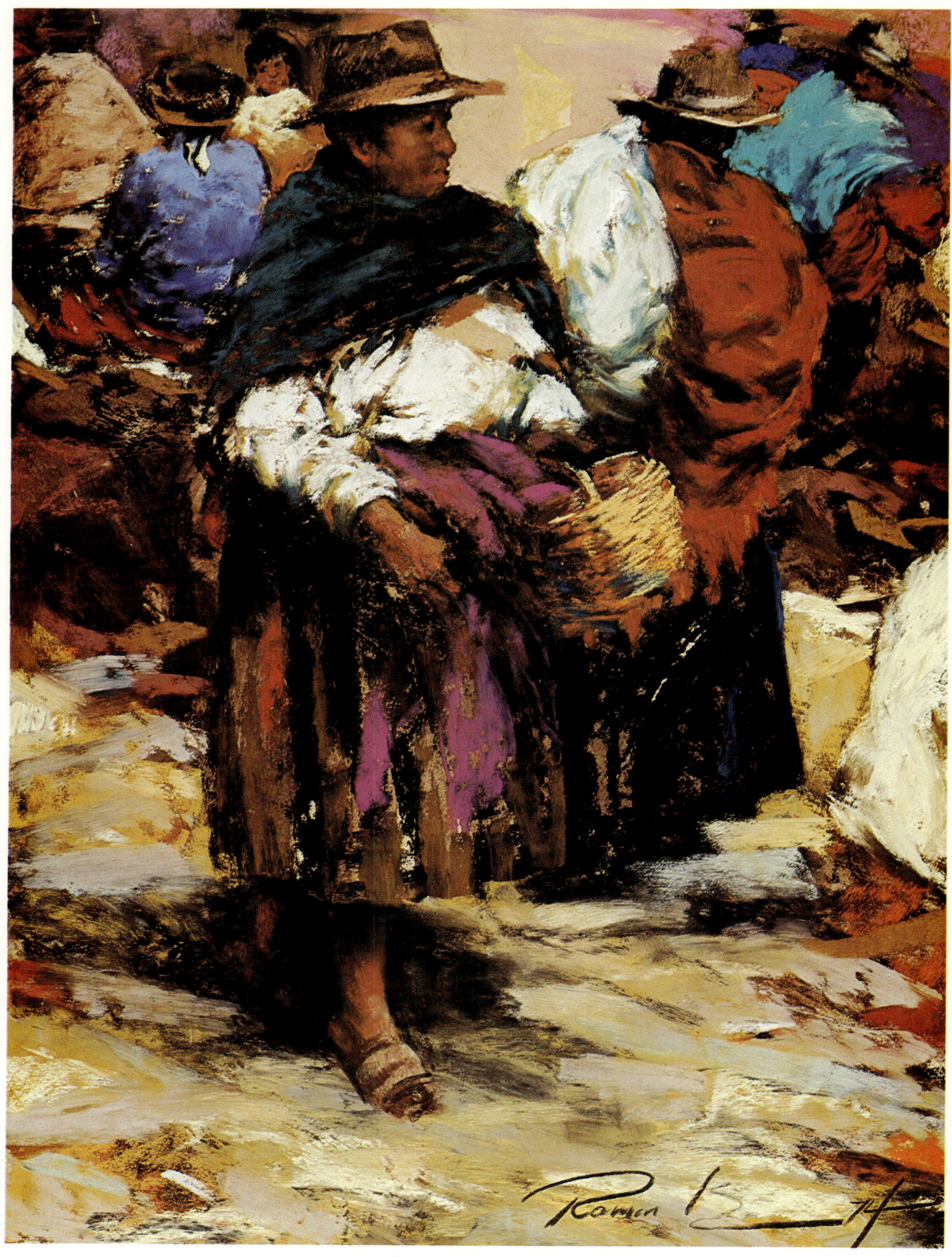

Inca Market. Pastel on rough sanded board, 16″ x 12″ (40.5 x 30.5 cm). The market places from Mexico and further south are very colorful and provide plentiful subject matter for the figure painter. I can spend hours there collecting material through sketches and photographs for future paintings. This market scene is based on one I saw in Guatemala, as you may note by the native dress. Notice the variety of colors in the clothing of each figure. The composition of this painting depends on an emphatic V-shape that focuses attention on the figure in the foreground. I selected these colors and figures from a dozen photographs when I composed this painting in my studio. I recommend that artists use photographs as sources of information and details; they shouldn't copy the whole photograph. Often a painting copied from a photograph ends up reproducing the mistakes of a poor photograph. It's then obvious to the viewer that a photograph was used and, furthermore, that the artist failed to compose his own picture.

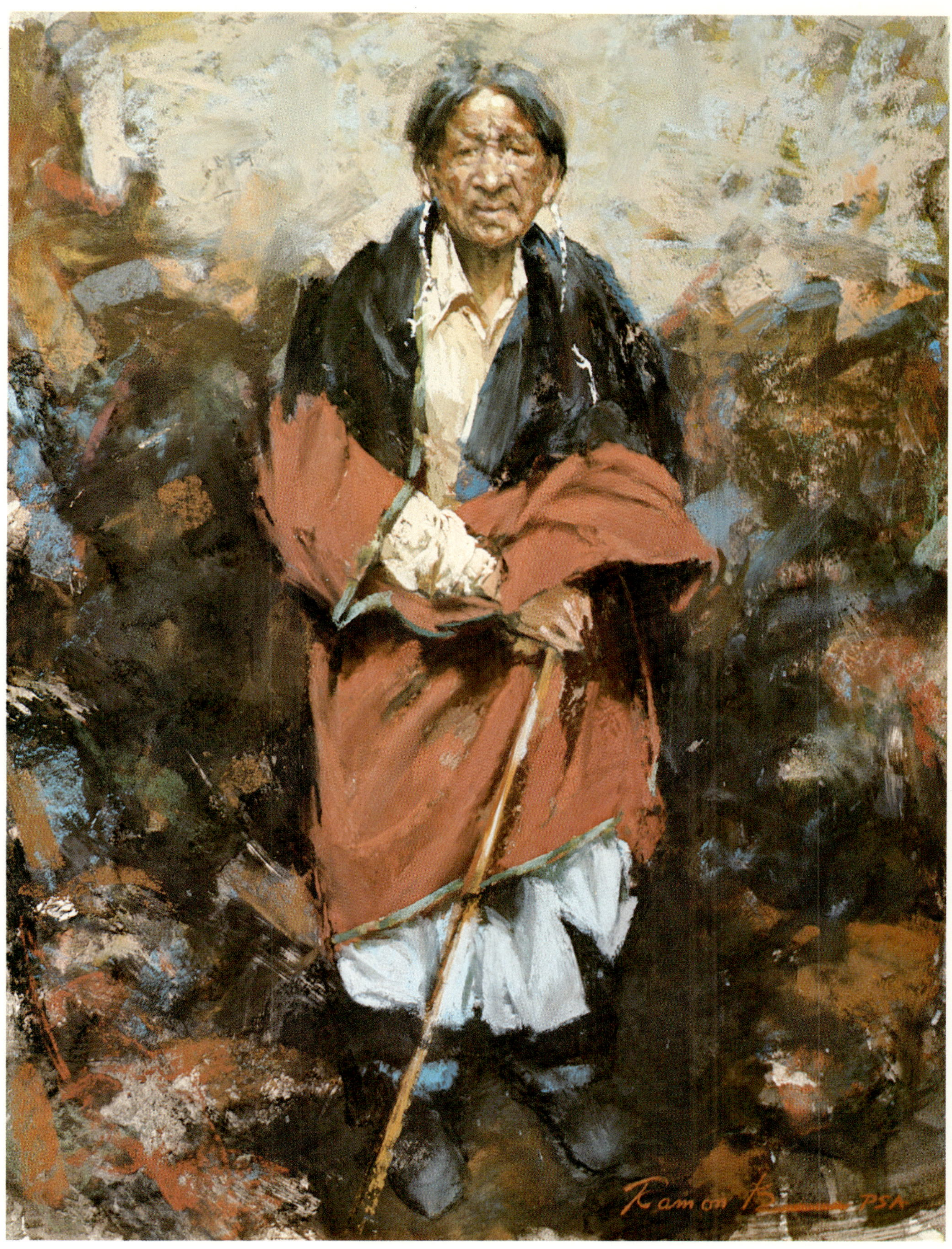

A Taos Elder. Pastel over watercolor on rough sanded board, 18″ x 14″ (45.5 x 35.5 cm). It was my good fortune one day in Taos to have this old gentleman pose for me as I sketched and took photographs. In this painting, the center of interest is the wide red band on the man's blanket. The background is divided into a light area at the top, which suggests an adobe wall, and a darker area that suggests the ground. The figure seems to emerge from these two abstractly painted areas. I painted the man and his clothes to a finished degree. I achieved a likeness of the model as a full-figured person, but I allowed the line of his cane and the edges of his robe to lead the eye to the face along an angular path. The colors used here are cadmium yellow, cadmium orange, cadmium red, cobalt blue, white, and black with touches of green and earth tones.

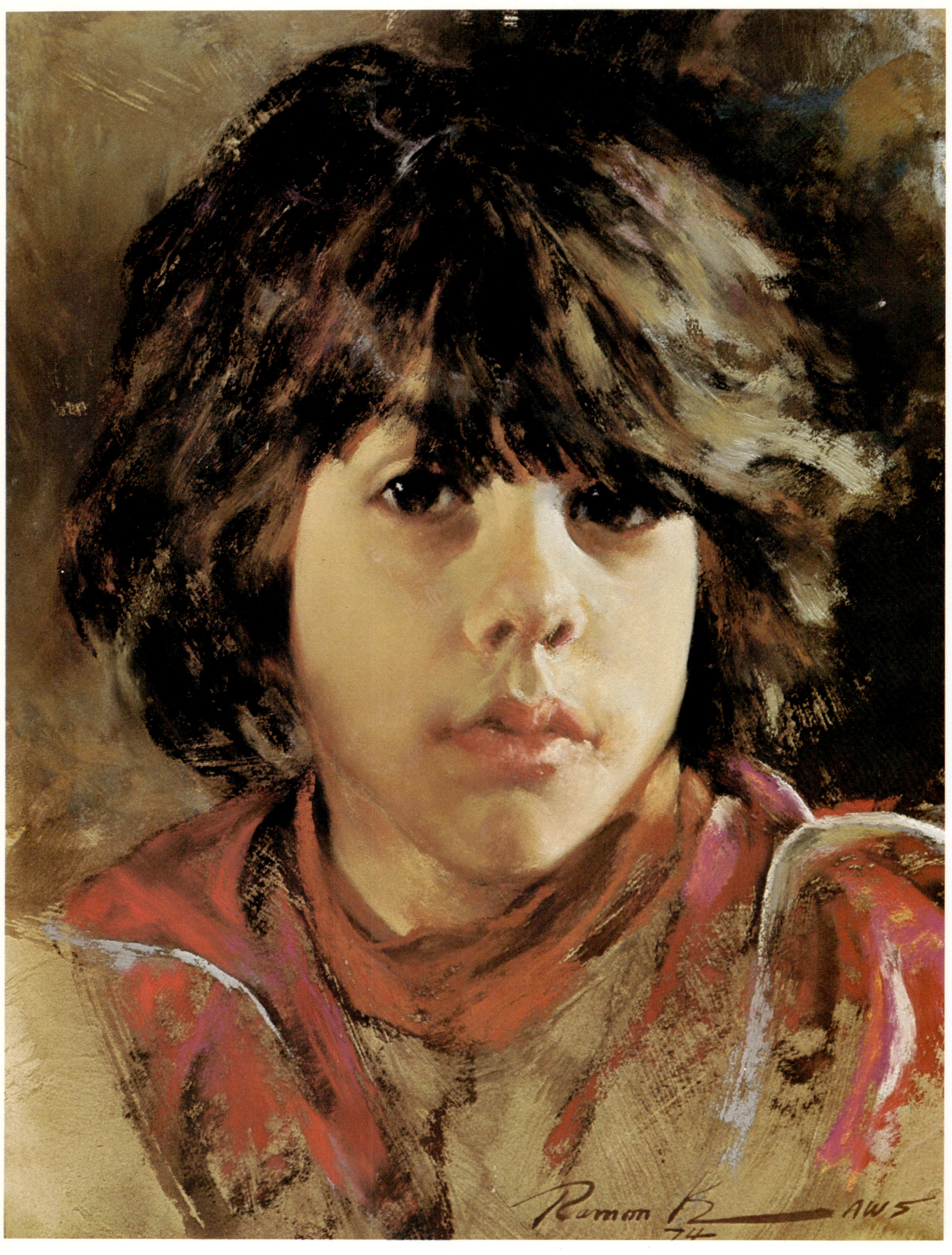

Ramon K------ AWS
74

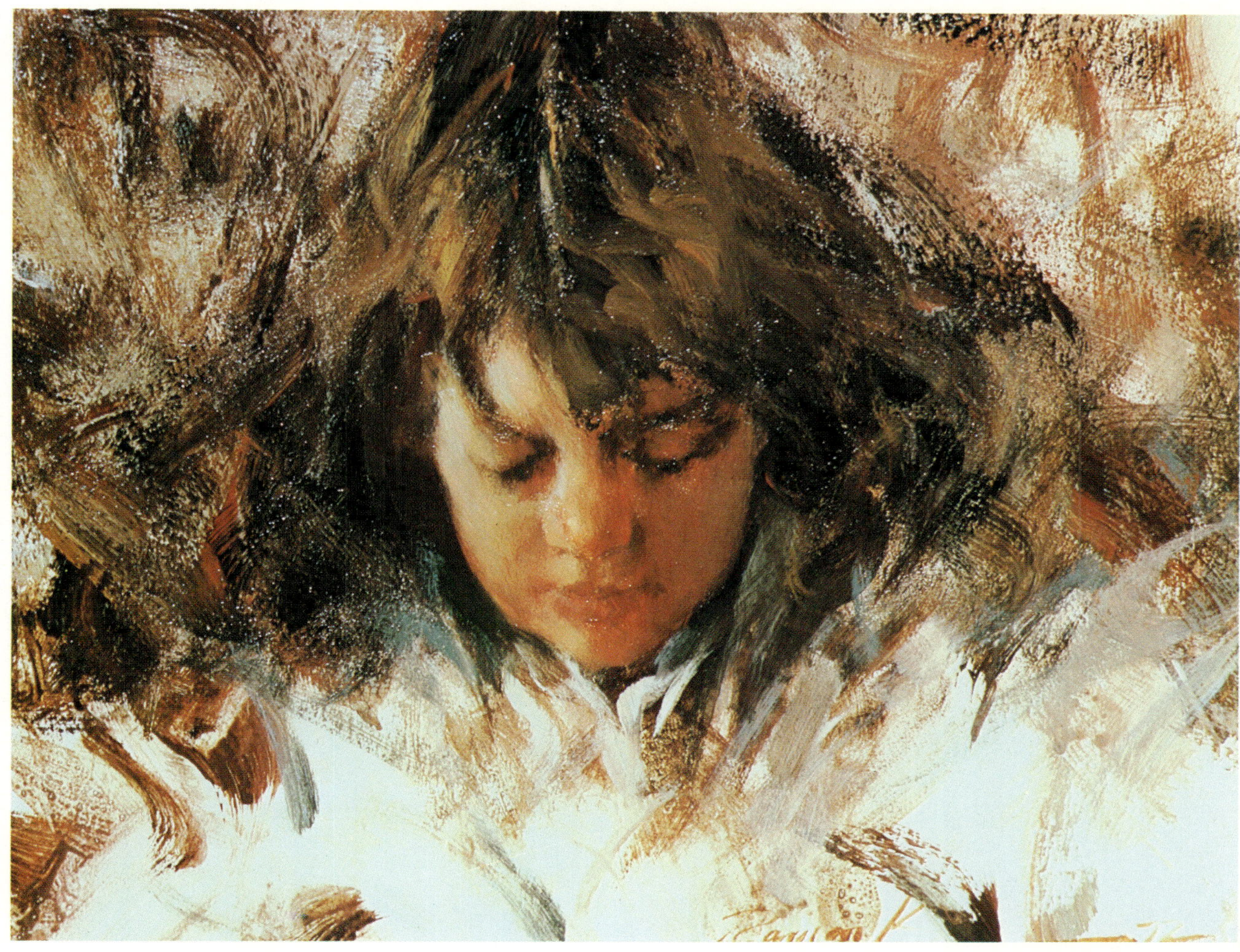

Adam (left). Pastel over watercolor on rough
sanded board, 14″ x 11″ (35.5 x 28 cm). When I do a
portrait, I not only try to create a likeness, but also
to make it work as a painting. Color, texture, and
the variety of pigment in watercolor and pastel all
play their part in this painting of my son Adam. I
toned the board first with a sepia watercolor wash.
Then with a dark overwashed shape, I indicated
the placement of the head. Switching to pastel, I
blocked in the features. The palette is set by the
colors in the face. Especially important are the
brown eyes; rosy, full lips; and warm flesh tones.
These colors are accented in the T-shirt and jacket.
Over the darks in the hair, roughly blocked in with
black, I used the reds and yellow skin colors for the
warm highlights, and blues in the cool highlights
for temperature contrast. I painted many soft,
feathered, blue strokes on the unobtrusive background to cool the area. Light coming from both
left and right makes this a complicated study of
light and shadow.

Little Antonia (above). Acrylic on illustration
board, 11″ x 14″ (28 x 35.5 cm). This painting was
hung in the Allied Artists of America Annual in
New York City in the National Academy galleries
in 1972 and led to my membership in the society. I
painted it quickly and directly. Since acrylic dries
fast, I was able to superimpose stroke over stroke.
The texture of the board grips and holds the paint
well. I enjoyed painting the brushwork on the hair
and I carried the free-flowing strokes into the surrounding background in an even broader way. I
placed opaque brushstrokes of yellow ochre and
cobalt blue on the hair and light cobalt blues and
grays loosely on the foregound. These brushstrokes help cool the very warm face. The unpainted board in the foreground takes on the shape
of the blouse. Areas of the white board also show
through in the background.

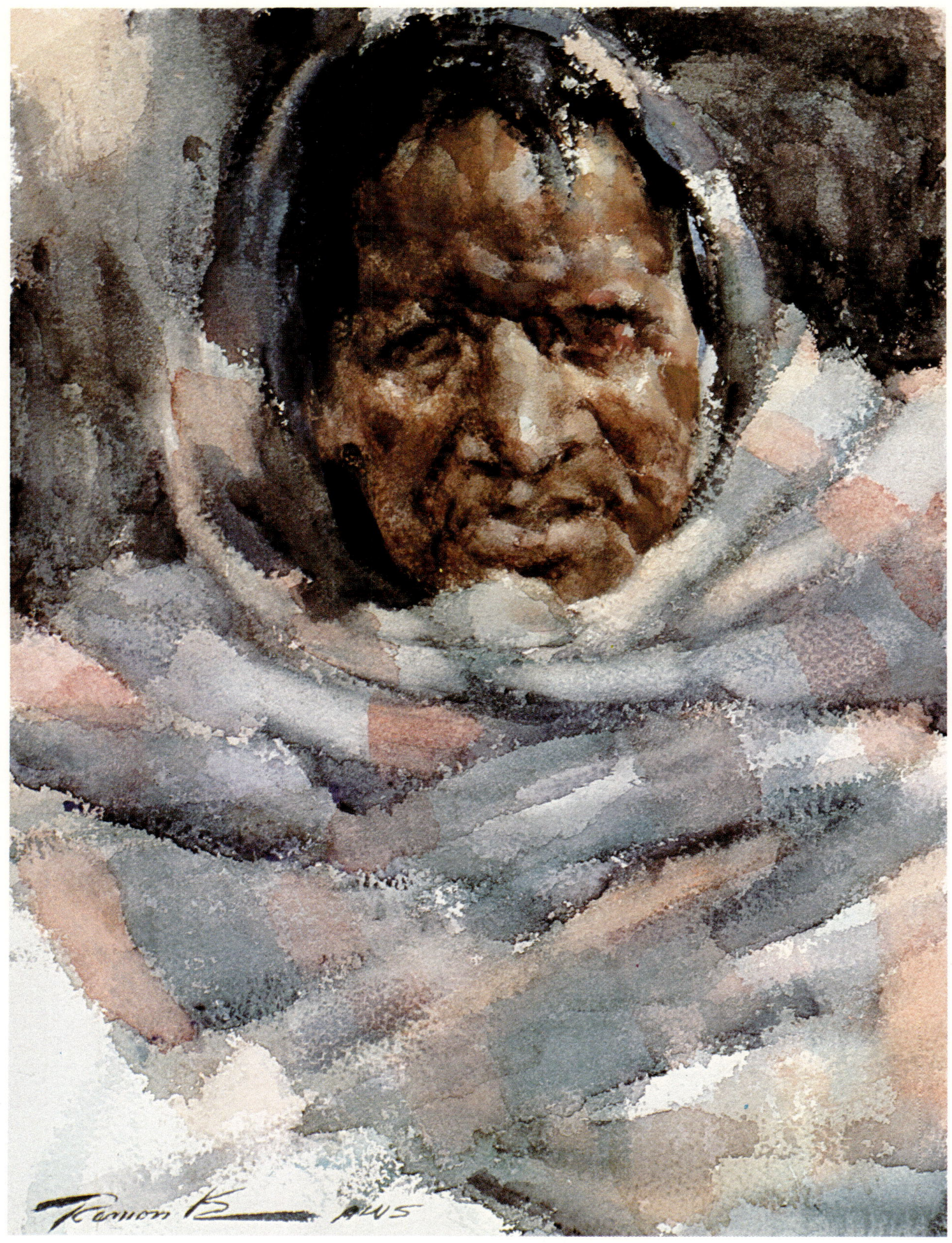

Joe Martinez de Taos. Watercolor with gouache on 300 lb Arches paper, 12″ x 9″ (30.5 x 23 cm). Because I wanted opaque passages on the face, I placed small strokes of gouache on the right-hand side near the eyesocket, on the forehead over the nose, and on the edge of the forehead just as it meets the hair in the center. Otherwise, this portrait study was handled like an ordinary transparent watercolor. I can't explain why I wanted to use gouache. I just felt that it was right.

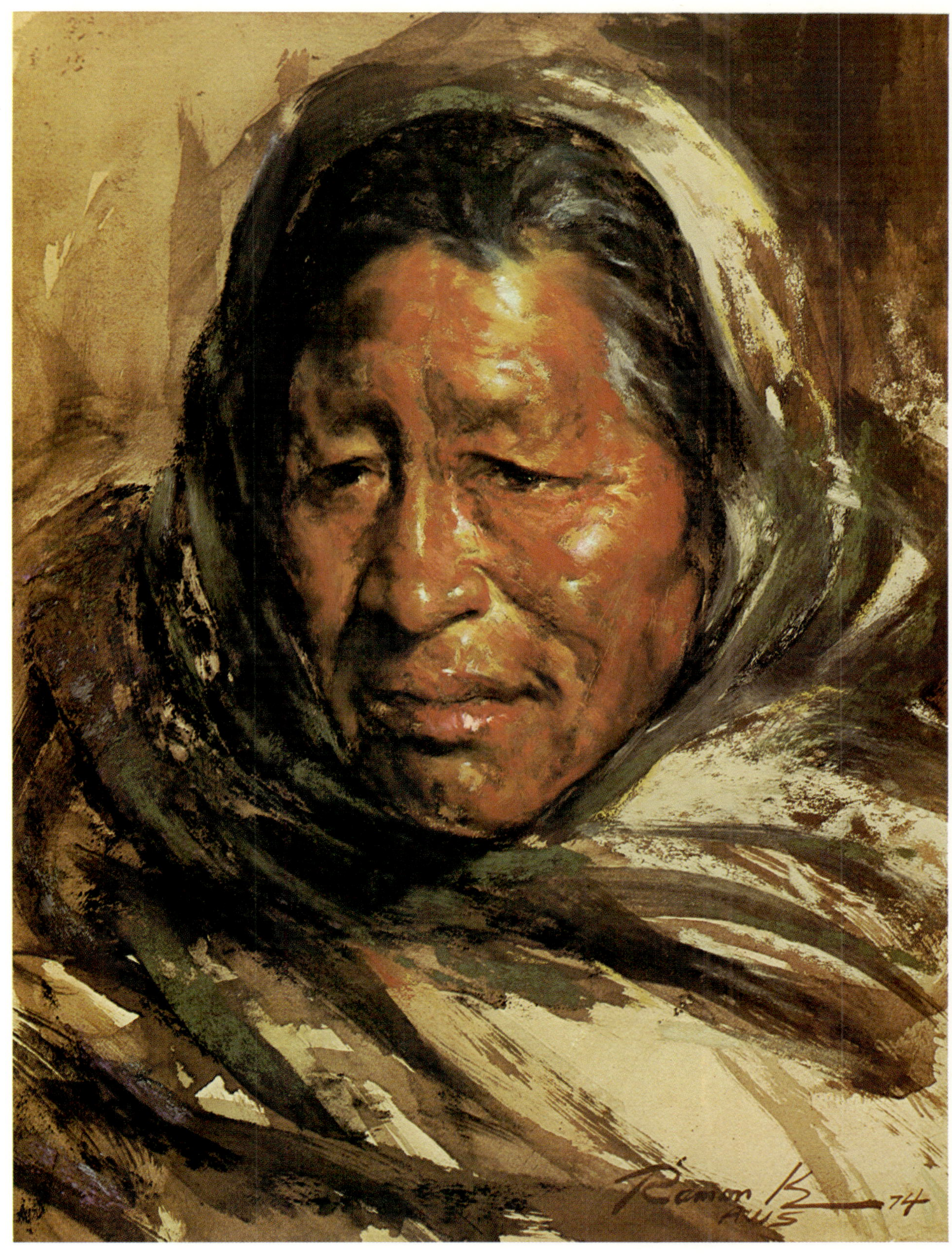

Juan Archuleta. Pastel over watercolor on rough sanded board, 14″ x 11″ (35.5 x 28 cm). It is customary for Taos Pueblo men to wear blankets wrapped around their head and shoulders. Working in the studio from a photograph and a pastel sketch, I was primarily concerned with likeness and facial expression. As I washed in the underpainting on this board, I placed the head immediately. Then, with a bristle brush, I loosened the sand grains slightly on the face and left shoulder and then quickly dried the board with a hair dryer to prevent buckling. It's necessary to use a minimum of water and work at great speed, but the result is a surface that accepts a greater amount of pigment than an untreated board. In the blocking-in stage of the painting, I used a medium value of yellow ochre and burnt umber. In the next layer, as I began modeling the form of the head with values, I put in the darks. Then I enriched the deep tones of the blanket that acts as a frame to the face. This gave me two references from which to develop the values on the face—the blanket and the warm brown washes on the background. It's essential, I believe, that an artist work all over the board and not isolate the face on a blank ground. All areas must work together in the final painting and should be brought along at the same time.

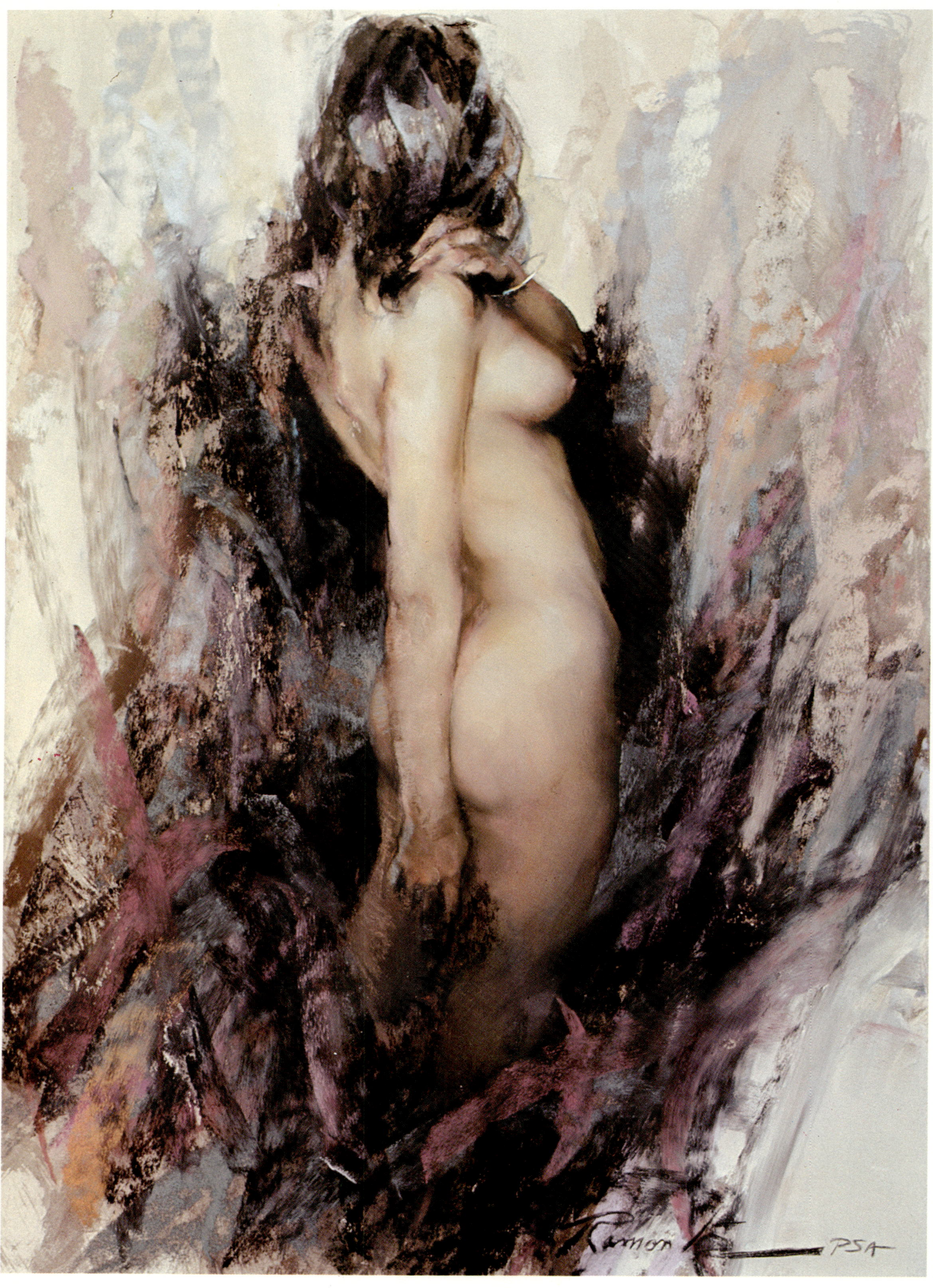

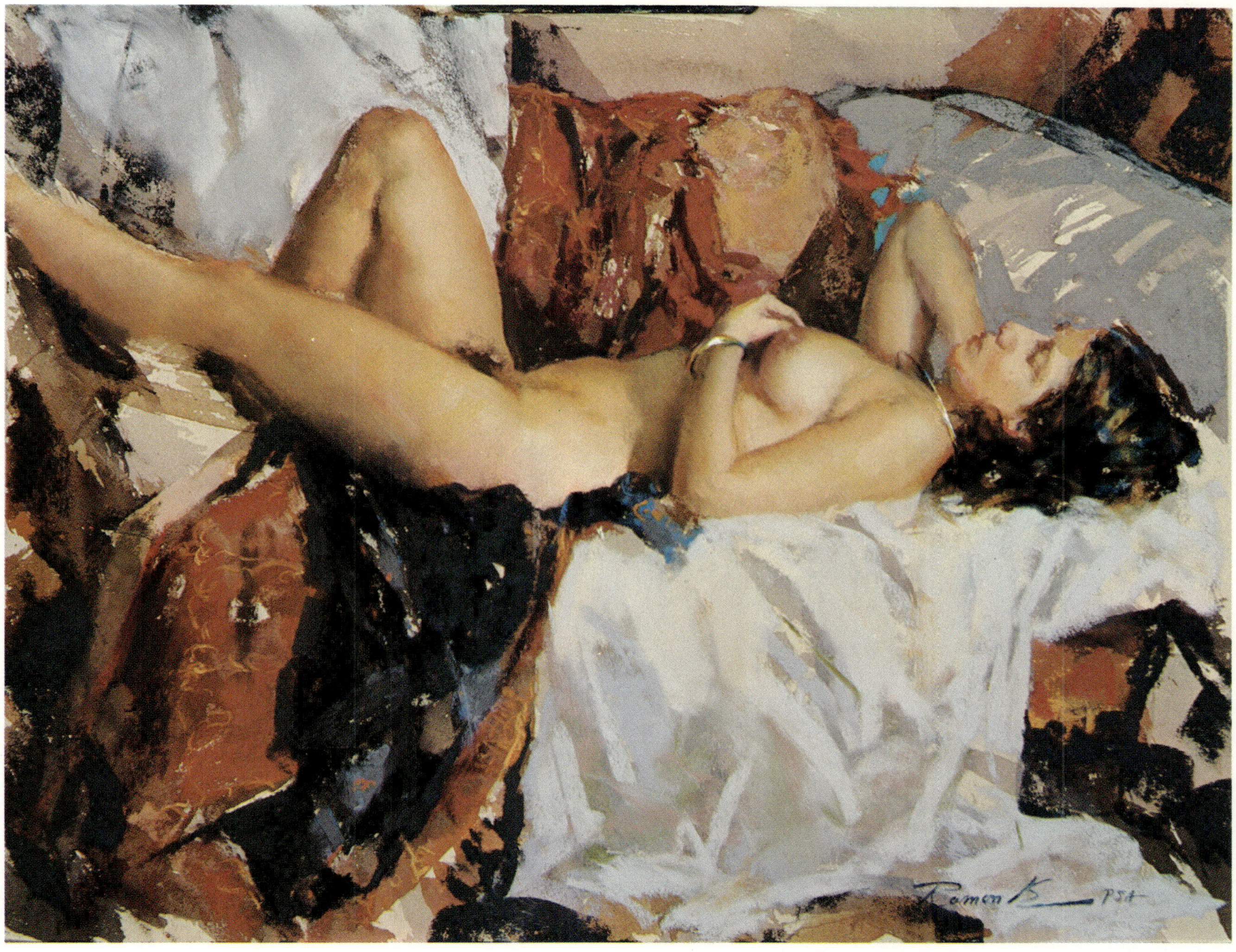

Standing Nude (left). Pastel over watercolor on rough sanded board, 16″ x 12″ (40.5 x 30.5 cm). I enjoy bringing a figure out of a dark shape. It adds a mysterious note to the painting and allows me to be entirely free in painting the textured, dense area around the model. By way of contrast, I painted this figure in porcelain tones, working toward a smooth surface. The model's pose is deceptively simple; actually it was a twisted pose and it was done over several sittings in the studio. I paid special attention to the details of the hands. Note the cool reflection at the edge of the little finger on the model's right hand that has picked up some of the cool tones in the background. I blocked in the hair with the flat side of the pastel and then used the point of the pastel stick to make finer lines. This linear quality is carried down into the dark background shape on the left. To create a vignette effect, I left the background simple on the top and at the right-hand side.

Nude (above). Pastel over watercolor on rough sanded board, 11″ x 14″ (28 x 35.5 cm). There are basically seven clearly defined shapes in this composition. Although this is a figure painting, I approach it much as I would a still life. The variously sized pieces of drapery and the concentration of darks make an arrangement that sets off the figure. For the patterned material, I used alizarin crimson, cobalt blue, and black—all cools—accented with cadmium orange. On the figure, the flesh tones are yellow ochre, cadmium red, and cadmium orange. I painted the highlights and other light values of the flesh tones with cobalt blue. To achieve the smooth pearly textures of skin, as I painted, I feathered the pastel with the little finger of my right hand to create a textural difference between the flesh and the surrounding drapery. I painted the drapery with bold, flat strokes and left them unaltered.

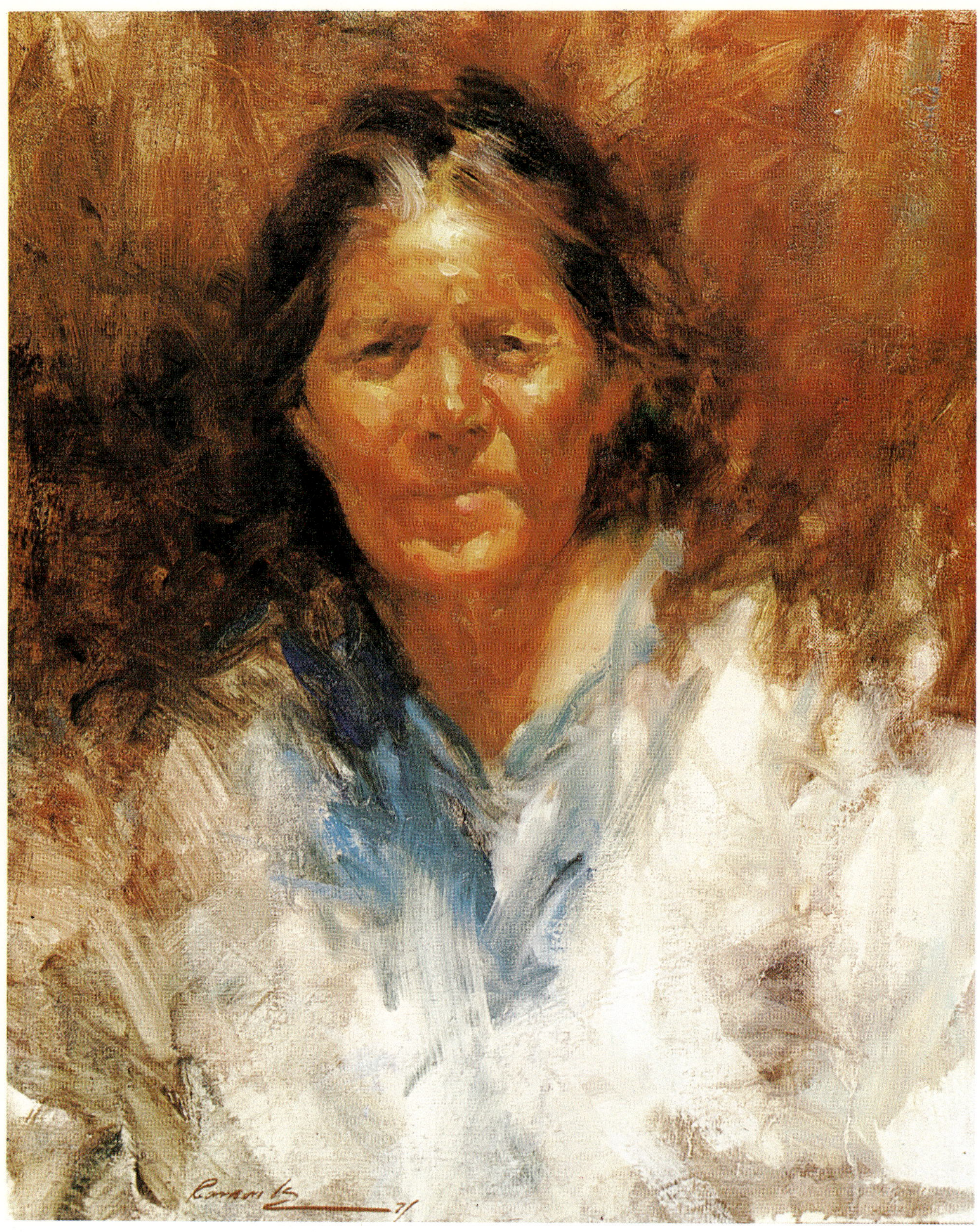

Pañuelo Azul. Oil on canvas, 20″ x 16″ (50.8 x 40.5 cm). I was near the seacoast in Mexico when I saw this Indian woman and stopped to photograph her. Her skin had the brilliant sheen that comes from hot sun and perspiration. From my photographs and color notes, I did this portrait later in my studio. I used diluted strokes of pigment and turpentine, working in a painterly style. The cool blue strokes of the scarf make an effective separation between the warm colors of the face and background, and the white blouse. I'm especially pleased with the subtle suggestion of white hair made with a flick of the brush on the forehead using thinner cobalt blue and white. Another interesting effect came from a quick upward swipe that I made on the blouse with a rag dampened with turpentine. Notice how it blended the white into the blue.

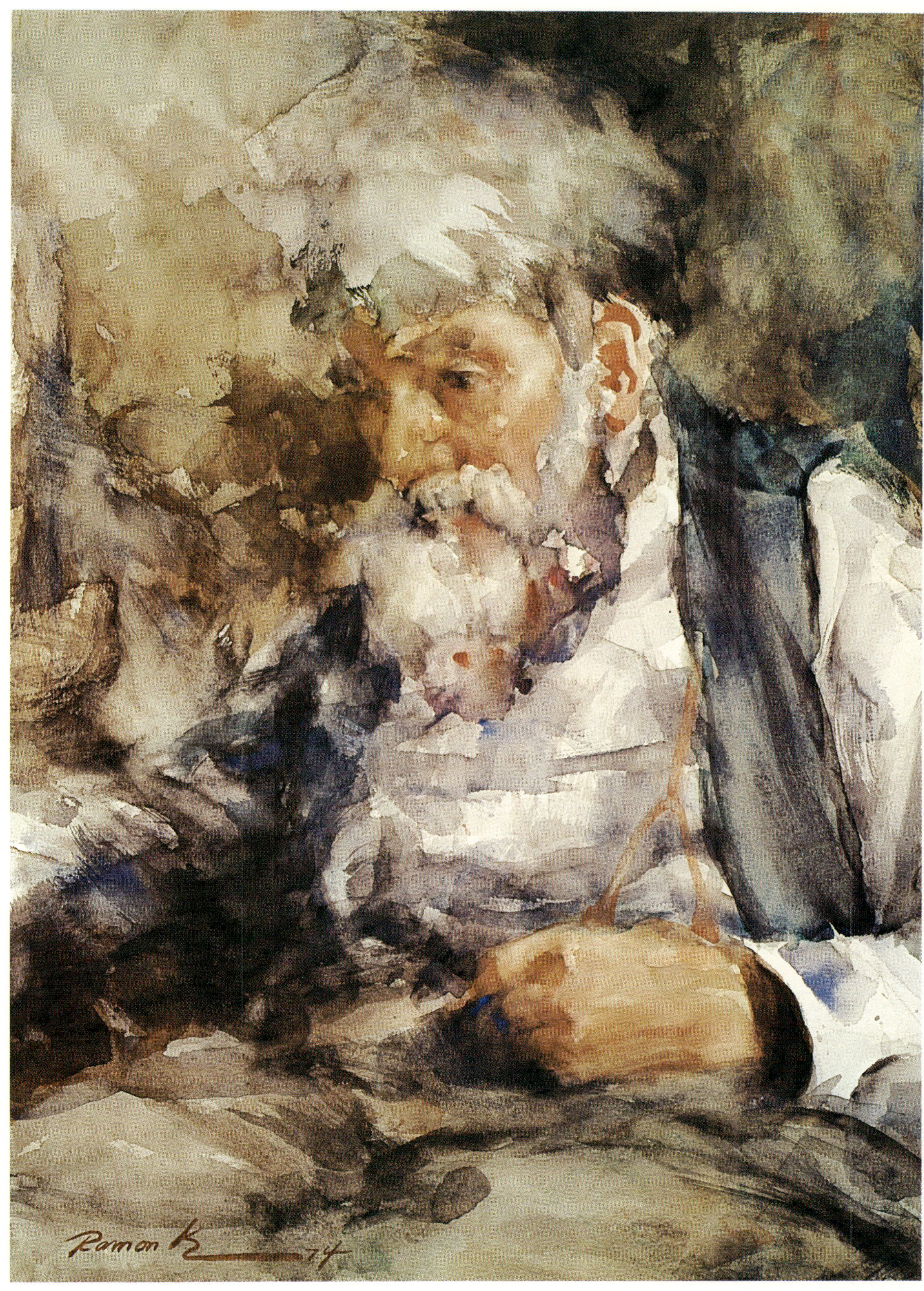

Grandfather Trujillo. Watercolor on illustration board, 24″ x 18″ (61 x 45.4 cm). I like painting on illustration board. First of all, watercolor washes tend to stay on the surface when they dry, clearly marking the boundaries of each wash. They don't run together as much as they do on watercolor paper, where they penetrate the fibers of the paper more deeply. It's easier to lift out light areas on illustration board, too, probably for the same reason. Note the effect of the flowing washes as they meet the dry washes in adjacent areas, and follow them downward. The wash on the upper part of the face meets the dark stroke below the nose and at the top of the mustache on the right—and then stops there. Below that, the washes of the mustache and beard are caught and held in the same manner. While the background washes flow into the upper part of the figure, where they meet the left side of the beard where it was dry, there's a definite, hard edge. I played with edges here, losing some and leaving others crisp. The edges on the arm and at the sides of the vest on the right are precise; those on the hand are softer and more fused. The dark section at the left is simply undefined space. My palette for this painting included cadmium red, alizarin crimson, and yellow ochre for the face and hand; burnt umber, ivory black, and cobalt blue for the background; and cobalt blue and Hooker's green for the shirt and vest.

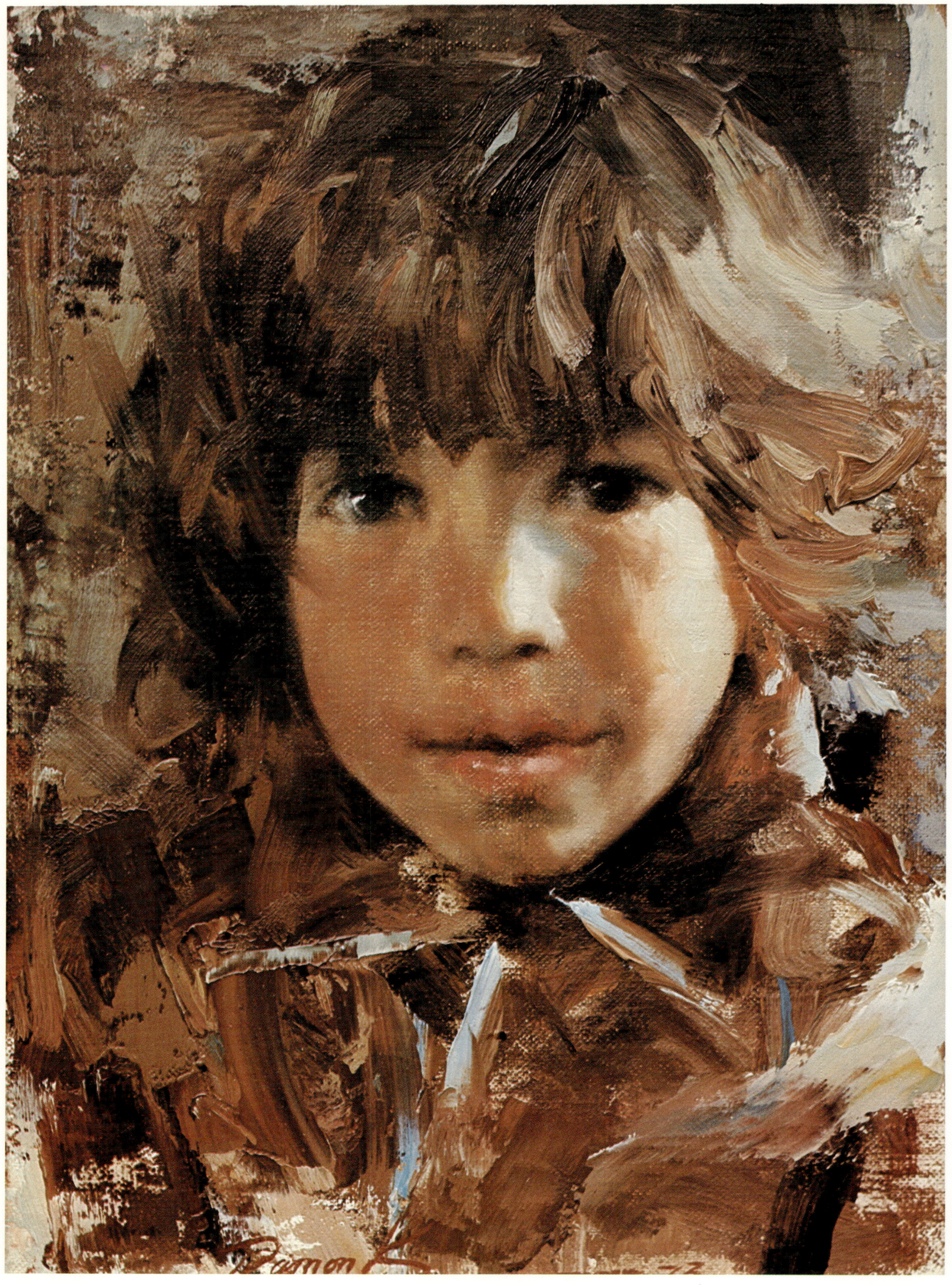

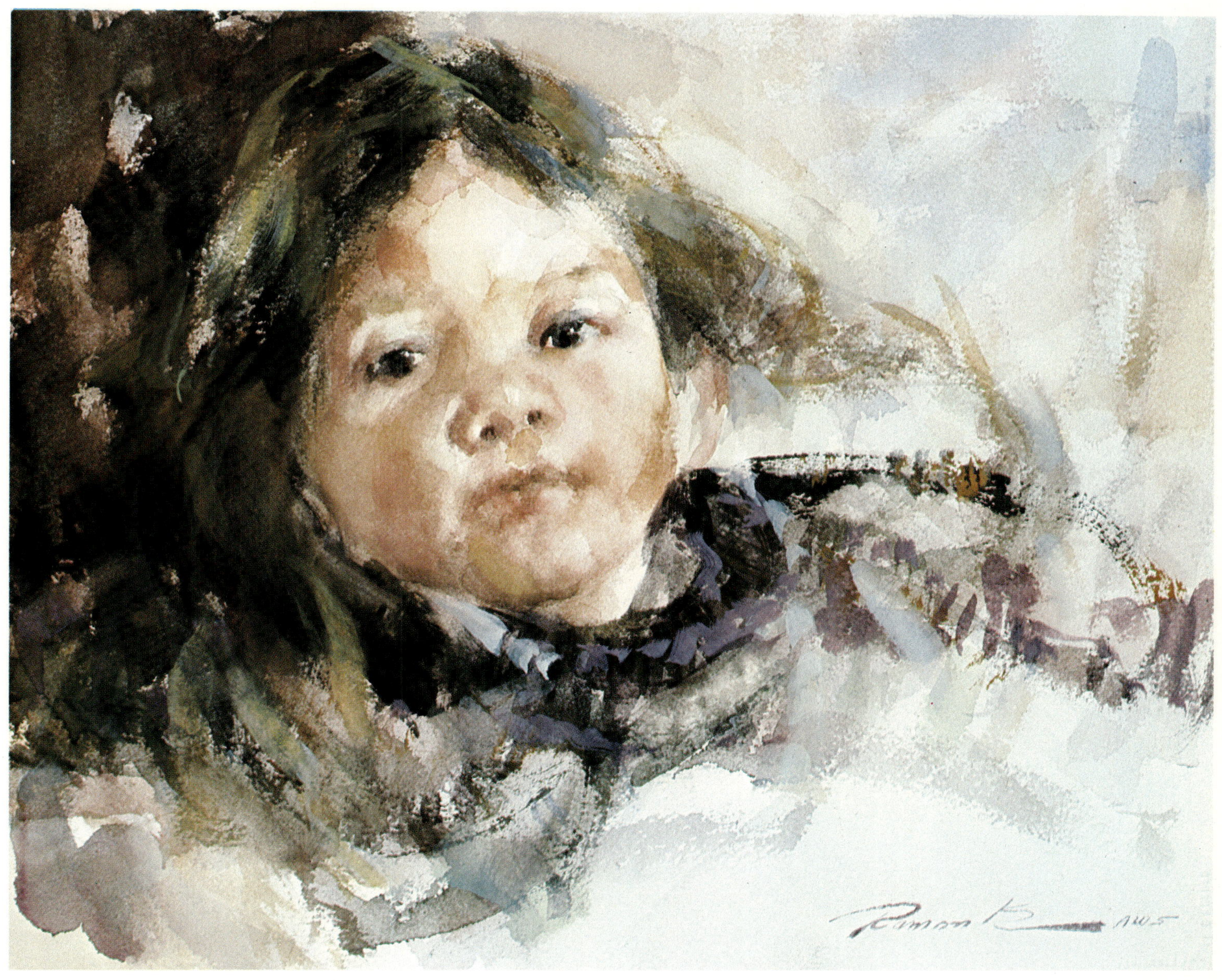

Ben (left). Oil on canvas, 12″ x 9″ (30.5 x 21 cm). I painted this portrait of my youngest son on a pre-primed English linen canvas called Herga, which has a medium texture. This canvas adapts to creamy, painterly brushwork, such as I've done on the face. I accidently discovered something I can do on this canvas that I particularly like. After laying a heavy palette knife cover in an area, I take a clean bristle brush and drag across it, leaving a trail that appears to be carved from the paint. There are several such strokes on the left side of Ben's hair.

Stephie (above). Watercolor on 140 lb Arches, 12″ x 16″ (30.5 x 40.5 cm). I painted this from life in several fifteen-minute sessions. Altogether I worked for about an hour and a half, much of the time from memory. The backward tilt of the child's head is an interesting gesture. I painted in watercolor directly on the dry paper without dampening the paper first. The brushstrokes, therefore, remain as unblended drybrush and are interesting in themselves. I concentrated the darks in a shape from which the child's head seems to emerge. I had to extend the darks to the right of the head in order to stabilize the composition. All the darks on the face were built up in layers. I left the light areas open until the end, when I washed them in with flesh tones. I cooled the flesh tones with mixtures of cobalt blue and cadmium red.

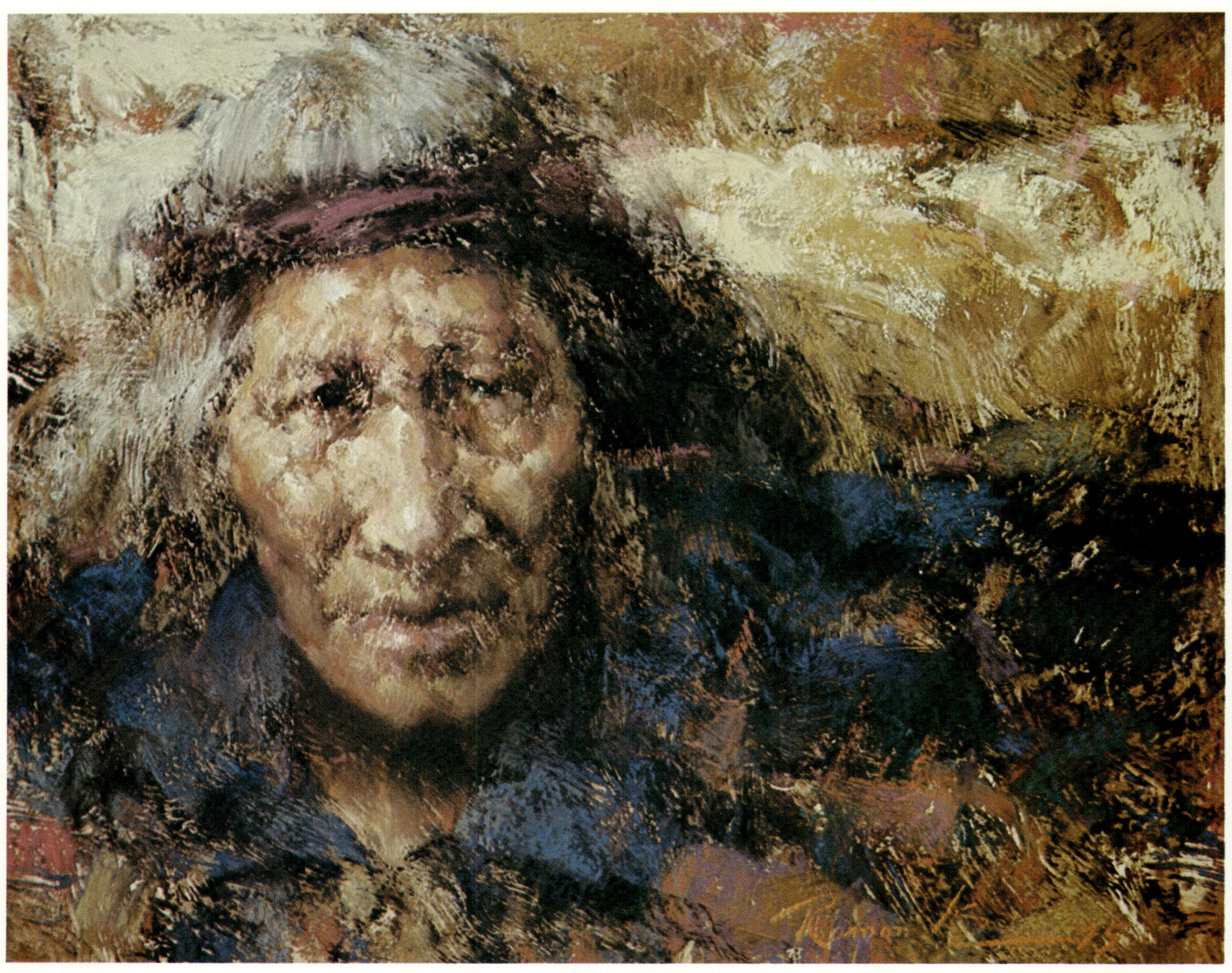

Old Navajo (above). Pastel over watercolor on rough sanded board, 11″ x 14″ (28 x 35.5 cm). This painting, which won several prizes in Mainstreams '76 at Marietta, Ohio, has an unusual composition. To place a portrait so far to one side and to use a horizontal format are both daring decisions, but I believe the portrait attracts the eye precisely because of its unique placement. I used a rough-textured board and applied pastel in a rich impasto. It's necessary to apply pigment lavishly in order to cover a sanded board well and to insure a handsome paint quality. I blocked the shirt in boldly, allowing the underpainting to show through in places. My attention was equally divided between the abstraction of the background and the light and shade modeling of the head. My two areas of concern—the background and the chiaroscuro modeling—are combined in the model's hair. There the cool gray of the hair fuses with the warm lights of the background.

A Taos Type (right). Pastel over watercolor on rough sanded board, 12″ x 9″ (30.5 x 23 cm). This is what I would call a studio study, painted alla prima. I concentrated on the construction of the Indian's features, with little work in the background. It's a pleasure to just let myself go, applying pigment with verve and speed. The edges around the head are crisp and clear. The wrapped blanket adds a textural and colorful accent without much definition. My attention is completely directed to realizing a three-dimensional form in color.

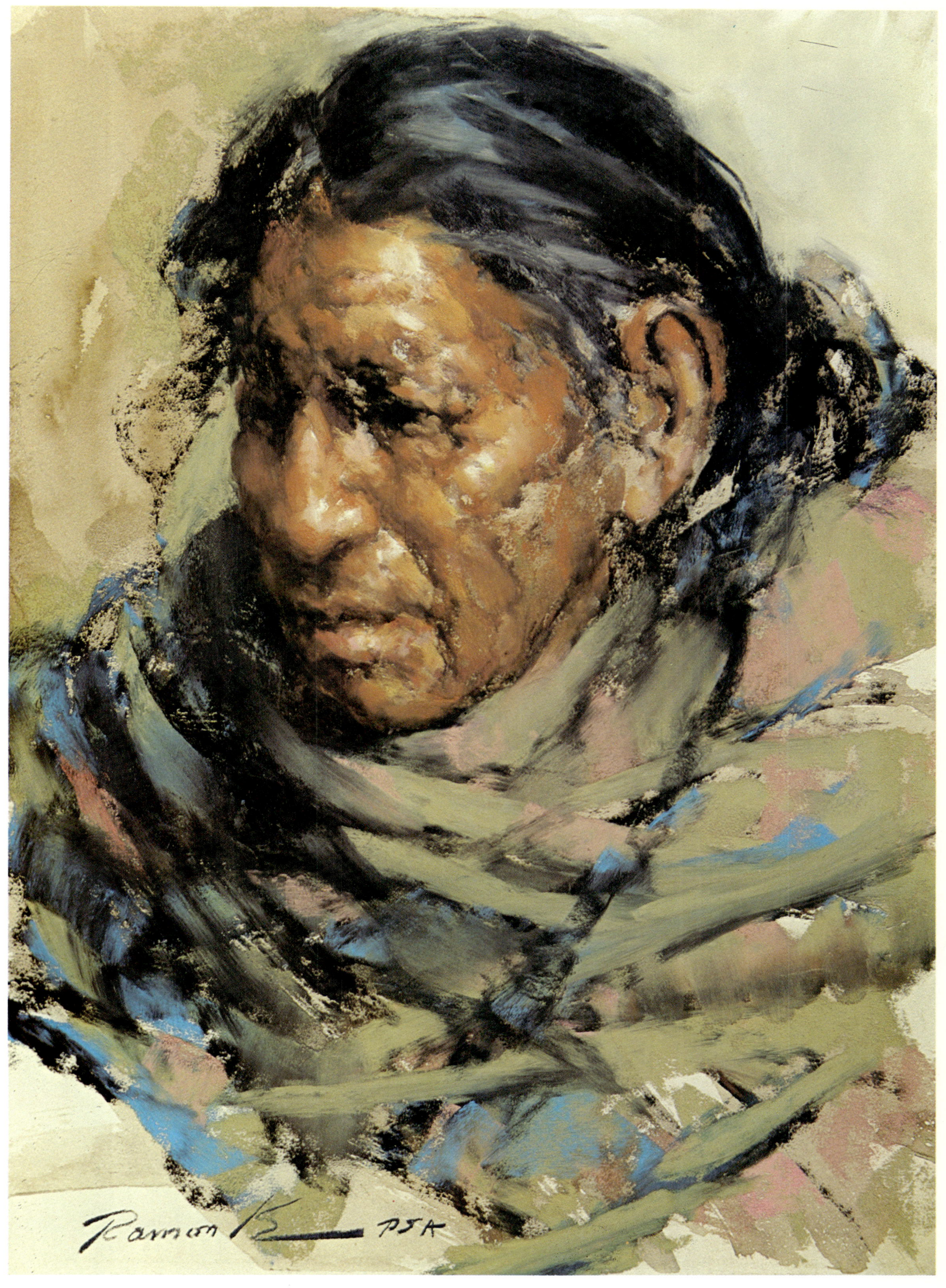

Ramon K—— PSA

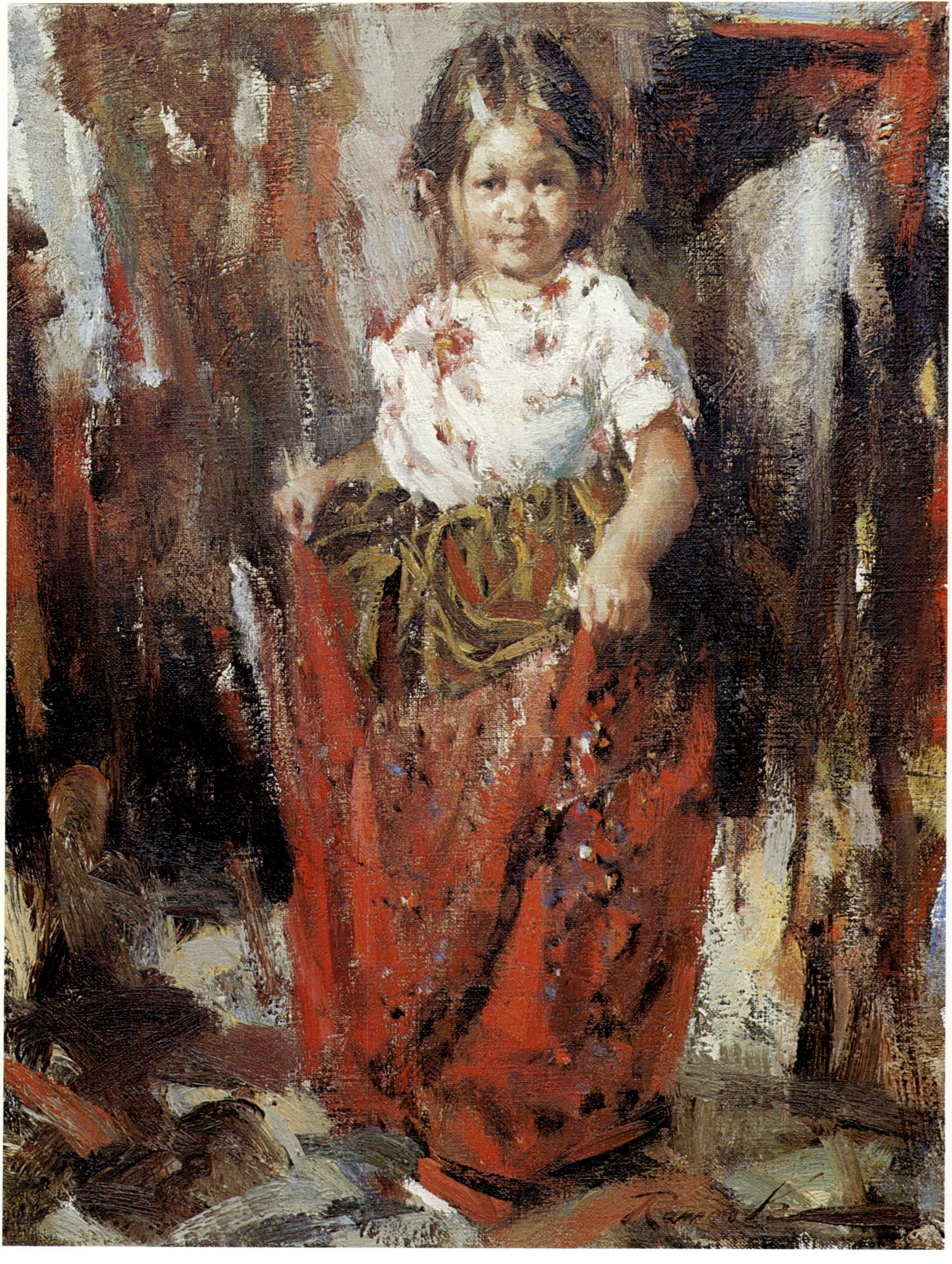

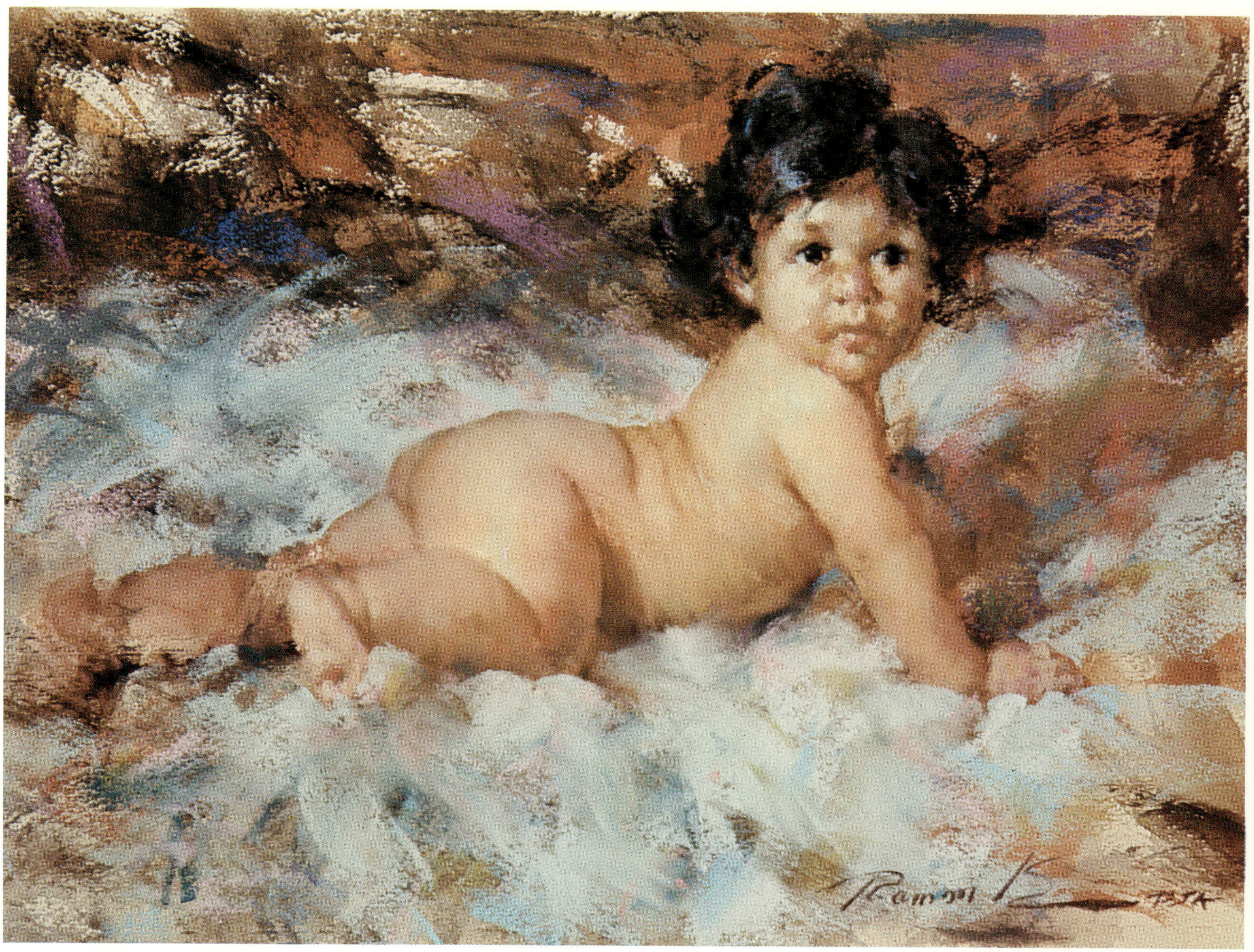

Little Stephanie (left). Oil on canvas, 16″ x 12″ (40.5 x 30.5 cm). This painting was done on a canvas I primed myself. I built up the texture with a 2″ (5 cm) brush when I laid on the white lead. Each artist has preferences in the method he uses to prime. I like to mix white lead and turpentine to a creamy consistency that retains the strokes of the bristle brush. I can always smooth these with a palette knife while they're still wet. The quality of paint in the finished work has a great deal to do with the underlying surface.

Stephanie (above). Pastel over watercolor on paper, 9″ x 12″ (23 x 30.5 cm). I've noticed that on the flesh tones of a baby, as opposed to an adult, the warm colors are concentrated on the upper torso, while the cooler colors are in the buttocks and legs. Therefore I used yellow ochre, cadmium yellow, cadmium red, and white on the back and chest. On the right arm I went a little cooler, especially on the right edge and into the hand, which tends to be a cool pink. On the flesh of the baby's buttocks and legs, I used cooler colors: alizarin crimson, cobalt blue, white, and a touch of cadmium red. However, the highlight was done with the same warm colors that I used on her shoulder. Stephanie has both Spanish and Indian ancestry and her hair is nearly black—I highlighted it with cobalt blue and white. The baby's coloration works well against the cooler colors in the sheet. I warmed the cool shadow with flesh tones on the right side of the sheet. To capture Stephanie's appearance I had to take numerous photos, since a year-old baby can't hold a pose.

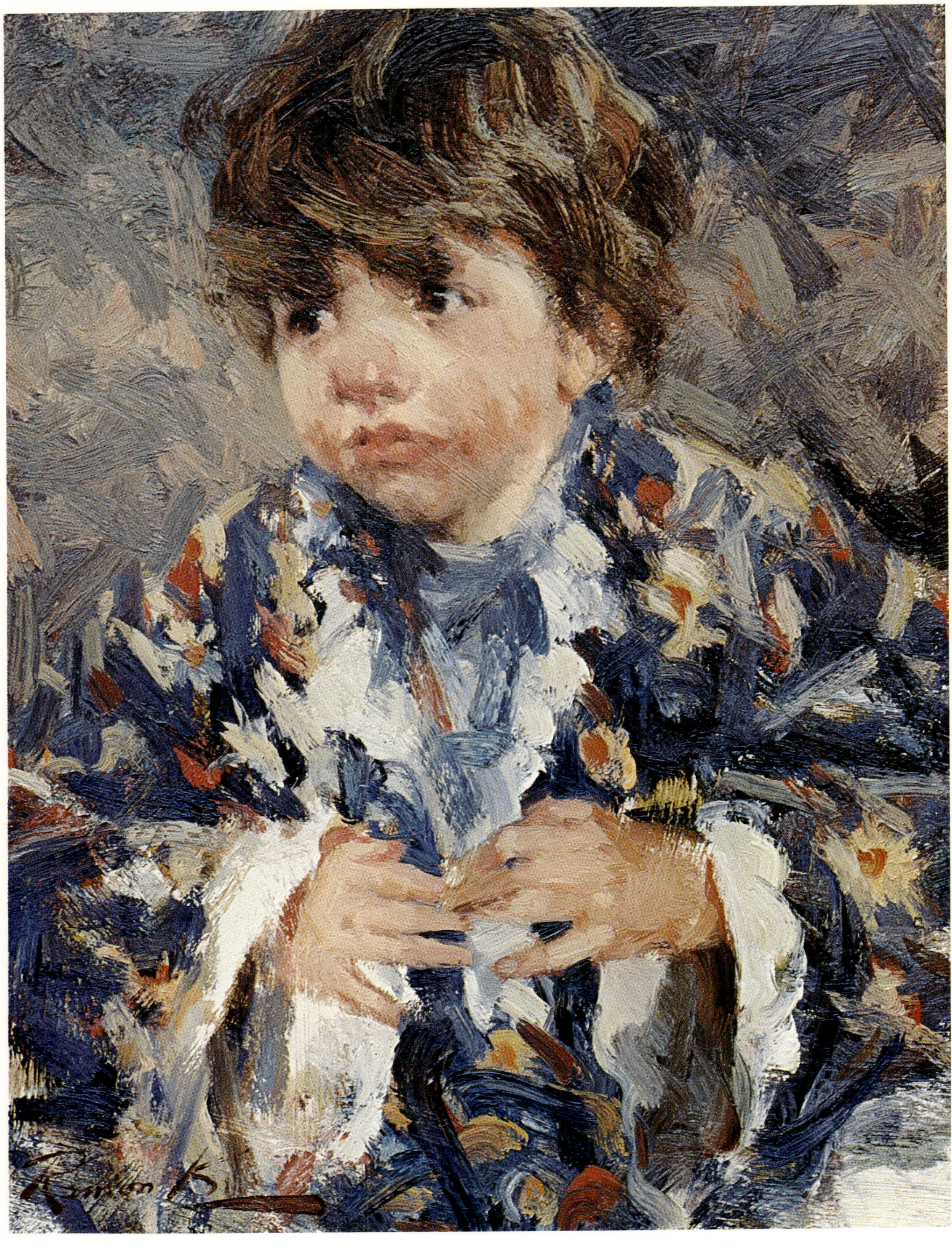

Little Girl with Robe. Oil on Masonite, 16″ x 12″ (40.5 x 30.5 cm). I painted this portrait in cool tones. I think of it as having two keys—a high key on the face and hands, and a lower one on the robe. There's a harmonious interweaving of blues and flesh tones, with a few bright touches of red and yellow. Working on Masonite, I tend to paint very directly, not depending on underwashes, since I find that transparent washes lack luminosity. I completely covered the surface here and relied on the sheen of the oil paint for luster.

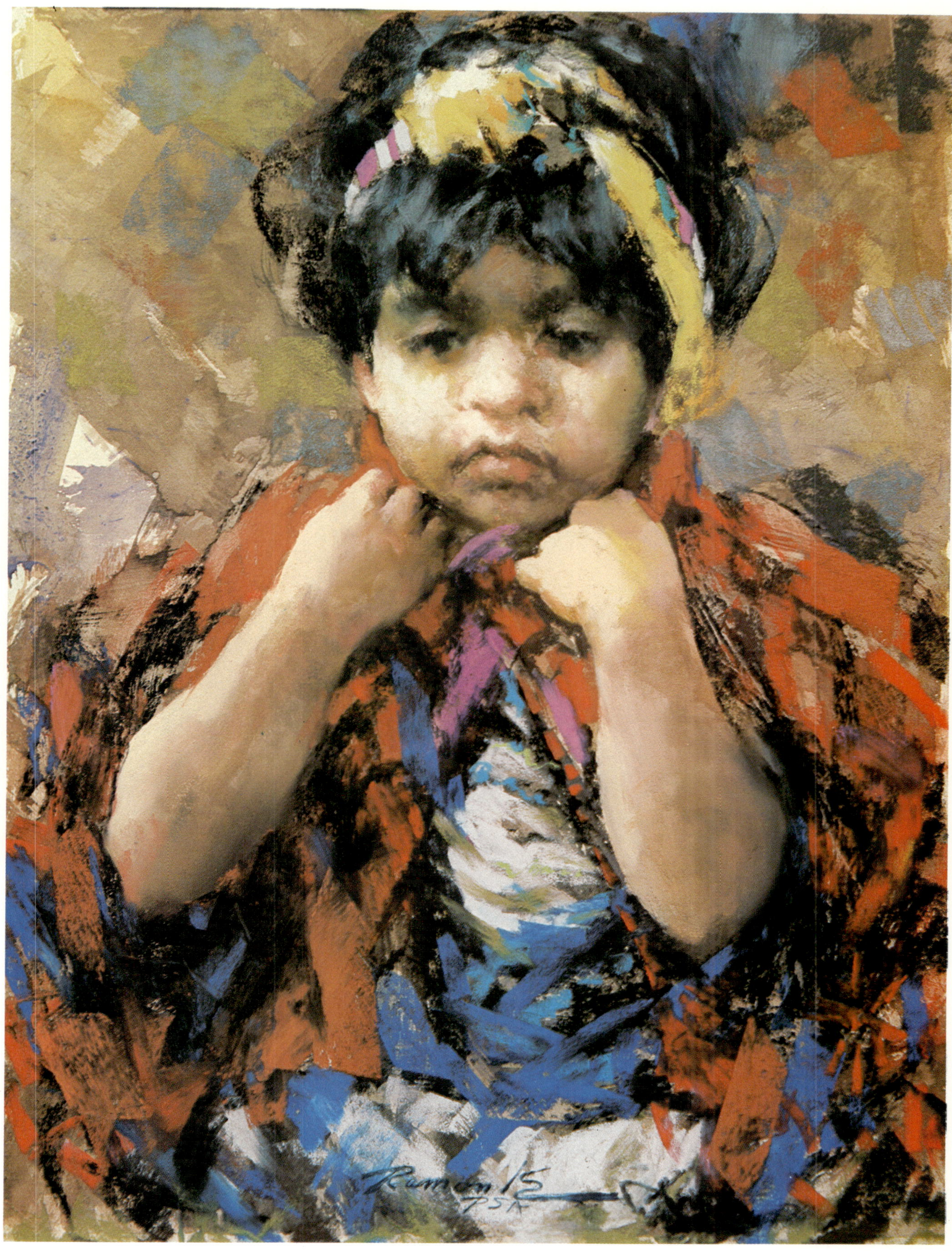

Caro. Pastel over watercolor on rough sanded board. 14″ x 11″ (35.5 x 28 cm). As an impressionist painter, I'm more involved with the colors and abstract patterns than I am with a realistic depiction of the model. I drew an outline of the face and arms with raw umber and left them open until later. I then gave my attention to building up the texture of the cape. I treated the background as a pattern of varied strokes that included the yellows and blues of the clothing, but only a few small touches of the red orange in it. Lastly, I went into the face and arms and developed them simply and quickly. Because the arms are on the surface of the painting, they seem to project toward the viewer. I heightened this feeling by shading each arm deeply under each elbow. This is an example of how I often try a new progression of steps to maintain an alert, creative approach to painting.

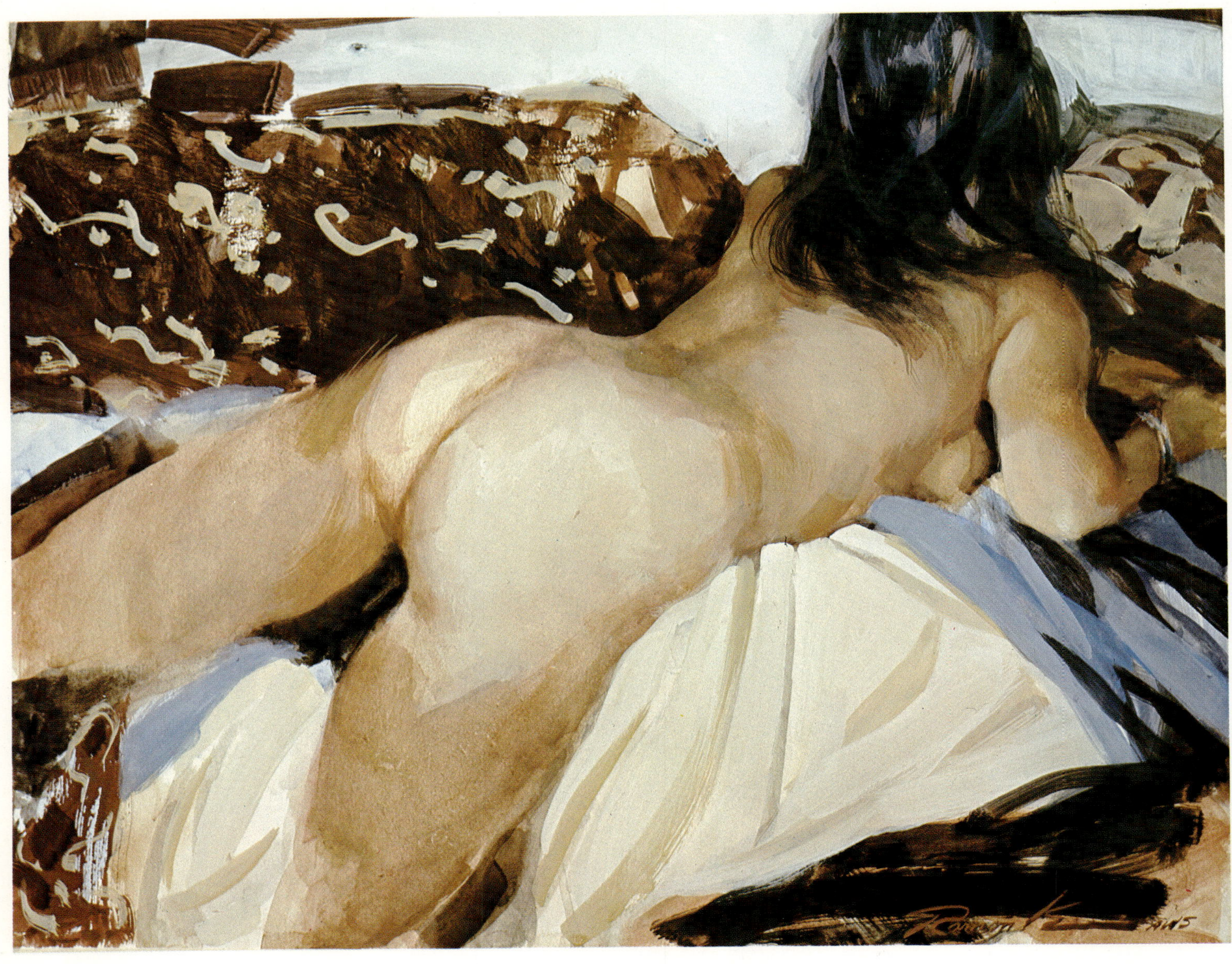

Nude. Watercolor with gouache on illustration board, 14″ x 18″ (35.5 x 45.5 cm). Two things demanded my attention here: the complexity of the foreshortened pose and the method I used to paint it. Using medium and small filbert bristle brushes throughout, I first blocked in the figure and background in simple, transparent watercolor underwashes. Then, as I usually do in watercolor, I went over them with additional washes. But then I took it a step further. I added an opaque gouache overlay to the interesting white shape at the upper side of the painting, to the rib cage, and to the right arm and shoulder of the model, to the creamy folds of the white sheet, to the blue drapery, and finally to squiggles in the design of the brown drapery in the background.

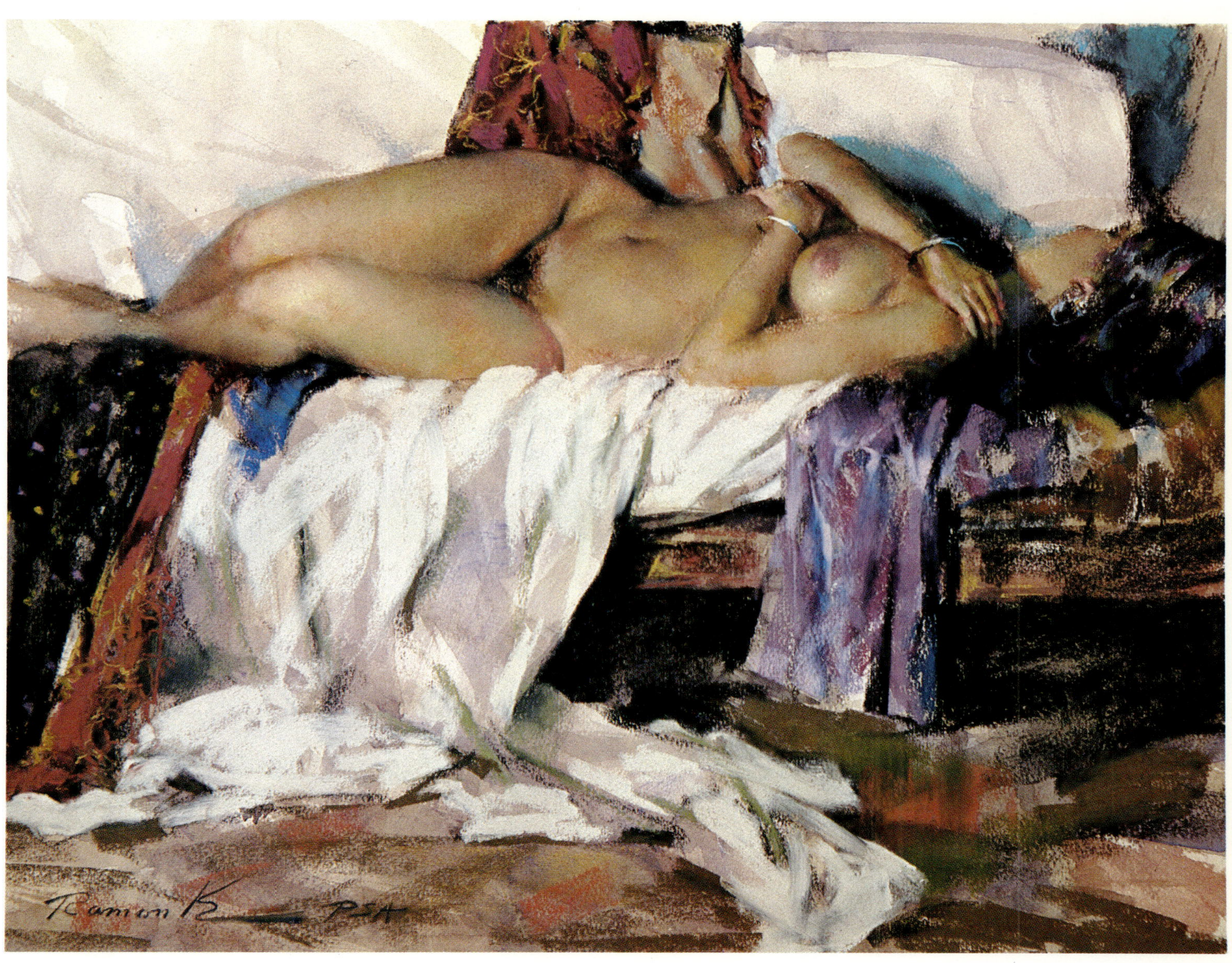

Nude. Pastel over watercolor on paper, 12″ x 16″ (30.5 x 40.5 cm). I brought this painting to a high degree of finish. Textures and color were of major interest to me as I sought to distinguish the different textures from one another—not just flesh against cloth, but against silk, cotton, and satin. Note the volume and weight of the figure as she lies on the couch. Details of wood and upholstery are clearly indicated and edges precisely defined, giving an unusually linear quality to the design. Although each piece of drapery has a different color, they complement the figure and never overpower it. By retaining a loose approach in areas of secondary interest, such as the immediate foreground, I've avoided the monotony of a painting that's brought to an equally polished finish in every area.

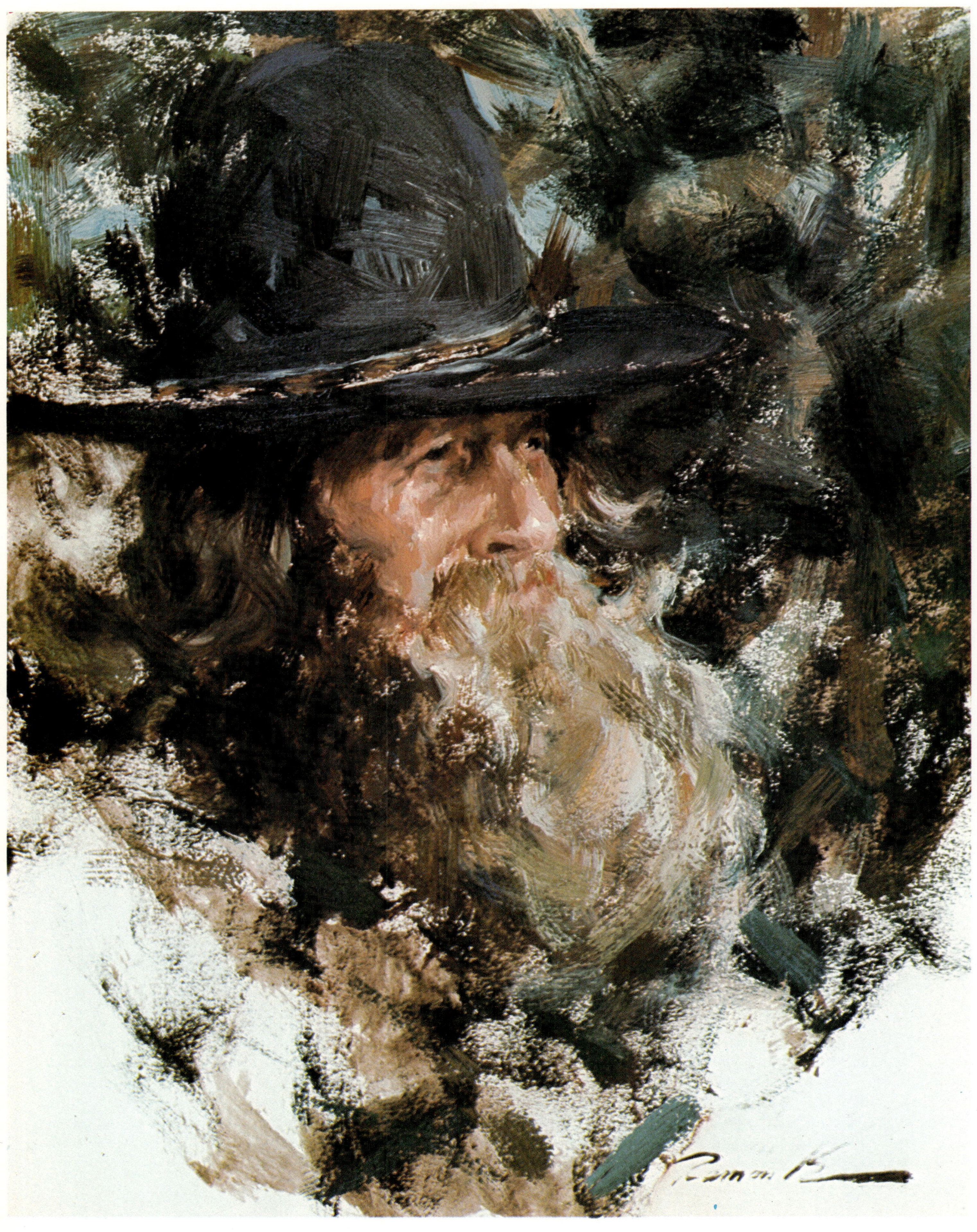

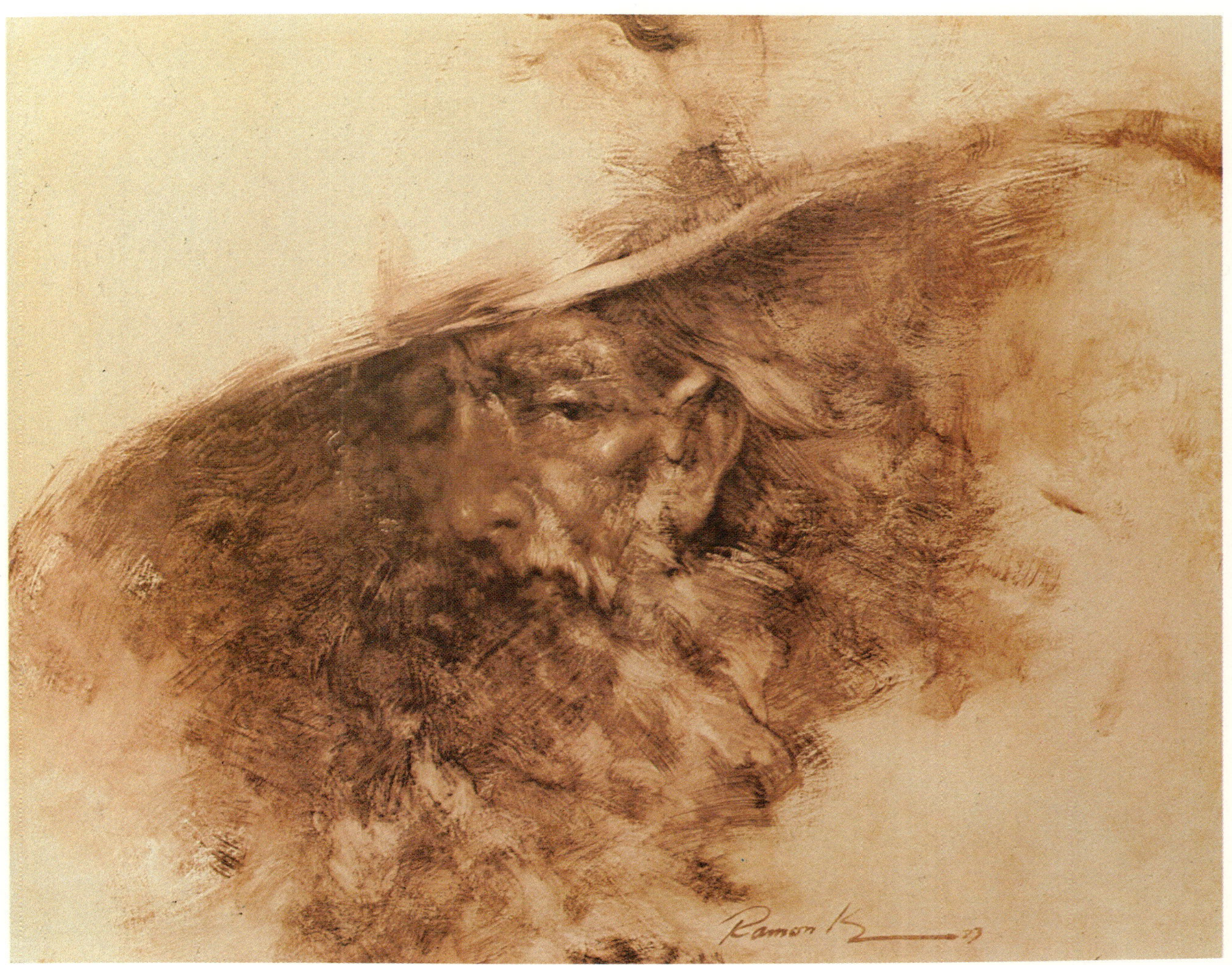

A Bearded Man (left). Oil on illustration board, 10″ x 8″ (25.5 x 20.5 cm). My palette here is meant to suggest evergreens and the snow of a cold Colorado winter. My model seemed to create the image of a mountain man, an effect enhanced by the high top hat—a studio prop. It was the beard that caught my eye and made me want to paint him in the first place. I needed to add the dark hat on his head in order to make the beard more prominent, lighter than it would have seemed had the hair been left in the light. On the cool, lighted side of the beard I used cobalt blue, raw sienna, and white. On the dark side of the beard, strokes of black are mixed with burnt sienna. This 100% rag illustration board was primed with 3 parts shellac and 1 part turpentine.

Mexican Shade Hat (above). Sepia oil on illustration board, 14″ x 18″ (35.5 x 45.5 cm). I first primed the illustration board with acrylic gesso that had been tinted a warm burnt umber. I then proceeded to paint this monochrome portrait with Van Dyke brown oil paint. The lifted out highlights are of special interest. Those on the face were carefully controlled and done with a single stroke of the same sable brush, now freshly cleaned, that I used to paint the rest of the painting. To make the highlights on the hatband and brim, I dampened each area with the brush, then wiped out the highlight precisely and carefully with a rag. The technique is similar to the one I use in my sepia conté crayon drawings.

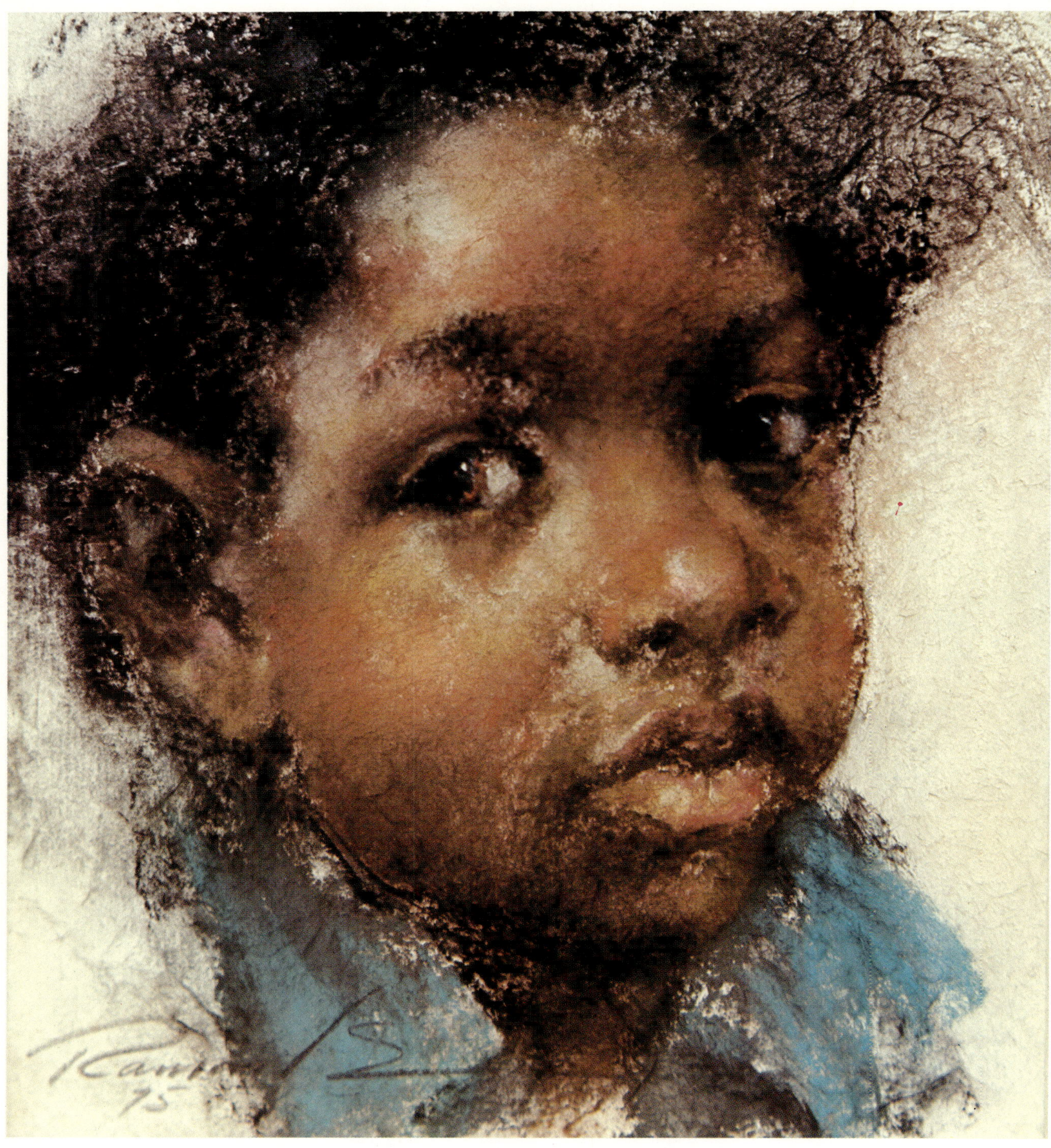

Little Mark (above). Pastel on rice paper, 10″ x 7″ (25.5 x 18 cm). This is strictly a portrait with no background. The fibers in the paper serve to texturize the painting; they're particularly effective in the hair. The left side is softer and cooler; the right side is warmer and more definite. On rice paper, it's necessary to be as direct as possible; the delicacy of the paper prevents much overworking. At almost every spot on the painting there are no more than two layers of pastel—including the distinctly modeled nose and lips. The cool blue collar of Tony's shirt provides a temperature contrast to the warm flesh tones I prefer.

Littlest Model (right). Transparent watercolor on illustration board, 28″ x 18″ (71 x 45.5 cm). The shapes of the areas in light and shadow make a curve that moves in a wide arc from the top left to the bottom left corner. The model exactly fits into this semi-circular space. Because the model is a Black, his flesh tones are warm with cool shadows. A network of brushstrokes from the underpainting is still visible in the lighted left side of the background. On the shirt and trousers I laid in darker washes with a number 6 filbert oil brush. Using this same brush on the background at the right, I laid dark washes over lighter ones and then added some drybrush strokes on top. With the bristle brush heavily loaded with paint, I painted the arms. I left open an area on the left wrist where it catches the light.

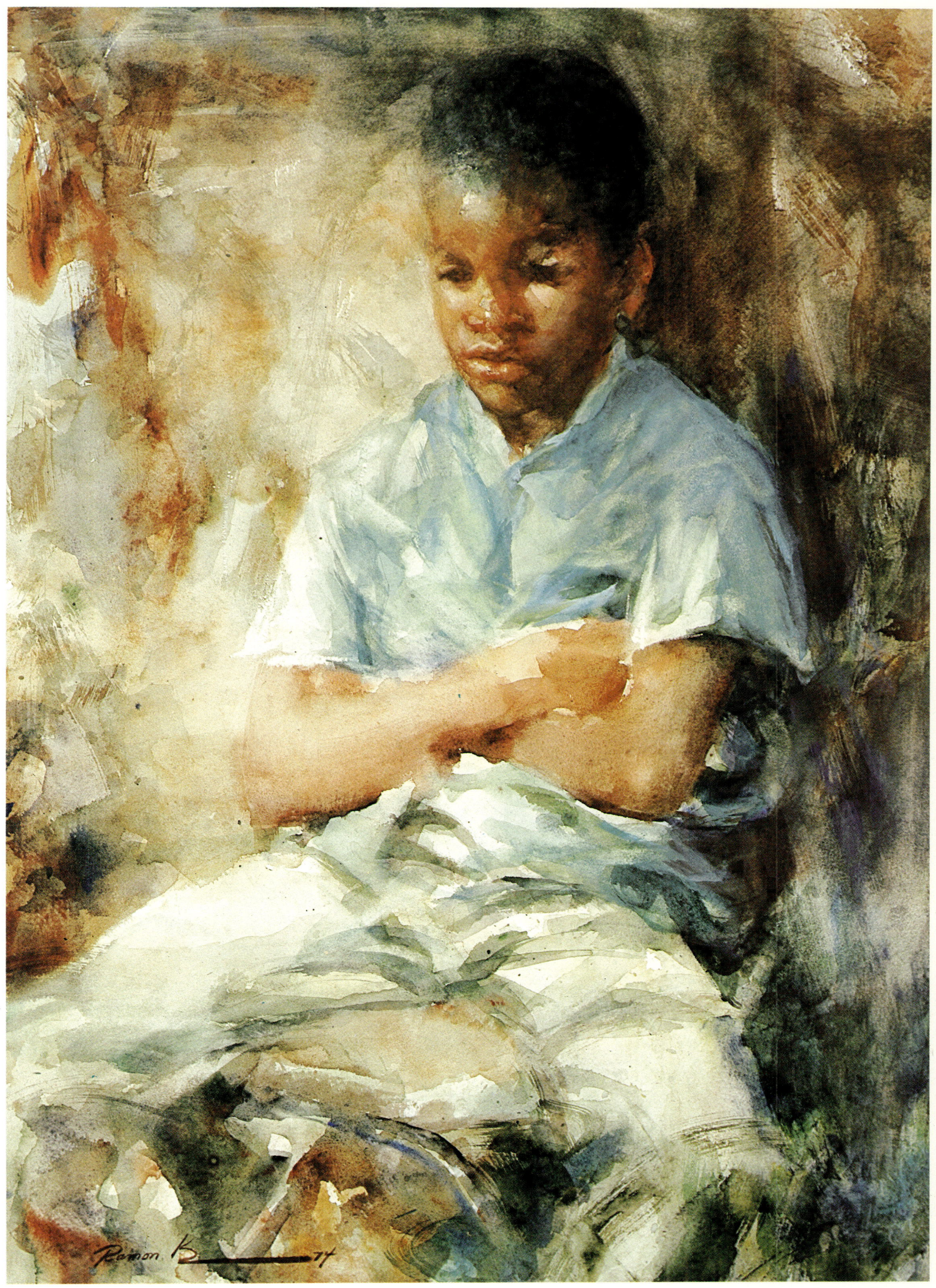

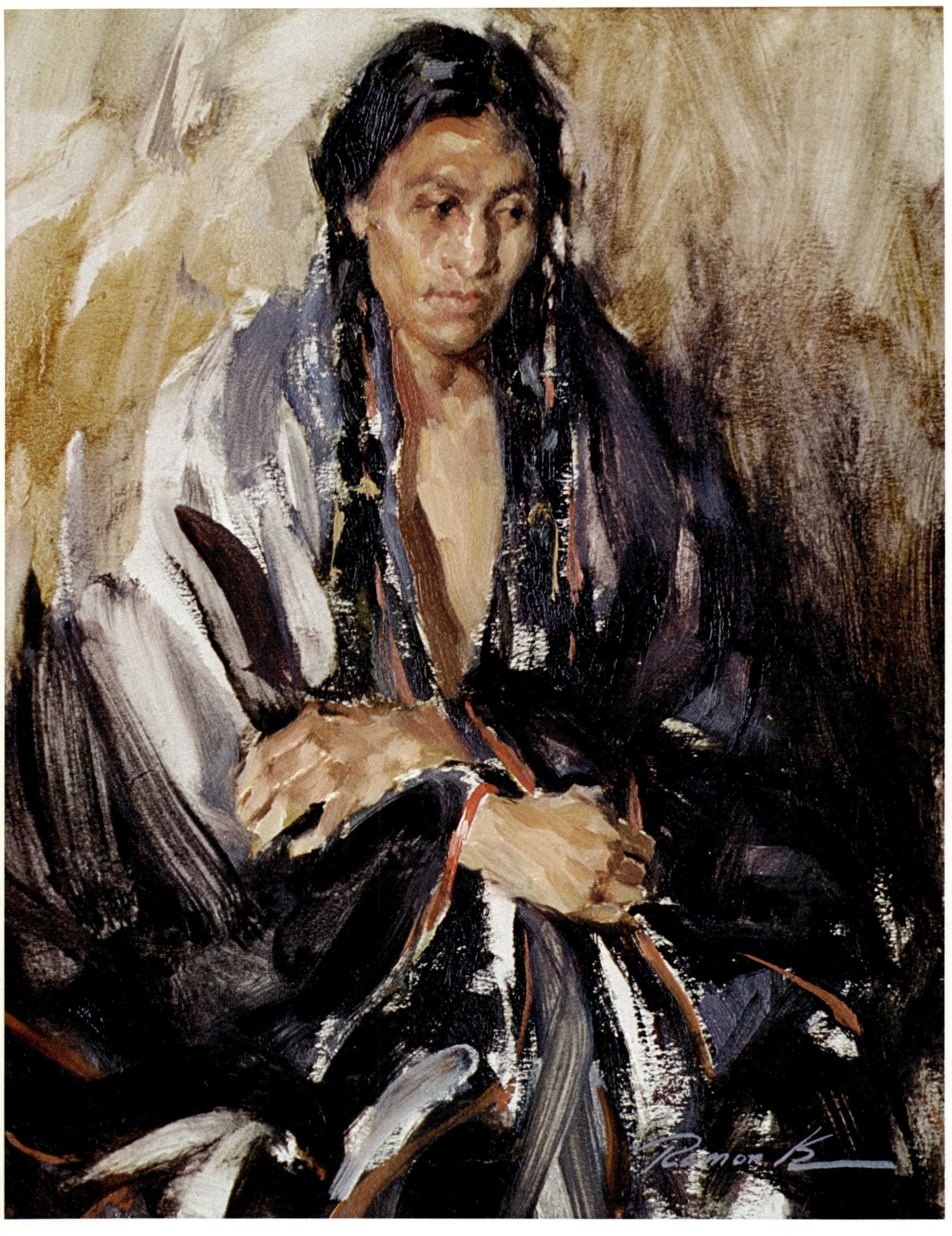

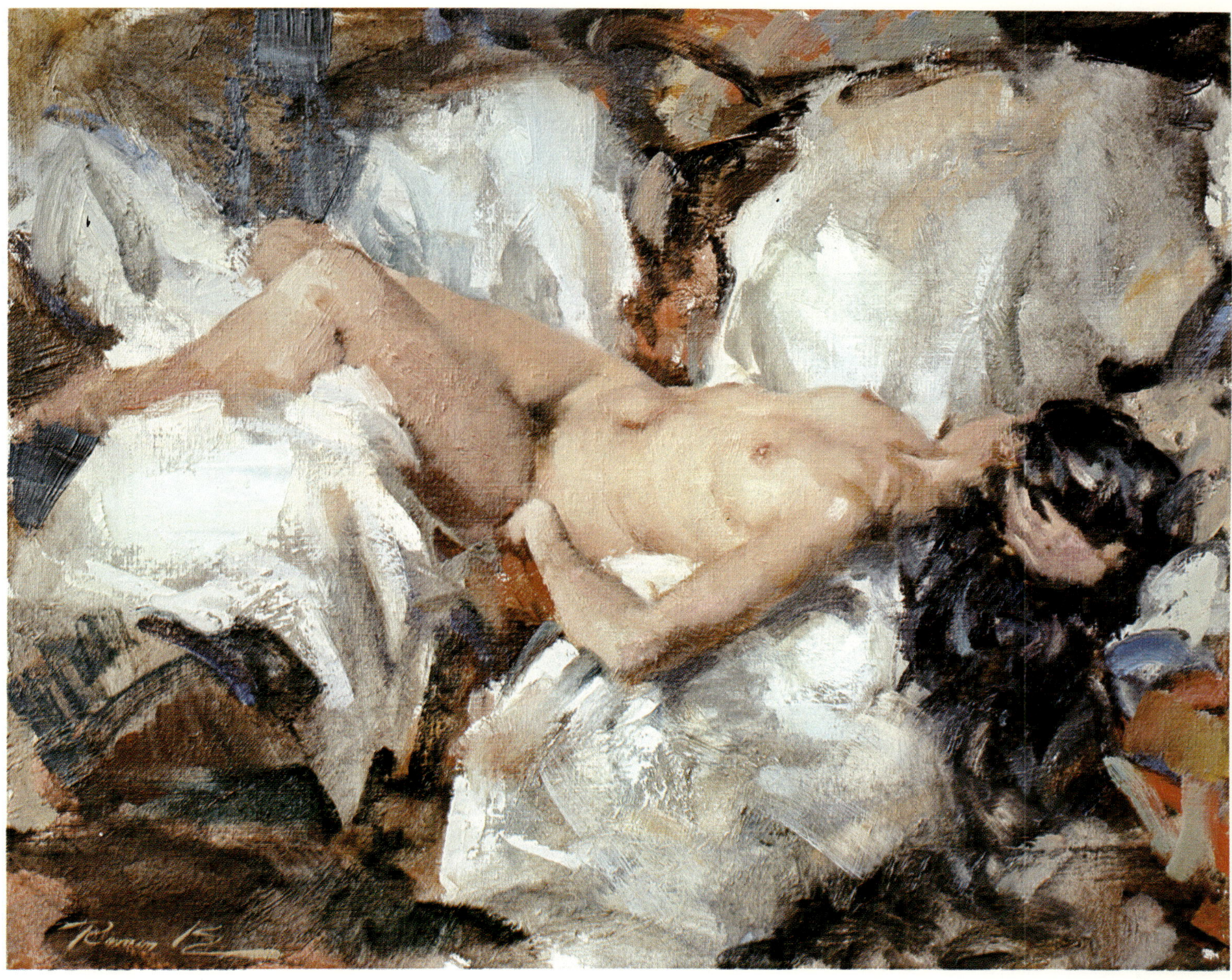

A Sioux Type (left). Oil on illustration board, 10″ x 8″ (25.5 x 20.5 cm). I began this small painting with diluted turpentine washes, which I then worked into with a clean brush. In the background, this initial layer is still visible. With creamier pigment, I established the local color of all the areas of the painting. With the third layer of pigment, I began modeling the features and the robe. To indicate folds on the lighted shoulder on the left, I lifted the strokes out with a clean brush; after each stroke, I cleaned off the brush with turpentine and dried it on a rag. Accents of red were made on the edge of the robe and I added some heavy white strokes to break up the dark foreground area. The painting was completed in about forty-five minutes.

Nude (above). Oil on canvas, 14″ x 18″ (35.5 x 45.5 cm). This is an example of an approach to oil painting that I use fairly often. I set up a strong composition based on an H which divides the spaces well and guides the eye to the figure. Rough brushwork on the drapery and background areas is in marked contrast to the smoother brushwork on the figure. For a fuller account of the technical aspects of this painting, see page 48.

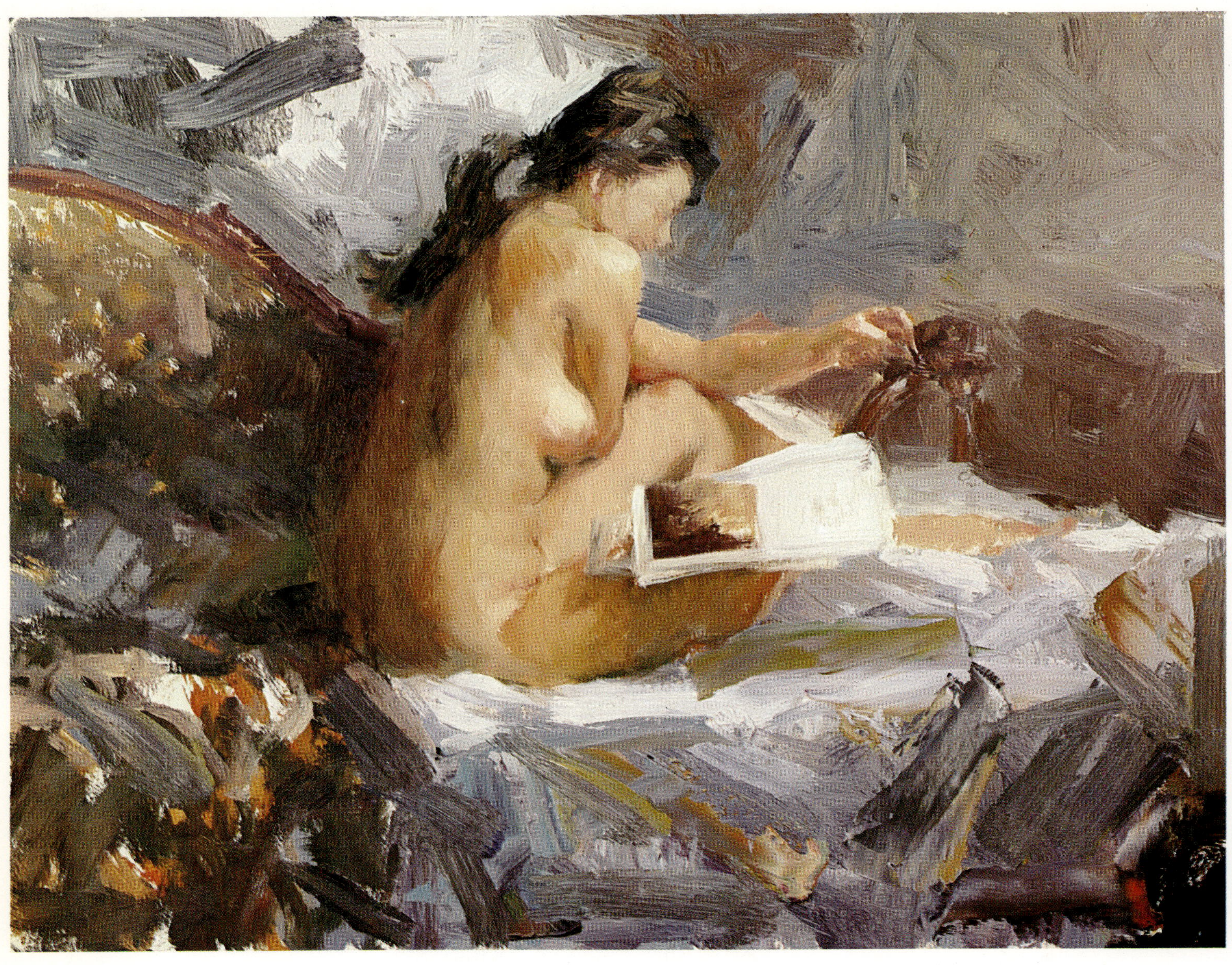

Nude. Oil on illustration board, 12″ x 16″ (30.5 x 40.5 cm). This is strictly a studio study painted from life for my own information and education. My experiment was with materials and methods, rather than with the pose of the model. I allowed shapes and ''happy accidents'' to occur spontaneously. When I finished the painting, I searched for useful ideas that I could incorporate into a later work. This is the kind of on-going practice that I feel is so vitally necessary to my continuing education as a painter. It is from such studies that I plan new approaches to paintings and maintain a sense of excitement and wonder about it. Experimentation is my lifeblood. I can't live without it!

Edited by Bonnie Silverstein
Designed by Bob Fillie
Composed in 11-point Palatino by Gerard Associates/Phototypesetting, Inc.
Printed in Japan by Dai Nippon